11/99

At the Hemingways

WITH FIFTY YEARS OF

CORRESPONDENCE BETWEEN

ERNEST AND MARCELLINE HEMINGWAY

At the Hemingways

WITH FIFTY YEARS OF CORRESPONDENCE BETWEEN ERNEST AND MARCELLINE HEMINGWAY

Marcelline Hemingway

With a Foreword by Michael Reynolds

UNIVERSITY OF IDAHO PRESS
Moscow, Idaho
1999

03 02 01 00 99 5 4 3 2 1
Library of Congress Cataloguing-in-Publication Data
Sanford, Marcelline Hemingway, 1898–1963.
At the Hemingways : with fifty years of correspondence between Ernest and Marcelline Hemingway / Marcelline Hemingway ; with a foreword by Michael Reynolds. — Centennial ed.
p.   cm.
Includes bibliographical references and index.
ISBN 0-89301-216-5 (alk. paper)
1. Hemingway, Ernest 1899–1961—Family.   2. Sanford, Marcelline Hemingway, 1898–1963—Correspondence.   3. Authors, American—20th century—Family relationships.   4. Hemingway, Ernest, 1899–1961—Correspondence.   5. Sanford, Marcelline Hemingway, 1898–1963.   6. Brothers and sisters—United States.   7. Hemingway family.
I. Hemingway, Ernest, 1899–1961. II. Title.
PS3515.E37Z82   1999
813'.52—dc21
[B]   98–16800
CIP
ISBN 0-89301-216-5

For permissions to print or reprint previously unpublished or published materials, the following are gratefully acknowledged:

Excerpt from "Little Giddings" in *Four Quartets*, copyright 1943 by T. S. Eliot and renewed by Esme Valerie Eliot, reprinted by permission of Harcourt Brace & Company.

Letter of May 20, 1921, from Ernest Hemingway to Marcelline Hemingway (Sanford) reprinted with permission of Scribner, a Division of Simon & Schuster, from *Ernest Hemingway: Selected Letters, 1917-61,* edited by Carlos Baker. Copyright © 1981 The Ernest Hemingway Foundation, Inc.

Permission has been received from The Ernest Hemingway Foundation, Inc., to publish all the other unpublished correspondence from Ernest Hemingway to Marcelline Hemingway (Sanford).

The John F. Kennedy Library, Hemingway Collection, provided the letters from Marcelline Hemingway (Sanford) to Ernest Hemingway.

Carol Sanford Coolidge, James Sterling Sanford, and John Edmonds Sanford provided permission to publish the letters of Marcelline Hemingway (Sanford).

At The Hemingways: A Family Portrait was originally published by Little, Brown and Company as an Atlantic Monthly Press Book © 1961, 1962 by Marcelline Hemingway Sanford.

*This book is for Carol, James and John
and for their children.*

Contents

AT THE HEMINGWAYS:
A FAMILY PORTRAIT, CENTENNIAL EDITION

The Hemingways Revisited:
Back to the Future

ONE hundred years ago, July 21, 1899, Marcelline Hemingway saw for the first time her younger brother, Ernest, the sibling with whom she was matched by her mother as if they were twins. In many ways, they were, growing up together in a world that no longer exists. Ernest, who later used almost every setting he knew well in his writing, never wrote about those early years in Oak Park, never wrote about the house on North Kenilworth or his older sister. Gertrude Stein once said that if Hemingway would write honestly about his own life that it would be better than his fiction. Here is part of that story told by one who experienced it as it was happening. It is a remarkable story, one that has deeply influenced all of the several Hemingway biographies.

A very young biographer once said that this book was Marcelline's effort to sanitize Oak Park. He may have even called the book a white-wash. As Scott Fitzgerald was apt to say, "That was not me. That was a man named Johnson who frequently masquerades as me." A somewhat older biographer is now more sympathetic with Marcelline's daunting task, for she presents the young Hemingway with more sympathy than most of his biographers have been able to muster. Despite all of Ernest's semi-fictional accounts to friends and strangers about how repressed he was in Oak Park, one sees here a far different story, one that leavens the bread. The exuberance that characterized Hemingway for most of his life bubbles up through these pages infectiously, evidence of that rare sense of immortality that protects the young. If he came back from the Great War no longer immortal and a little disillusioned with the political rhetoric that sent him there, it was not Oak Park's fault.

Children, as Fitzgerald again said, cannot believe in the youth of their parents; how much more difficult is it for strangers like us to recapture the young Hemingway born into an Oak Park before automobiles, phonographs, motion pictures, and telephones completely restructured small and large town America. Republican, progressive, and intellectually enlightened, Oak Park was morally conservative and socially advanced with one of the best school systems in the nation and a rich cultural life. Here the Strenuous Life preached by Teddy Roosevelt was as written in stone as any of the commandments. The sons of Oak Park, armed with a sense of duty, went out into the world to make it a better place. In high school, Ernest made a written promise to himself and signed it:

> I desire to do pioneering or exploring work in the three last great frontiers: Africa, central South America, or the country around and north of Hudson Bay. I believe that the Science, English and to a certain extent the Latin that I am now studying in high school will help me in this object. I intend to specialize in the sciences in college and to join some expedition when I leave college. I believe that any training that I get by hiking in the spring or farm work in the summer or any work in the woods which tends to devel-

op resourcefulness and self-reliance is of inestimable value
in the work I intend to pursue. I have no desire absolutely
to be a millionaire or a rich man but I do intend to do something toward the scientific interests of the world.

He may never have become an explorer, but these ambi-
tions, fostered by his father's love for the natural world and
confirmed by the life of Theodore Roosevelt, bore
remarkable results. Hemingway's interests in natural history, instilled in Oak Park and fleshed out at Walloon Lake,
were with him all his life. He studied the habits of fighting
bulls, African predators, Gulf Stream marlin, and the most
dangerous game, his fellow man. He never got to college
to study science, but he never stopped learning about it,
either. Before he died he spoke reasonably fluent French
and Spanish, could make himself understood in Italian and
German, and had a smattering of Swahili. All that he
absorbed in the Hemingway home and its surrounds
would stand him in good stead, but nothing he took away
with him was more important than his life-long belief in
self-reliance and resourcefulness—Oak Park virtues that
never went out of fashion.

Between the turn of the century and the end of World
War One, Oak Park worked very hard at the moral and
cultural education of its young. Above all it taught its sons
that, whatever the game, winning was important. The
Strenuous Life was the Village code and the high school
athlete's model. Wherever one listened in Oak Park—
church, civic clubs, or the newspaper—he was told that
physical, mental, and moral condition correlated: better
body, better grades, better boy. For the football team of
Hemingway's youth that came to mean unbeaten seasons;
a single loss was almost unbearable. Young Hemingway,
who was a slow-footed athlete, became a life-long, fierce

competitor. Twice he ran the high school cross-country race. Twice he finished last. But, he always finished. Whatever he did in life—fishing, hiking, hunting, writing, loving, learning—it was a competitive venture, a challenge match to be won or lost. So, too, do many of his fictional characters behave as well. The competitive trait runs deep in the American vein, one that we admire still, a trait that Hemingway learned by heart in the heart of the country.

The Village, as Oak Park called itself, also changed during his growing up. What began as a haven from which to escape the threat of Chicago fires and Chicago vice, was no longer isolated from the temptations of the Loop. Five different trolley lines connected husbands to their downtown jobs, wives to Marshall Fields and the Art Institute, and teenage boys to whatever teenage boys found most alluring. Cows that once grazed in the vacant Oak Park lots disappeared along with the lots, which were filling up with houses. The area south of the tracks was being developed by people like Ernest's Uncle, George Hemingway, whose name can still be found carved into his office building. And, lord help us, apartment units with flat roofs were being built for young people who could not afford houses of their own. Some old-timers were positive that such apartments would be the doom of the village. If the developers didn't ruin the place, Hollywood movies were doing their best to undermine the moral fabric of the young people. The Censorship Committee worked over time to keep the youth of Oak Park innocent, but of course it was an impossible task. Their stringent movie code kept the most pernicious Hollywood influence just outside the Village limits but those boundaries were becoming less and less effective. On a sweltering July day, an Oak Parker could not buy a cold beer within the village limits. But hot movies and cold beer were only a nickel trolley ride away.

Or if you could not spare the nickel, you could walk across the avenue into Cicero where all manner of forbidden activity was possible. But not in Oak Park. Not yet. At least not in public.

The last time he actually lived in the Village was the spring of 1919 when he limped about, sporting his war-wounded leg like a badge of honor and making guest appearances at the high school and local churches to tell how the Great War had been won. As Marcelline and the family could not help noticing, Ernest returned from the war grown-up, changed, different. A trench mortar shell leaving him without a knee cap and his companions dead has a way adding years on a young man's age. Hemingway returned from the war to find the Village blacksmith dead, and the horses that clopped down the streets of his youth replaced by automobiles; the Village was electrified and up to date, very modern. No matter how conservative their national Republican politics might be, Oak Parkers were always progressive. Their streets were paved and lighted when parts of Chicago were still muddy; their water system was the most sanitary possible; the hospital, the library, and the high-school were all of premier quality. Of course the older generation, as usual, was certain that the Village was on its way to perdition, and there were signs of the times to support their view. Young girls, like Marcelline, were bobbing their long hair short as sin, raising their ankle length skirts almost to the knee, and listening to phonograph music that shocked their parents. By 1919 young men and women could, at certain country clubs, actually dance to the new jazz. The girls were wearing lipstick and some were smoking cigarettes in public. The times, as Bob Dylan would tell a much later generation of parents, were changing, even in Oak Park.

When he left town at the end of March, 1919 , no one

but his family and a few friends noticed his departure. *Oak Leaves*, which in those days kept pretty close track of all Village arrivals and departures, did not mention his name when Ernest drove out of town. He never again lived in Oak Park, but he took the Village with him to the four corners of the world. By mid-century the story was being told that Ernest hated Oak Park, but there is little evidence in this memoir or any other to support the charge. "I gave Oak Park a miss," he once said, using the metaphor of trap shooting. No other important American author has been so kind to his home town. Whatever else Ernest Hemingway became when he left home, he remained a loyal and native son who never fouled the nest. Look past his modernist facade and you will find virtues and standards straight from the Village. Without drawing wider conclusions, Marcelline's memoir takes us back to those formative years, the period historians now call the Age of Innocence. As an important afterward, you will find the letters between sister and brother printed together for the first time. Read them aloud to get their full flavor. Hear two voices speak across the century, telling us how things were when a native son and author was growing up. Read carefully and you will find, beneath the surface of this narrative, the resources upon which Hemingway drew to reconfigure American fiction for all time.

MICHAEL REYNOLDS

Foreword

by

EDWARD WEEKS

IN THE AUTUMN of 1940, shortly after the publication of *For Whom the Bell Tolls*, I was on a lecture tour in the Middle West; and at Oak Park, Illinois, where I was to speak about the importance of some of the new books, I gave first place to the Hemingway novel. I was unaware of the fact that this was the novelist's birthplace, and at the conclusion of my talk it was something of a surprise when the chairman introduced me to Mrs. Hemingway, Ernest's mother, a tall, white-haired, imposing figure. Mrs. Hemingway said that she was glad to hear that I was such an admirer of her son's work, but as we talked it was not quite clear to me whether or not she had read his latest book.

Some years later when I was speaking at the Town Hall in Detroit I had an agreeable meeting with Hemingway's older sister, Marcelline Hemingway Sanford; I sat beside her at the luncheon which followed, and it was there that I got her talking about her parents and their family life at Walloon Lake, Michigan, where they had their summer cottage, and about Oak Park, where she and Ernest had graduated from high school in the same class. Her description of her doctor father, rugged, dark-haired, and so fond of hunting and fishing, and of her talented mother, whose first love was music, and of the independent and spirited upbringing which they had given to their six children was so lively and colorful that I said she ought to make a record of such things. She replied that if she did, it would be for the sake of her children and grandchildren, and that it would be a family chronicle about her parents and grandparents and all the children, not in any sense an exploitation of her famous brother. "That's the last thing Ernie would want me to do."

This was in 1955. The early chapters began to flow in to us a year later, and they continued coming until by 1961 we had in hand a book of substantially the present dimensions. What Mrs. Sanford has given us is essentially the picture of a happy family whose parents were strong-willed, highly opinionated, and each gifted in his own right; a chronicle of the years of innocence. Because they were older and because of their mother's planning, Marcelline and Ernest shared in a rather special life until their graduation from high school. For years she was the stronger and taller of the two; she watched him grow, helped him with his music, read the same books, and wrote for the same high school papers. Her intimate observation of her whole family tells us things which I believe readers and critics alike will be curious to know.

Illustrations

At the Hemingways

A FAMILY PORTRAIT

I

Oak Park

WHENEVER I looked out of the big front window of Grandfather Hall's house on North Oak Park Avenue through the Nottingham lace curtains, I could see the white clapboard home of Grandfather Hemingway directly across the street. We were Number 439 and they were Number 444. The families were that close in space and affection.

Oak Park, in 1900, was a small, well-to-do suburb ten miles west of Chicago, and here until I was seven my mother and father, Ernest, Ursula, Madelaine (called Sunny) and I lived with our grandfather in a three-story Victorian house. Grandfather Ernest Hall, after whom my brother was named, had built it in the 1880's when turrets were in style — and of course our house had one too. Within the little tower was a circular room, a part of the attic, where my young doctor-father kept his medical specimens on high shelves out of the reach of us children. There were six bedrooms and a bath on the second floor, and partway down the front stairs, off a little landing, was my father's consulting office. It was to the office that Ernest and I were called for punishment when we misbehaved. The parlor on the first floor was a large room with a bay window facing the street, and a shiny brown tile fireplace with carved golden oak pillars supporting the mantel, above which hung a big mirror. On the floor was a red and pink flowered Brussels carpet. Behind the parlor heavy folding doors, which slid into the wall, opened into the dining room, and behind that was the rather dark kitchen, with its huge and well-blacked coal stove from which tantalizing odors emerged.

To the north of the kitchen on the main floor was a small library, where my Grandfather Hall and our Great-uncle Tyley Hancock, Grandmother's brother, smoked their cigars and pipes after dinner every evening. I used to crack open the door and whiff the fragrance, but when they saw me, I was told to shut it quickly, lest the odor of tobacco reach into the parlor. It wasn't my mother who minded, but my father did not smoke, and though he would not criticize his father-in-law, he disapproved of tobacco in all forms and was frank about it.

At the rear of the house behind bushes of flowering pink weigela stood the old outhouse, screened by latticework from the view of the street and used only for emergencies when our single bathroom was overcrowded.

Our Grandfather Hall, who was to figure so impressively in our youth, we called Abba from the phrase in the Bible, meaning "Father." Abba had the first electricity installed in any house in Oak Park, and the contract he made with the electric company was for the flat sum of twenty dollars a year, no matter how much electricity we used. But with the few dim bulbs of that time, often only one to a room, the company probably made money. Grandfather also owned one of the first telephones in town. The black instrument was set high on a golden oak stand on the wall of the library, and we children would have to get up on tiptoe to turn the black metal crank at its side to call central.

Each morning Abba went downtown to see about his investments. Long before I can remember, he had retired from the firm of Randall, Hall and Company, wholesale cutlery, which he and his brother-in-law, William Randall, had established in Chicago, with branch offices in New York, in Manchester, England, and in Germany. In his retirement, he was interested in the stock market, and once, for a matter of a few hours, Mother told us, Abba had something called "a corner in wheat" and was a potential millionaire. But in a short time he had lost it all and, disappointed, returned to his more modest investments.

Grandfather Hall, who had been born and educated in London, was in appearance a typical English gentleman. His pink cheeks, blue eyes, thick black eyebrows contrasted with his thinning white hair and fluffy white muttonchop whiskers. He always wore dark clothes, of excellent material but extremely loose fit. He said he could not bear to have his clothes touch his skin, so he bought suits, collars, and overcoats much too large lest he feel bound in any way. I always remember Abba wearing immaculate gray gloves and a black derby or a high top hat, and I can see him walking along the street, with his little white woolly Yorkshire terrier, named Tassle, by his side.

Both Ernest and I were devoted to Tassle. He looked like the frayed end of a rope, his hair in his eyes, his coat curly, fluffy and creamy white when he was clean, matted and yellow-gray when he needed a bath or had been rolling in the coal bin. He slept in Abba's room at night, and it was Abba who gave him his Saturday bath in the laundry tub in the basement. We were never allowed to attend this ceremony, but we often stood at the top of the cellar stairs, listening to Tassle's moans and yelps as he underwent the tortures of yellow soap and water. After the bath, Abba would dry Tassle and carry him up the stairs wrapped in one of his worn brown bathrobes; the dog would be placed on the register to dry, with only his shining black eyes peeking out of the bathrobe. Those big floor registers were wonderful things! The comfort of standing over a register when you came in from the cold, and the joy to a little girl of having the hot air make her skirts fly out around her like a ballet costume, are things few children of this day can fully appreciate.

Abba always had his breakfast late, after the family meal was over. When we heard his bedroom door open, Ernest and I would run to the foot of the staircase to wait for him as he walked down with his leisurely tread, about nine o'clock. At breakfast he wore his neatly belted brown wool dressing gown over his white shirt, topped with a stiff white collar and black bow tie. In his brown leather slippers he walked with his feet turned slightly outward, like a very gentle duck. "Only red Indians walk with their toes pointed straight ahead," Grandfather once said.

We would take hold of his hands and walk with him to the dining room, where he sat alone at the head of the table. The cook would bring in his crisp bacon, his toast on an open toast rack, and the white stoneware jar of Dundee orange marmalade, and there he would sit reading the paper and drinking leisurely cups of coffee.

If we were very quiet and didn't bother him until he got through with the financial pages, he would give us snips of bacon. This was the time Abba would tell Ernest and me stories about a pack of little dogs who had a series of exciting adventures. He would add to this tale endlessly. Other times he told us about the old days in Chicago, when he rode on the horsecars, or of his early life on the farm in Iowa, which he hated. Once he told us about meeting Charles Dickens on some of his walks about London, years before.

Grandfather's parents, Charles and Mary Miller Hall, had left London and sailed to the United States in 1855, along with their daughter and son-in-law, the William Randalls, and their other children. The Randalls bought a large sheep and cattle farm in Dyersville, Iowa, and it was here that the Halls' three sons had their first taste of farm work. Of the boys, it was Ernest who most disliked his chores, and one day when he was seventeen, after many long, hot hours of plowing, his resentment was such that instead of watering the team, as he had been told to do, he angrily drove the horses into the river, where the swift current caught them and they were drowned. Abba ran away from home, not meaning to return until he had saved enough money to pay for the team. He had reached Louisiana and was helping a contractor build slave quarters on a plantation when he learned that war had been declared between the North and South. Then he knew he must get back to Iowa as quickly as possible, and traveling by night, sleeping in haystacks or barns during the day, he finally made his way home, where he was welcomed and forgiven. Soon thereafter he enlisted in an Iowa regiment in which he served throughout the four years of the Civil War. To the end of his life, he carried a bullet in his body. In later years, when he was offered a pension by the United States Government, he firmly refused it, saying proudly, "I gave my services to my adopted country. I did not sell them."

After he returned from the Civil War, Ernest Hall married Caroline Hancock, who like himself had been born in England. She was of Welsh and English parentage. She had come to Dyersville with her widowed father, Captain Alexander Hancock, a retired sea captain, her younger sister Annie, and small brother Tyley. After the death of his wife, Caroline Sydes, Captain Hancock had disposed of his home at Clifton Downs, near Liverpool, left England,

and taken his three children around the world on his cargo ship, the barkentine *Elizabeth*, but before the long voyage was over it was obvious to him that this was no life for his young family. He decided to sell his ship and settle in Australia, but neither he nor his children were happy there, and he was soon persuaded by friends from his own village in England to join them in Iowa.

The Hancocks came by ship from Australia to the Isthmus of Panama, crossed the Isthmus partly on foot, then took passage to New York, and finally entrained for Dyersville in 1854.

All over Grandfather Hall's house there were reminders of our grandmother, who had died four years before I was born. A large gold-framed portrait of her, her hair piled high on her head with curly bangs over her forehead, hung on the north wall of the parlor. Her sheet music, with her name written in her neat, spidery handwriting, stood on the fretwork music rack of the square piano. A small mahogany rocking chair she used to sit in stood in the corner of the living room. Her perky little velvet bonnets, some trimmed with bows and others with curled ostrich feathers, were nestled in paper boxes in my mother's closet, and Grandmother's hoop skirt, its red cotton tapes connecting the five collapsible hoops to the tiny waistband, was also in that closet. It was this miniature hoop skirt that made me realize how very small Grandmother had been — just four feet, eleven inches. She was only forty-nine when she died of cancer.

Grandmother Hall's melodeon stood against the wall in the library, and sometimes Mother would sit down and play it for us. She told us that this was her "little mother's" most treasured possession. Captain Hancock had ordered it from Chicago, and there was great excitement in Dyersville when the wooden crate arrived and was finally opened. It was the first organ in town. On Sundays it was transported to church, where Caroline played for services. She and her melodeon went to every party in town. When she married Ernest Hall it accompanied her to their first home in Chicago and was one of the few things saved from the flames at the time of the Chicago fire. It still remains in the possession of one of our family.

Grandmother Hall was unreal to us, almost like a character out of a book. But her younger brother, Benjamin Tyley Hancock, was close at hand and a beloved member of our household for many years. Grand-uncle Tyley was a traveling salesman for Miller Hall and Sons, the factory owned by Grandfather Hall's brother, Uncle Miller, from whom my brother Ernest received his middle name. Uncle Tyley sold a stylish line of brass and iron beds to homes and hotels all over the Middle West. His twinkling blue eyes, squeezed up at the corners, showed he was smiling even though his sweeping mustache nearly covered his grinning mouth. We children looked forward to his return from every trip. He would bring delightful surprises, an Indian doll, a pair of slippers, or a carved animal — and himself; he was such fun. Uncle always greeted Ernie, Ursula or me with a big hug, a firm kiss, and "How's my little darling today? Did you miss me?" Uncle's homecomings brought excitement to our house. As soon as he removed his coat Ernest and I would be struggling to get on his lap, and Uncle would be off on the story of his adventures since he had last seen us. He never talked down to us. He treated us as though we were adults.

Sometimes Uncle took us with him to a special treat in Chicago. Once when I was about six, Uncle took me to the Boston Oyster House all alone, and seated me as he would have seated an older lady guest. That was my first taste of raw oysters, but because Uncle enjoyed them, I too liked the flavor, slippery as the oysters felt. Another time Ernest and I were escorted downtown to Henrici's Restaurant, where we had wonderful red snapper, and afterward Uncle Tyley let us stop to pick out our choices of the iced and nut-filled *Kohlsaat* coffee cakes in that famous bakery's windows.

Uncle Tyley was a great storyteller. His adventures on his father's ship made a terrific impression on our childish imaginations; especially the time he was left behind because he disobeyed Captain Hancock's orders not to leave the ship at a New Zealand dock, and mischievously hid in the center of a huge coil of rope on the wharf. How frightened he had been as he suddenly realized that the ship had left without him.

"But what happened? How did you get back?" we would ask.

Uncle shifted us on his knee and answered calmly, "After he thought I'd learned my lesson not to disobey him, my father turned the ship around and came back for me. But not until some hours later. I can tell you children, I did just what I was told after that, yes sir!"

"Now tell us another story!" Ernie would beg, and often Uncle would oblige with a tale of the lumber camps up north.

One story Uncle told us has always stayed in my mind. We were talking about birds, and Daddy was planning a hunting trip down at Uncle Frank Hines's farm near Albion, Illinois.

"Speaking of birds," Uncle Tyley said, "did you ever see so many of them at once that they darkened the sky? I did. They were passenger pigeons. I remember out in Iowa when I was a boy how the pigeons went over. We all got out with shotguns and pulled the triggers as fast as we could load. Pigeons came over by the thousands. When they had gone we filled barrels and hogsheads with the dead birds. Some of the barrels were shipped to the city. We ate what we could and the rest we just threw away or buried. Nobody ever ate anything but the breasts. The rest of the birds were fed to the hogs."

Daddy couldn't stand it when Uncle got to this part of the story. Even though he had heard the tale before, he still became indignant at the thought of that awful waste of game.

"And to think they are extinct now," Daddy said. "It's wicked!"

Our first bedroom in Abba Hall's home was the nursery, where Ernest and I slept in our twin white cribs. Our beds had high spindle sides that could be let down, and I remember that one side of my bed was left lowered because I was older, but Ernest's crib sides were both at the top.

Ernest must have been two or three years old when he began naming himself for various animals. I remember at one time he did not answer us or our nurse unless we called him "Bobby-the-squirrel." We had all just gotten used to saying Bobby instead of Ernest when one day he turned on me in great anger and said:

"*Not* Bobby. My new name Carlo-gleaming-fiery-eyes coming-through-the-dark." He had taken the name and personality of one of the characters Abba had told us about in his stories about little dogs. Ernest had a small black woolly dog with a red cloth tongue and shiny shoebutton eyes which he called Carlo. In his own mind, apparently, he and his toy dog were brothers. We called Ernest Carlo after that until he gave himself a new name the next week.

Abba Hall loved Ernest very much. He was proud that Ernest was named for him. When Ernest was five, his vivid imaginative stories of things he had done or would do were so real to him that less understanding parents than ours might have punished him for telling lies. One day, after a particularly big exaggeration by Ernest — about how he had caught a runaway horse all by himself — Grandfather Hall turned to my mother and said, in his soft gentle way:

"Chumpy dear, this boy is going to be heard from someday. If he uses his imagination for good purposes, he'll be famous, but if he starts the wrong way, with all his energy, he'll end in jail, and it's up to you which way he goes."

My mother noted those words and often quoted them to my father in afteryears. I don't think she was reassured about which direction her older son was going until after he was married and started on his newspaper career.

We used to go for walks with our Grandfather Hall, and I remember that he would carry lumps of sugar in his pocket or sometimes an apple in a paper bag which he would feed to any horse he might see standing on the street. Abba's love for animals was very real. On one occasion he saw a junkman brutally beating his skinny old nag as it stood helplessly hitched to the junk cart. Grandfather was incensed, and he insisted that the man stop.

"It's none of your damn business!" the man shouted. "I'll beat him if I want. He's my horse."

"How much will you take for that horse?" asked Ernest Hall, exerting all his self-control.

The junkman named a figure that seemed extraordinarily high to my grandfather, but he never hesitated. "I'll pay it," he said.

"Let's see the color of your money," said the junkman.

Abba got out his checkbook, but the man would have none of it. "I'll write the check and cash it at the bank.

You come along with me." And they went to the bank, where Grandfather paid off the man and the horse was his.

Back on the street the junkman unharnessed the nag and started pushing his cart away. Grandfather Hall then led the old veteran to a livery stable and there made arrangements for the horse to be taken to a farm to the west of Oak Park. There the old animal was put out to graze, and there it stayed until it died, getting fatter by the month while Grandfather paid for its board. Mother thought that he was making up to this horse for the death of the pair he had let drown in his youth.

Every winter Abba Hall went to California, where he stayed at the Abbottsford Inn in Los Angeles. He often visited with his lawyer son, Leicester, who lived in Bishop, Inyo County, where Uncle Les, a graduate of Amherst, was county attorney. Letters from Abba came to us frequently, and though we were too young to read, Ernest and I loved receiving them. Uncle Leicester Hall had been in the Klondike in the Alaska gold rush, and my mother wrote down my three-year-old childish reaction to this news. Sunday school was new to me at that same time, and the family was most amused, Mother noted, when small Marcelline sang loudly, while thumping on the parlor organ:

Jesus is in Heaven, Uncle Leicester's in the Klondike,
Jesus is in Heaven, Uncle Leicester's in the Klondike —

meanwhile pumping hard on the pedals and playing any keys she could reach.

Each spring when Abba came back from California, there was great excitement. He always brought us presents.

Sometimes it was a Mexican hat with bobbing cotton ball fringe around the brim or a fan or a Mexican basket. Sometimes he brought us candy made of orange peel, and once Ernest was given a Spanish costume with a short jacket and long tight trousers, but he outgrew it almost before he had time to wear it, and it was added to the family costume trunk.

My father became the head of the house during my Grandfather Hall's absence, but he always seemed delighted to have Abba return home to resume his leadership of family prayers, saying the blessing at the table, and giving household orders. Everyone we knew said grace at the table before meals. Though sometimes different prayers were said, the grace used most often at our house was: "For what we are about to receive, may the Lord make us truly thankful, for Jesus' sake, Amen."

Sometimes when we were hungry we said it very fast. In later years Ernest jokingly used to say it quickly from just the sounds and rhythm. It turned out to be: "Mrump mi raw, m'ree ma m'raw, m'raw, m'raw amen." But that was never a joke to my mother and father. If they heard this short cut going on, we had to start right over again, bow our heads, close our eyes, and say it correctly before we could touch our food.

Abba was a sincerely religious man. God was a person he knew intimately. On Sundays he attended the Grace Episcopal Church, and almost every day we had family prayers. I remember Abba kneeling at the center table in the parlor. The table had light-colored fluted legs with a scroll design. On its shiny varnished top my grandfather opened a small thick book, with gold edges on the leaves, called *Daily Strength for Daily Needs*. He read a passage out of this brown-leather-covered volume every morning, while the family and servants sat in dining room chairs 'around him. The cook came in from the kitchen and the nurse-girl left her bedmaking and came downstairs to join us. This simple service was always directly after breakfast. My father was of course excused if he had to leave early on his medical calls.

My father and mother and each of us children, as well as Uncle Tyley, sat quietly listening while Abba led us in worship. After Abba had read the lesson for the day, we would all rise, turn, and kneel down on the carpet in front of our chairs, resting our elbows on the black leather seats, while Abba knelt at the center table. But instead of closing his eyes or bowing his head as the rest of us did, he raised his head, his eyes upward, as though he was talking to God, right above him. I can still see Abba's shiny pink and white head, his white muttonchop whiskers and the white fringe of his neatly center-parted hair, his beaming smile and those lovely deep blue eyes looking up to God as he prayed. I liked to watch Abba through my fingers, because he seemed so surely to be talking right to his friend God.

There was a great affection between my parents and Grandfather Hall. Abba admired my father's scientific and medical abilities, his prowess in hunting and fishing, his cheeriness with patients, his outgoing manner and many friends. Grandfather Hall called him "dear boy," and in talking about him to others he often said, "the blessed doctor." My mother's close, congenial friendship with her father and with her Uncle Tyley Hancock made it a very happy and loving household. My grandfather could do no wrong in Mother's eyes. Father and daughter had their love of music and the theater, of literature, and religion in common. They had a similar sense of humor and a certain British deliberateness and neatness that was quite different from my father's quick ways, casual lack of orderliness in his care of his possessions, and his usually sober and serious point of view. But Daddy glowed under Grandfather Hall's affectionate approval. The Hall family jokes and lighthearted conversation and the good-natured teasing at table were new experiences to him, and he enjoyed them very much. It was his wish as much as my mother's to name their first son for Ernest Hall.

2

My Father, Dr. Hemingway

I ALWAYS felt especially close to my father, for he personally brought me into the world on January 15, 1898. From the time I was three I can remember my parents retelling me the story on my birthday.

"It was a cold, snowy day," Daddy would begin, "and I was several miles away in my office."

Then Mother would add: "It was the worst snowstorm of the winter and I sent Sophie on the Chicago Avenue streetcar to get your father and to tell him to hurry back quickly. I knew you were going to be born very soon. We didn't have a telephone then."

"I sent Sophie right back to your mother," broke in Daddy, "while I picked up Dr. Lewis, who was to take care of you and Mama."

Daddy had promised Mother that she would feel no pain, so he administered chloroform to her in her bedroom while Dr. Lewis readied himself for the delivery. But before it was completed Dr. Lewis had a sudden heart attack and lost consciousness. My young father, tense enough with worry over his wife, had to lift the old doctor out of the way and administer first aid to him, keep the necessary anesthesia going for my mother, and then perform a high forceps delivery. There was no nurse present, only Sophie singing at the top of her voice in the kitchen so as not to hear anything that was happening on the second floor. The cumulative effect of this repeated tale gave me a sympathetic feeling for my mother, who was so frightened of being left alone or in pain, for poor lovable old Dr. Lewis, who was sick, and for my father, who had performed under such tense circumstances.

"Marshmallow," Daddy would say as he gave me a whiskery birthday kiss, "nobody's known you any longer than I have. I gave you the spank that made you breathe your first breath, and you've been makin' a big noise ever since, haven't you?" and Daddy would give me a pretend spank, one for each year of my age, and one to grow on. We both understood that these were love pats.

Daddy's father, Anson Tyler Hemingway, was born in Plymouth, Connecticut, but in his childhood he and his parents came by train to Chicago, where his father (my great-grandfather) Allen Hemingway as a representative of Seth Thomas opened the first wholesale clock business in that area in 1852. A. T. Hemingway was a serious man, deeply religious and rather formal in manner. He was a friend and close associate of Dwight L. Moody, the evangelist; he was employed as a general secretary of the Y.M.C.A.; and with his wife and six children, he lived very modestly in a small one-story house, which was all his salary could afford. His four sons and two daughters were brought up in the stern religious discipline of that day, and the discipline and near poverty both had a lifelong effect upon my father. When his salary became plainly inadequate for the education of his children, Grandfather Hemingway resigned from the Y.M.C.A. and set out to establish a real estate firm under his own name in Oak Park; it prospered, and at last he was able to move away the little house they had outgrown and to erect on the same site the spacious white clapboard house which I used to gaze at as a child.

Grandfather Hemingway was rather fastidious about his dress; I remember his manicured fingernails, gray beard, and his dainty way of holding his fork or knife at the table. Grandfather was rather proud of his descent from Jacob Hemingway, who had fought in the Revolution. He told Ernest and me that the first Hemingway in America was named Ralph, and that he came from England in 1634 and settled in Duxbury, Massachusetts. He also told us the family legend that the first student at Yale was a Hemingway.

The ancestors of Grandmother Adelaide Edmonds Hemingway also went back to the Revolution. John Plum, from whom she was descended, received a grant of land from the government and a veteran's pension after the colonies were free. He moved West, and his Edmonds descendants settled on a farm along the Rock River in Illinois, where Adelaide Edmonds was born. Her father, John Wesley Edmonds, was named for John Plum as well as for the founder of Methodism.

Grandmother was a pretty girl with dark hair and flashing brown eyes. She was one of a large family of children on the Edmonds farm, and as was natural a hundred years ago, the boys had first chance at an education. But Adelaide and one of her sisters, Cordelia, saved enough to enter Wheaton College, Illinois. Twice she had to drop out of college and teach school to earn money for her education. It took her nearly six years to get her degree.

So many students had deserted this small Congregational institution during the Civil War that Adelaide and Cordelia Edmonds were the only two left in their graduating class. A clipping in a family record reminds me that Adelaide gave the Valedictory Address and the Class Poem, and her sister gave the Welcome and the Class Prophecy. In their last year, Anson T. Hemingway, recently discharged from the Army, where he had served as a lieutenant in charge of colored troops, entered the freshman class at Wheaton. Though he was a couple of years younger than Adelaide, his maturity, his beard and his experience in the Army made him feel quite ready for marriage to his charming fellow student.

In college Grandmother Hemingway had specialized in botany and astronomy. She taught her son, my father Clarence Edmonds Hemingway, and her other children the names of trees and plants and showed my father the stars when he was a very small child.

When I was less than five I remember Grandmother holding me on her lap and showing me a flower she had taken from a bowl on her dining room table. "Do you see this flower?" she said.

"Of course I do, Grandmother," I answered.

"But do you *really* see it?" Grandmother insisted. "I want to show you how wonderfully it is made."

Starting at the base of the blossom, Grandmother pointed out the green cuplike section which she named for me — the calyx. Then she showed me the corolla, stamens, the pointed pistil, amid the yellow pollen. I learned these names, calyx, corolla, stamens and pistil, like rhythmic song. Suddenly the flower was a whole new wonderful creation to my childish eyes. Grandmother explained the reason for the golden pollen. She told me how the bees helped to create new plants and flowers by carrying it on their feet as they visited the blossoms of other similar plants. She explained that God had given the bees a special sense so that they never carried the pollen of one variety of plant to a dissimilar one, but always kept to plants of a like variety or to tree blossoms of the same kind when they were on their honey-collecting rounds.

Grandmother was by way of being an astronomer too. She had studied all the books available to her on the subject of the stars and planets, and by her stories she made the heavens come alive for us. It was no wonder that my father should have a tremendous love of nature.

Even during her overworked days in the crowded little house, Grandmother was never too busy to talk with her children about the world of ideas — the things that really mattered. She continued to be a confidant of her sons and daughters in their adult years and was a warm friend of her grandchildren.

Later, after the lean years when she had had to run the household on such a narrow margin, Grandmother Hemingway naturally enjoyed the latitude that was hers in the big new house. But she had too much common sense ever to lose her perspective. When one of her neighbors protested that the Hemingways' new lawn was being ruined by her four sons, who were playing ball on it, Adelaide Hemingway's remark was characteristic: "I don't mind a bit," she said. "You see, I am raising boys, not grass."

As a boy Daddy often spent his free hours after school delving into old Indian mounds along the Des Plaines River. He hunted for arrowheads, clay bowls, spear heads and other remnants of Indian life for his growing collection of Indian artifacts. He found some stone ax heads, and he had a remarkable collection of flints which he showed to us when we were children. He could make fire with the flints as the Indians had done.

Though my father was needed to help his mother and his older sister Nettie at home, he still found time to look for many of the wild plants both edible and medicinal which he pointed out to us years later when he took us on hikes along the river. His great joy in the few week ends of summer vacation when he was not needed to help at home was to take his three younger brothers and drive with them through the countryside in a wagon hitched behind Nellie, the old family horse. Ed, my father, pretended that he and his brothers were members of a mythical tribe of Indians, whom he christened the Skowhegans. Ed was big chief and his brothers, George, Will and Alfred Tyler, had other names appropriate to the tribe. In later years, they used to tease their little sister Grace by telling her that they had Indian blood in them — "Skowhegan blood." The youngsters traveled slowly, with the ancient horse making no more than five or six miles a day in her leisurely way. Nellie stopped often to crop grass, and nothing the boys could do would induce her to hurry. But even at this slow pace the four young Hemingways felt they were entering a life of adventure with a capital A. Young Ed and his brothers slept in haystacks and cooked their own food over open campfires, roasting the meat Grandmother had packed for them on green sticks over the blaze.

For these trips he devised a bent sheet iron reflector with which he baked an appetizing johnnycake. The boys made applesauce from green apples they picked along the country roads, and they cooked the sauce in a tin pail hung by its handle on a green limb across two upright sticks that were stuck into the ground.

In telling these tales my father once admitted to us in a smiling but somewhat shamefaced way that one day he and his brothers caught a farmer's red cow and milked it without permission. Then, lest we children consider this the right thing to do, Daddy always hastened to add that in later years he took care of that same farmer's children when they were sick, and that he did not charge the family for his services; so in his own mind he had more than paid back what he owed for the cow's milk he had appropriated.

Father's conscientious desire to do what was right and to serve where he was needed made it impossible for him to neglect home duties, just as later it was impossible for him to turn down anyone who needed him professionally no matter how tired he was. From the time he was a small boy, my father's emotions were touched by the need of any wounded bird or animal, and he used to put splints on a wounded creature's leg or wing. Often he would feed a tiny orphaned animal, trying to help it into healthy, independent adult life. When he was very small, he thought he might like to be a doctor for animals, but by the time he was in high school he knew that being a doctor of medicine and a surgeon was the one thing he must do in life. To this end he took all the science courses possible in high school and at Oberlin College he specialized in premedical work.

He attended Rush Medical College in Chicago, later to be known as the College of Medicine of the University of Chicago, and he was helped in his entrance to professional life in Oak Park by his older friend and mentor, Dr. William R. Lewis. It was Dr. Lewis who suggested shortly after Daddy's graduation that he disguise his apparent inexperience by growing a mustache and Vandyke beard. Whiskers and medical knowledge were practically synonymous in the minds of the public at that time.

Before he entered medical school my father had one delightful last fling with adventure while he was still a student at Oberlin. He was invited to go on a geological expedition to the Great Smoky Mountains, then a largely unexplored area of the south. Ed Hemingway wasn't a geologist, but he did know how to cook and that is why the geologists wanted him. The four young men from Oberlin started for North Carolina, their belongings carried in packs on their backs, and with them they took fishing equipment, guns and tents. Until this first official expedition from Oberlin, the Smoky Mountains were well known only to a few mountaineers and to the Cherokee Indians, whose land this had been. The expedition lasted most of that summer, and the stories of my father's experiences were the delight of our childhood. Over and over Daddy told us about the time he was alone in the camp while the three geologists were off on their scientific explorations. Daddy heard a slight rustling and looked up to see a giant mountain lion (or puma) crouching in a tree crotch just over his head. Ed Hemingway pretended he did not see the animal, and gently edging his way to the tent, was able to reach inside, grab his trusty rifle named "Old Ed," and shoot the creature just as it sprang toward him. He told us this tale over and over and always ended with the phrase, "Pretty good, eh?"

Another tale we loved to hear was the one about the surprise dinner Ed Hemingway fixed for his three friends on that same trip. The young men had stayed in the mountains longer than they had first expected to, and their store-bought supplies were running low. They had made a few friends among the shy, clannish mountaineers, but these people had mighty little surplus food to sell. Father was determined to give his companions a good meal that night, and he went out with his gun to find some game for supper. Luckily he roused and killed some partridge and then shot a few squirrels. He was on his way back to camp when he saw bees flying in a straight line toward a hollow tree. Ed Hemingway suspected this meant a store of honey was nearby, but how to get it was the problem. He wet his felt hat, lined it with wet leaves, dampened in a nearby creek, then piled dry grass and small twigs on top of the leaves, lit this dry mass with a match and threw other damp leaves over the top. Holding up his hat full of this burning, smoldering mass from which black smoke poured out, Ed approached the bee tree and thrust the smudge on a branch close to the opening. The device worked. Soon he could see the bees dropping inert, and the combs of wet honey were near enough to the opening so that he could grab a few handfuls and stick the comb in the front of his shirt, which he pulled out from under his belt, like a little bag. With his game bag and gun in one hand and his other hand supporting the sticky mass of honey in his shirt, he told us he ran like hades to get to camp before the bees woke up from their stupor, or before the honey leaked through his shirt front and ran down his legs.

He reached camp in time to surprise his friends. He dressed out the game and cut up the partridge and squirrels into pieces for frying. He made biscuits and baked them in the reflected heat of the bent sheet iron next to the camp-fire. He dipped the meat in corn meal and fried it in bacon drippings. When the game was done he laid the brown pieces aside to keep warm, near the biscuits, and finally he cooked a blackberry pie. His hungry friends ate every bite of the biscuits and meat and then, as the crowning touch, he produced the pie. It was crusty brown on top and dripping with purple juice.

"How in blazes did you ever make a real pie?" they asked.

Ed was smug. "Well," he said, "I picked the blackberries this morning. I got the honey from a bee's nest."

"But how did you make crust that looks like this?" one of the boys asked.

My father always grinned as he told this part of the story.

"Oh, it was easy," he said. "I just rolled out the dough on a log and I used a beer bottle for a rolling pin."

His friends shouted with laughter.

"Imagine our Ed using a beer bottle," they said. "What did you do with the last of the beer?"

"I poured it out on the ground," said my father, primly. "All I wanted to use was the bottle." He was then a teetotaler and remained so all his life.

Thinking back to my childhood, I can see my father with his dark beard and mustache, and his eyes twinkling when he was in good humor. He was tanned and powerful — he had played football at Oberlin — and now he seemed to be always rushing to or from an appointment, out to the back yard to feed his chickens or down to the basement two steps at a time to put coal in the furnace. We knew when he had finished, for he slammed the furnace door, dashed up again to his office, grabbed his black leather medical bag and his hat and tore out the front door, closing it again with a slam, to leap into his buggy, cluck to the horse, slap the reins up and down, and start the horse at a fast trot down the street.

Daddy had little patience with anyone who merely sat down in a room. He understood you had to rest if you were sick, and he believed in getting to bed early at night, but he could never understand how any of his children or even the maids could just sit down in a chair with nothing to do. Many times if he came into the living room from his office in the front of the house and saw any of his children leaning back in a chair looking at a magazine, or just stretched out on a davenport reading or thinking, he would stop abruptly in the doorway saying, "Haven't you children got anything to do? Haven't you any studying or mending? Well, if you have all that done, why don't you

ask your mother what you can do to help her?" Sometimes we didn't want to do anything. We just longed to sit
for a few minutes.

For us children our bedrooms were a haven. It wasn't
possible to read or concentrate in the living room. Mother
had her music room, where she could lock the door and
do her composing or writing. Daddy often did analyses in
the small lavatory built behind his home office, and of
course he was busy with his patients in his office hours or
keeping his records. But when he was free he liked to be
with his family. He always had one or the other of us, and
frequently several children, with him in the back yard or
helping him in the workroom, where he stored and
chopped the wood for the fireplace. He wanted his youngsters with him even in the basement, where he showed us
how to can fruit or how to mold bullets or make candles
in an old candle frame. He liked physical activity and almost resented anyone's taking time for resting or for
purely mental occupations. It was hard for him to understand how we could be busy unless we were moving about
This love for physical activity was one of my father's
most charming attributes. He was always ready to go
somewhere and do something. "He's got a self-starter," he
once remarked in describing a family friend, but the phrase
applied even more to my father.

As we grew up, Daddy tended to avoid decisions by
automatically saying "No" whenever we suddenly asked
him for permission to go somewhere or do something. We
learned to work up to these questions gradually. By presenting a project first to Mother, and getting her to mention it casually to Daddy a day or so ahead of time for his
decision, we had prepared the doctor to say "Yes" easily
instead of letting him take refuge in an abrupt "No,"
which he almost always did when he was taken by surprise.

When I was in high school I was often asked by the younger children to intercede for them.

"Please, Mazween, make Daddy" (or Mother) "let us go!" I heard that a thousand times. Often I could help them by talking to my parents.

In Daddy's office were many nonmedical things he valued highly and often showed to us. In his cupboards he had collections he had worked on for years. One was his collection of ancient coins; another his stamps, which included some rare issues of the early Colonial period and sheets of valuable uncanceled stamps, which he told us might one day help to put us through college; and another was his collection of Indian arrowheads, flints and other Indian artifacts he had found along the Des Plaines River where the Pottawatomie tribes had once lived. He also had a box of beautifully beaded moccasins, a bowie knife in its case, and articles of decorated deerskin and baskets worked in quills and sweet grass. Many of these had come from the Dakotas, where the twin sisters of my Aunt Mary (Uncle Will Hemingway's wife) taught in an Indian mission school.

One special item he showed to us meant more to our father than any of these relics of an older time. This was a pair of shiny steel forceps my father had invented himself. They were called laminectomy forceps, and we were told they were the first of their kind.

Not too many years before he first showed them to us, young Dr. Hemingway, twenty-three years old, had sat in the audience of seniors at the June, 1894, Rush Medical College graduation. Dr. Nicholas Senn of the faculty was addressing the graduates upon "The Progress and Needs of Medicine." After he had mentioned improvements that had taken place while these young men were studying, he touched on the many continuing needs of the profession.

One of those he singled out was the lack of adequate surgical tools which he felt must be invented to make more delicate spinal surgery possible.

"We can't go on with this crude hammer and chisel business much longer," Dr. Senn told the young graduates. "Maybe one of you men sitting here will be the person to invent an instrument to replace this primitive technique. We must have new and better surgical instruments. We must have better anesthetics."

Somehow Dr. Senn's phrase about the hammer and chisel stuck in young Dr. Hemingway's mind. He had had some experience with crude instruments during his training, and now as he thought about the matter he told two other people of his own longing to invent such a needed instrument. One was his mother, Adelaide Edmonds Hemingway, and the other was Grace Hall, the girl who lived across the street. Young Dr. Hemingway was seeing her frequently while he assisted in the care of her mother. One day when he was sitting on a grassy bank beside the Des Plaines River suddenly a design for the spinal forceps flashed into his mind. Taking a pencil and an old envelope out of his pocket, he sketched the outline of what were to be the laminectomy forceps. He presented his design to Sharp and Smith, the instrument makers in Chicago, who were immediately interested in the possibilities of this new instrument, shaped somewhat like a pair of stork scissors with a hinged cutting surface on the lower part of the beak.

Using his sketch, they made up a model of the forceps, and my father tried them and slightly modified his design. Sharp and Smith began manufacturing the laminectomy forceps just as young Dr. Hemingway designed them, and the Rush Medical School faculty were delighted with them. Though the instrument company suggested that my father patent his design, he indignantly refused to do so in the belief that anything that was for the good of humanity should be available to all. Similarly he later refused to patent various medicines he originated, including a most efficacious cough syrup with pineapple as its base.

My father's desire to help was expressed in many ways. He taught nature lore to boys' clubs. He had a Sunday school class for young men at the Third Congregational Church. He did a great deal of charitable medical work in Oak Park and surrounding communities of the Chicago area. He not only took care of his parents and other relatives, including some of his wife's relatives, without charge, but he sent no bills to many of his patients who were in strained financial circumstances. For years and years he took care of two widows and their children, in the Forest Park area, each of whom used to do laundry for our family in return for his kindness to them. He did plastic surgery operations on several babies born with facial deformities. I remember one time he constructed a nose for a baby born without one, when the family was too poor to afford an operation. Another time he made a chin for a new baby and fixed its protruding ears.

He gave his services to Hepzibah Home, an Oak Park orphanage, where he and other local doctors took turns taking care of the children without fee. My father took his month of assigned time at the home very seriously. He dropped in daily to see the children and often had his pockets full of peppermints or suckers or balloons for the little orphans. The Hepzibah staff knew they could call him any hour of the day or night. They never had to worry about his being annoyed if he found a child's condition not as serious as those in charge had believed it to be. No one could be more gentle than my father or more considerate of a patient. Many a time he sat all night watching over a seriously ill patient at the hospital or in the patient's own home. For him, it was not a question of being paid; he really cared for the person. Patients confided in him. He carried their personal troubles on his mind.

But my father had another side to him. With his own children he was by turns indulgent and also a strict disciplinarian. In our youth he would make no compromise between what he considered right and wrong. He believed in physical punishment. Even as a very small child, I remember that Ernest and I and the other children were soundly spanked when we had infringed some rule of conduct my father considered essential. He kept a razor strap in his closet, which he used on us on some occasions. But he was never cruel. He and Mother did what they felt was best for us. Mother often disciplined us, but the hairbrush was her instrument. My father's dimpled cheeks and charming smile could change in an instant to the stern, taut mouth and piercing look which was his disciplinary self. Sometimes the change from being gay to being stern was so abrupt that we were not prepared for the shock that came, when one minute Daddy would have his arm around one of us or we would be sitting on his lap, laughing and talking, and a minute or so later — because of something we had said or done, or some neglected duty of ours he suddenly thought about — we would be ordered to our rooms and perhaps made to go without supper. Sometimes we were spanked hard, our bodies across his knee. Always after punishment we were told to kneel down and ask God to forgive us.

My father was insistent upon our being on time. He was punctual himself, and he expected everyone else to be. It did not occur to us to be late getting home for meals or after school, and if we were we knew we could expect the inevitable punishment.

Sometimes my Father used to stand on the front porch and whistle loudly. Then he counted how many seconds it took us all to come running from the various neighbors' yards where we were playing. He was proud when we could make it home in two minutes. We had a family whistle. I think my father was the first one to use it, though both he and Mother called by the same shrill notes. The whistle sounded like the bobwhite call. We used to paraphrase it, "Whee — you-whee-ee-ee," with the last note rising. Very early in our lives we learned to come instantly when we heard this call.

Daddy liked to have groups of young people around him. He would lead us on picnic hikes through the woods along the river, and he organized Ernest's and my eighth grade class into an Agassiz Club, named for Louis Agassiz, the famous naturalist, whom he greatly admired. Agassiz Club field trips came usually on Saturday. Some twenty or more boys and girls, including Ernest and me, went on these weekly hikes along the Des Plaines River both north and south of the North Avenue Bridge.

Daddy could make any walk a pleasure because he knew how to look at nature. He could make you see things you had never known were there. Instead of just seeing a tree, we learned from him to look between the branches of the tree and see the birds' nests cleverly hidden in the crotches. Often he would let us climb up very carefully and look into a bird's nest, but he never let us touch the nest or the eggs for fear the fluttering mother bird would not return. Often in springtime we walked in the rustling leaves, and Daddy would stoop down and push the leaves aside and show us the budding wild hepaticas, pinkish lavender in contrast to the blue bells and brighter pink mayflowers growing nearby. Yellow dogtooth violets with their spotted lilylike leaves and the wild yellow and lavender violets and the pungent white May apple blossoms on what we called umbrella plants were easily recognized. But the tiny white "Dutchman's britches," with their dainty fernlike leaves, and the rare dead-white "Indian pipes" were becoming very scarce even then. We were thrilled when we found a plant of either species. We did not pick them or dig them up. Our father taught us to leave wildflowers to seed themselves.

He also taught us to be quiet in the woods. He would cock his head sideways, raise his index finger in the air, saying "Sh-sh-sh" and whisper "Listen." At first he heard nothing, then gradually we would begin to hear the birds calling, small twitters, little cheeps and even tiny wing flutters of which we had been totally unconscious while we had talked and laughed among ourselves. So we learned to know varieties of warblers and recognize their songs. We found scarlet tanagers, Baltimore orioles, rose-breasted grosbeaks and other varieties of birds we had read about and identified in the illustrated bird books at home. We had looked at these and learned the names of the birds long before we went with the nature study groups to the woods.

Daddy taught us that wild onions pulled from the ground and smoothed through one's fingers to remove the clinging black earth made a wonderful sandwich with plain bread and butter prepared at home and brought along for this purpose. In the fall Daddy pointed out squirrels and chipmunks picking up the wild black walnuts and hazelnuts and beechnuts, carrying them in their distended cheeks and rushing off to bury them for food for the coming winter. Then, too, Daddy would take time to show us the V formation of the ducks and geese as they flew south in October and November. Sometimes he would show us the dens of some of the small wild animals. Once we found a foxhole and another time a woodchuck burrow. One time, I remember, Daddy took us some miles south of Chicago on the prairie and showed us muskrat houses in a swamp. He told us how smart the muskrats were to have the entrance far under water, where it was inacessible to predators, while inside the house itself the little animals were warm and dry above water level.

Because my father himself liked to cook, he encouraged us to learn cooking and even to experiment with new recipes and unusual concoctions. He did not like anything wasted and would raise quite a rumpus in the kitchen if he felt good food was being thrown into the garbage pail or down the drain. But he was extremely generous in providing for his family, and if we were trying something new in the cooking line he never complained of the outcome. He liked *initiative* in us, whether in trying a new recipe or starting on some other idea.

Years before the word vitamins came into use my father had his own theories about food. While we were still nursing babies and before we were six months old he fed all of us fresh vegetables, orange pieces and orange juice, cut up tomatoes and shredded meat in gravy and broth form. Mother wrote down in my baby book how annoyed she was that my father brought the new baby to her to nurse "with onion on her breath."

We all teethed on celery stalks instead of teething rings. We chewed on carrots and green onions, and when Mother used to protest and say that nobody else's children had such primitive food and that all the neighbors were kind enough to cook the food for *their* children, her husband replied that he was going to prevent rickets if he possibly could and that there was something in fresh tomatoes and oranges and vegetables that he felt sure made bones grow straight and kept babies healthy. Even mother's milk isn't enough for a strong body, he preached. Daddy also believed that large quantities of meat and fish and eggs were needed by small babies.

His theories were shocking to his contemporaries in the medical profession. I remember when I was six or seven a fellow physician, whom Daddy and I encountered at a drugstore in Oak Park, called out teasingly, "Well, Doctor, are you still killing babies with steak and tomatoes?"

My father bristled. It wasn't funny to him. "Just look at *my* patients six years from now," he answered. "If you can find a case of rickets among them, I'll eat my hat. Someday you'll be prescribing the same thing."

The other doctor laughed derisively and walked off. Daddy turned to me and said, "No more children that I take care of are going to grow up with pigeon breasts and bowlegs if I can help it."

My father wanted us to eat all kinds of foods and enjoy them. Whenever he introduced a new food to us, some of us disliked the new taste intensely, but there was no escaping it. Each of us had at least to try each food, and though we might not like it the first time, Dad had a theory that eating it in a small quantity educated one's taste buds to the point where on the fourth time one began to enjoy it. Often he was proved right. It was in this way that I learned to eat and like not only ripe olives and pâté de foie gras but mayonnaise made with olive oil, boiled cabbage, salsify — which Daddy always called vegetable oysters — and other foods, including some of the stronger cheeses. I am sure my brothers and sisters had the same sort of experiences. We were not allowed to get emotional over food. No fuss was made about our eating it, we were just expected to finish what we were served at the table. Usually this was no problem at all, for we had healthy appetites. But on the rare occasions when, for instance, I turned up my nose at one of the family's favorite Saturday night dishes, a homemade vegetable soup, boiled with a meat bone and lots of pieces of meat in it, my parents would merely say, in a casual tone, "Oh, don't you care for our good food, Marcelline? Then apparently you are not hungry and we'll save it for you at breakfast." I was then excused from the table. Cold vegetable soup was much less attractive the next morning, so I quickly learned to "like" it.

We had venison at times. We ate fried squirrel. Sometimes we had turtle meat and turtle eggs, and it was a sort of family game to identify the parts of the turtle that tasted like other familiar meats.

"Almost like chicken, isn't it?" Daddy would say, taking a bite. With the next mouthful, he'd say, "Here, try this. Isn't it like pork?" Using our imaginations, we agreed. Woodchuck we found tasty, delightful, much like stewed chicken, and of course frogs' legs were a great delicacy. We ate opossum, baked with sweet potatoes around it, when Daddy brought it home from hunting trips in southern Illinois. We ate all kinds of fish, of course, cooked in every conceivable way. Though they had to be shipped in to Chicago, we often had ocean fish too. We had red snapper, oysters, codfish, clams, shrimp and lobster when the season and the budget allowed.

One of the stories Daddy told us about his own childhood was of the time he was sent with his brothers to visit their mother's brother, Uncle Hiram Edmonds, and his wife, Aunt Helen. He was then about ten. Uncle Hiram and Aunt Helen were referred to as "close," and they certainly worked the Hemingway boys hard on the farm. Even the youngest ones put in several hours' labor in the barns before breakfast. When the boys came to the table, they were given a bowl of yellow corn meal and water, boiled to a thick mush. They had to eat the first bowl plain. If they could get through this, Dad told us, his Aunt Helen then let them each have a second bowl, with blue skimmed milk. Those were my father's exact words. If their appetites were still unsatisfied, my father and his brothers could then have a third bowl of mush, with milk and sugar. My father told me he never saw cream and rarely butter on that farm. Most of the farm produce apparently was sold. As a result of this long-endured visit my father had a great aversion to the name Helen and said that it should be spelled with two *l*'s.

He always liked to have a good supply of food on hand; the kitchen shelves and our basement fruit room bulged to overflowing. Neither our own family nor our friends were ever denied after-school snacks, nor food at any time we thought we were hungry. We used to be the envy of many of our schoolmates when we brought them home to play after classes. We would descend on the kitchen for bread and butter and peanut butter or brown sugar after school, or we took our guests with us down to the bricked-in fruit room in the basement where they could help themselves from the barrels full of apples my father always kept on hand. The fruit room shelves were laden with jars of crisp pickles, jelly and jam. Much of our winter supply of preserves Dad and our cook put up during the long summers from June to September when we were at Walloon Lake. But the pineapple he cooked in Oak Park. Every spring Dad brought home a crate or two of fresh pineapple from the South Water Street market in Chicago, and often he got up early the next morning and peeled, cut up, cooked and canned the fruit before it was time for breakfast. Then he would lead us all to the basement to admire the dozens of gleaming quart jars of golden cubed pineapple lined up on the laundry table. He was as proud as though he had painted a picture.

Daddy taught us our natural history. A prehistoric dinosaur bone had been dug up in Forest Park when a new part of the Forest Park cemetery land was being leveled. Daddy took us out to see the huge bone and told us about what life must have been like when these giant beasts had roamed the continent. We were so fascinated by his stories and his descriptions of how coal was made from giant ferns of prehistoric times that he took us to the Field Museum of Natural History, then housed in the only remaining building of the Columbian Exposition of 1893, which Dad and Mother always spoke of as the "World's Fair."

We took the elevated Lake Street train downtown, transferred to the south side el and got off near the University of Chicago, where the museum stood. It had once been a building on the midway of the fair. Though the outside plaster of the building had cracked and the light cream color outside paint was peeling, inside we entered an exciting world. Here we saw whole skeletons of prehistoric animals. We looked at exhibits of precious stones, and of stuffed animals looking lifelike in their original hides, with their glass eyes shining out at us, just as though they could see us the way we could see them. Trips to Field Museum were among the most stimulating experiences of our childhood. Each time we went we tried to see more and different exhibits, but we always ended up seeing the prehistoric animals' skeletons. I believe they were as fascinating to my father as they were to us.

Daddy always made a point of explaining to us that though God created the world in seven days, according to the Bible, and we were not to doubt that statement, nobody had ever explained how long a day was. He also told us that the men who wrote the Bible explained natural history the best they could, but that now through research we knew much more about how things must have been made thousands of years ago. He told us that our new knowledge only added to the truths we learned in Sunday school.

Collections of ancient coins we saw at the museum tied in with the stories of ancient civilization Daddy had told us when he showed us his own rare coin collection at home. Greek and Roman coins brought out stories of Zeus and Mercury and the caduceus, the physician's symbol, with its wings and stick with twined snakes on it.

Interesting and kindly as my father was in most ways, the rules he had in his own mind as to what was right and what was wrong were very rigid. With him it was black and white with very little gray between. As a young man he had been taught and had come to believe at Oberlin that social dancing, card-playing and gambling were wrong. Smoking he did not approve of, and drinking alcoholic beverages was not only forbidden but looked down upon with scorn by my father. We all knew Mother did not entirely agree with Daddy on all these matters. She was as strict as he as to what was right or wrong, but her interpretation of which items belonged in the "wrong" category was much more lenient than his.

To Mother a lie was wrong, but dancing was just healthful exercise. Cards were a pleasant pastime and not wrong in themselves — she only disapproved when cards were played for money. Mother liked games, and we all played dominoes and checkers after dinner in the living room. Even Daddy enjoyed dominoes, and Grand-uncle Tyley

Hancock was the family expert. Mother used to tell me that Daddy's idea that dancing was a bad thing was because of "dance hall girls." Who these persons were or where my father had known them, I never heard.

My father's abhorrence of playing cards prompted him to destroy a pack he found in the room of one of the maids we had at one time. I believe it was a cook named Mary Beck, who liked to play. Daddy had another reason to disapprove of Mary Beck — she liked a wee drop on her day off. She was Irish, black-haired, pink-cheeked, with a loud jolly laugh, and she was a good cook too. She had a great fondness for Ernest and was always bringing him special presents or giving him some extra tidbit in the kitchen. On one occasion she came home late after her day off, rang the bell at midnight, waking Daddy from sound sleep to let her in, and she stumbled up the third floor stairs singing loudly. We all woke up at the noise, and when we asked Daddy what was happening, he just told us to go back to sleep. We never knew exactly what happened, but I remember that my father rushed out in the second floor hallway and after the noises subsided there was a strong smell of coffee in the air. Mary stayed in her room the next morning, but by afternoon she was back at work, a little pale and rather quiet as she stood by the sink fixing the vegetables for dinner. We did not ask any questions. There was no more trouble for several weeks. But the second time Mary came home singing, with whiskey on her breath, she left our house abruptly, and a gift she had brought to my brother was packed in her bag and left our house with her. She got no chance to give it to Ernest. My father could not compromise.

If he was stern with others, Daddy was fully as disciplined with himself. He had great courage, not only where moral issues were concerned but in enduring physical pain.

One time Dad was on a fishing trip in the early spring near Horton Bay, Michigan. In some way, I think through a fishhook being caught in his arm, my father developed blood poisoning in his left arm while on that trip. He had no medical bag with him, and the fishing camp where Daddy and young Wesley Dilworth, the blacksmith's son, and some other men were staying was at least a day's trip from a town or any medical help. The infected arm had bothered my father, he told us later, but he thought that hot compresses would reduce the swelling and make it possible for him to stay with the others until their fishing jaunt was over. But the night they were to leave the camp to return to Horton Bay, his arm was not only red and swollen but it became hard and began to throb. He was too good a doctor not to recognize these symptoms of danger. He knew an operation to drain the arm was necessary. He knew just what to do, but he wondered if he would have the physical stamina and endurance to plunge a sharp knife into his own extremely painful arm. He decided there was only one way to find out and that was to do it. As he described the scene, we could almost see the kerosene lamp burning, lighting up the plain kitchen table and the sharp hunting knife, red-hot from the fire, sterilized and ready. Daddy admitted it was the hardest thing he ever had to do. He instructed Wesley and the other men to hold him tightly and keep his left arm on the table. With his right hand he raised the knife and plunged it into his own arm.

"It's a good thing the boys were holding me," he told us when he returned to Oak Park later. "I screamed bloody murder. I couldn't help it and the spurt of pus hit the ceiling. The boys had to duck. I was mighty glad the knife was red-hot because it cauterized the incision and I couldn't have stood it to have to do anything else to that arm just then. I'm not ashamed to say it, Gracie," he told my mother as all of us children listened too, "I cried like a baby when it was over, but I knew if I let it go another day I might lose the arm."

"Oh, Clarence, how awful! I am so glad you are all right. Don't tell any more," my mother almost moaned. "I just can't bear to think of anybody being hurt like that."

"Well, it was no picnic, I can tell you," said my father. "And now," and here Daddy changed his tone of voice, "come and see what I've brought you." He opened his satchel and said, "We'll have brook trout for dinner."

"Brook trout!" said Mother. "How could you bring trout to Illinois? I thought it was illegal to take them out of Michigan."

"Sh-sh-sh," said Daddy. "Don't say a word. They are all packed inside my bedroom slippers." And sure enough, he brought out his newspaper-wrapped slippers from his suitcase. Ferns were sticking out of the brown leather edges, and inside of each slipper were nestled half a dozen brook trout, all gutted but with their heads and tails still attached. We had them fried in butter that night, and somehow my admiration for my father's courage in the operation combined with my memories of Horton Bay to make the fish taste better than ever trout tasted before.

Daddy's fishing for trout was not confined only to the early spring season. He often took Ernest and me with him, and in later years the other children too, on trout fishing expeditions during our summers at the family cottage on Walloon Lake, Michigan. He fished in Schneider's Creek as well as Horton's. But a great deal of his summer fishing was "right in our own front yard," as Daddy used to say. There was good perch fishing off the weed beds a few hundred yards offshore in front of our cottage, between Bacon's Point on one side and Murphy's Point, called Illinois Park on the maps, on the other.

I remember one time Dad had taken Wesley Dilworth and two of us children on a long row up through the Narrows into the west arm of the lake near a picnic spot we called Crackin, where fishermen went less frequently and where he had promised Wesley they would find some big ones. The day was cloudy and rain was forecast. Before we had had our lines in the water long enough to get more than a few fish, it began to rain. Daddy wasn't one to run for shore just because of a little "heavy dew," as he put it; the fish were biting well and both he and Wesley wanted to keep on fishing. But when lightning and thunder began and a real deluge descended, Dad hauled up the anchor and rowed quickly toward shore.

"We'll make a fire and I'll have you kids dried off in no time," he shouted as he dipped the curved bladed oars into the water faster and faster.

When we landed, we were shivering in our wet shirts and overalls, but I still remember Daddy saying, "Both of you get down under that umbrella." It was the old black cotton one Mother always kept in the boat to protect her from sunburn, and it was faded and had several small holes.

"How are you going to make a fire in the rain, Daddy?" I inquired.

"I'll show you," he shouted above the thunder. "Here, bring the umbrella over this way." Dad was bending over an old rotted log, busily scraping out some dry, dusty, reddish material from inside the log. Dad always carried a flint in his pocket in those days. He took it out and rubbed it on his trouser legs and put it back in his pocket.

"Marce, run quick and get some loose pieces of birch-bark over there on that tree. Ernie, pick up some little twigs, and Wes, you get some small bits of cedar," Dad ordered. "Hold them under your clothes and bring them here as fast as you can."

While we followed orders, Dad was crouched over a small group of flat stones he had pushed together, balancing the umbrella over the dry punk wood of the old log with one hand.

"Here, hold the umbrella," he said, "and give me your stuff. Now watch!" We peered over his shoulder in the rain, crowding as close as we could under the partial shelter of the umbrella.

Daddy built up a little pile of the bits of fuel we had brought to him; then, sheltering it carefully, he struck the flint. It made sparks, and finally one of the flashes caught in the dry red punk wood. Daddy protected it with the palm of his hand and his hat and blew on it gently until the tiny tongue of flame sprang up.

"Feed it slowly," he'd say. "Little piece of bark, birch is always best, then any of the pine or hemlock or cedar pieces. They have resin in them. It catches quickly. Never smother a fire with big pieces or too much fuel at once. A fire has to breathe oxygen. You can't start it big. Start it little. Feed it slowly. Let it get air and you can get warm and cook food in any weather."

The rain didn't last long that day, but before it ended we had warmed our chilly bodies and eaten our lunch in comparative comfort.

My father was a great stickler for cleanliness. He was particular about everything important being almost surgically clean. Not only did this apply to food and its preparation, but it extended to clothing and bodily care and everything to do with the disposal of waste.

"Use it up or burn it up," he'd say. "Don't let anything decay." He was almost fanatical in his determination to avoid infection through careful food preparation, sterile jars for canning and personal cleanliness. Our underwear and linens were always boiled. But Daddy enjoyed wearing old rough camp clothes at the cottage, patches didn't bother him a bit. In fact it was all Mother could do to make him give up some of his wornout trousers and old flannel shirts. He would wear them until they almost fell apart. He seemed to have an affection for old stained felt hats and ancient trousers with rounded knees so that he'd wear them in preference to the newer, neater clothes hanging on hooks in his bedroom at the cottage. But when our father did dress up in his light-colored summer suits, or in his neat, dark wool city clothes, wearing his starched turned-down pointed collar and four-in-hand tie — usually a bright one — he was a handsome man. Neighbors and farm friends who saw him in his old clothes chopping wood or skinning fish at Walloon Lake found it hard to recognize him when they saw him in his city outfits. It was as though he lived two lives, one as a woodsman and the other as the dignified professional man.

Daddy always had a sense of the dramatic, and I remember how this showed itself at the time my sister Ursula was born in 1902. Mama had told me about the coming baby, and I had watched her fix the bassinet, which she said was to be the little nest for the baby when it came to our house. She told me she hoped it would be a baby sister for me, but it might be a baby brother for Ernie.

One evening there was increasing tension in our house on Oak Park Avenue. Our nurse-girl, Lily, hurried us through our supper and put us to bed without letting us kiss Mama goodnight. There was a strange new nurse wearing a cap, hurrying up and down the second floor hallway. Her starchy skirts rustled as she passed us on our way to bed. I begged to be allowed to say my prayers in Mama's room as I often did. She said "No" and she brushed past us as though we didn't live there at all. I could hear people talking in the hall before I fell asleep.

It was still dark when Daddy wakened me by a gentle shake on my shoulder. He put his finger to my lips and whispered, "Sh-sh-sh! Don't wake Ernie. I'll get your clothes and we'll go downstairs." He carried me barefoot in my nightie to the warm kitchen, where he had a good fire going in the black iron stove. His eyes were twinkling.

"Marshmallow," he said, "you have a baby sister in Mama's room. Her name is Ursula."

"Oh, Daddy, can I see her?" I begged.

"Not now," said Daddy. "She's asleep and so is Mama. Let's go and tell the printer about your new baby sister. Maybe he can finish the baby cards in time to get them in this morning's mail. Wouldn't that be fun?"

I put on my clothes as fast as I could and Daddy did up the back buttons. He helped me with my coat and peaked bonnet and we tiptoed quietly out the front door into the exciting darkness, where the arc light was still burning in the street. Just as we got to the sidewalk the milkman came along, his horse clop-clopping and the ironclad wheels of the milk wagon creaking on the wooden block pavement.

"Hi you, Doc. What gets you out so early this morning? Somebody sick?"

"No," said my father. "It's good news today. Got a new little girl at our house, and we're going to walk down to North Boulevard and get the baby cards out, if we can rouse the printer in time. How'd you like to give us a lift, if you're going that way?"

"Hop in," said the milkman, and that was the beginning of the most exciting ride of my life. The milk wagon looked way up in the sky to me. Daddy gave me a boost and the milkman swung me onto the driver's seat beside him as Daddy followed. It was the highest place I had ever sat, and as the milkman clucked to his horse and slapped the reins on its back, I felt as though I were on top of the world. It was even more exciting when the milkman turned to me and said, "Well, Missie, how would you like to drive for a while?" I held on to the greasy black leather reins while the horse clattered along briskly toward the printer's shop several blocks down the street.

When we got out, Daddy thanked the milkman and we hurried over to the printer's. The owner lived upstairs and Daddy knocked on his door.

"Good morning," he called up the stairway. "Sorry to get you up so early," Daddy said when the printer appeared, "but we got our baby last night and now you can fill in the name and date and weight on those cards. She's a pretty little girl named Ursula. Do you think you could add the name and April 29, 1902, in time for me to get the envelopes into the post office before the mail goes out this morning?"

The printer agreed that he could try and Daddy and I went over to the livery stable nearby, where our family horse was boarded. We watched the livery stable boy feed the horse, curry him, and hitch him up to Daddy's black buggy with its little round glass windows on each side of the black curtained top. By the time Daddy drove out of the stable, the printer had the cards ready. He had had the birth cards all set up except for these last details Daddy had given him, and Mother had addressed and stamped all the envelopes several days before. Daddy and I took the boxes of cards and envelopes with us in the buggy, drove up to the post office, and sat there stuffing the cards into the envelopes and licking the flaps as fast as we could.

"There," said Daddy as the last one was finished. "We've done it! I'll bet a lot of folks in this town will be surprised to get a birth card the same day a baby arrived. It's never been done before!" There were a few cards left over. "Let's address one to Mama!" he chuckled.

"But Daddy, doesn't she *know?*" I asked innocently.

Daddy laughed uproariously. In fact, he kept chuckling all the way home to breakfast.

3

My Mother

OPPOSITES are said to attract, and surely no two young people could have been more opposite than my father and mother. Grace Hall was the talented, somewhat pampered daughter of Ernest Hall and his wife, the former Caroline Hancock, both of whom had been born in England and had come to America in their early youth. During her girlhood my mother and her younger brother Leicester Campbell Hall had lived on Fulton Street in Chicago, in the house where Mother was born on June 15, 1872. Like so many other Chicago families in the Seventies, the Halls had lost almost everything in the Chicago fire, but in the ensuing years Ernest Hall did so well in the Randall, Hall cutlery business that he was able to give his children many advantages.

Mother was twice taken to Europe by her parents; in other summers the family went to the mountains of Colorado or to White Sulphur Springs and repeatedly to Nantucket Island. The Halls were a musical family, and both Grace and her brother Leicester studied the piano. Grace also played the violin, but her greatest gift was her remarkable contralto voice. With her mother, Caroline Hancock Hall, she sang in the choir at St. Paul's Episcopal Cathedral in Chicago, where the family worshiped, and at the Apollo

Club, where both mother and daughter were soloists. Grace came naturally by her musical ability, for among her ancestors were a Doctor of Music of Oxford University — William Miller, the organist and composer, of Doncaster, England (Rockingham, one of his best-known hymns, is still in use today) and his son William Edward Miller, organist, violinist and pupil of Paganini, who was later disinherited when he became a Wesleyan preacher.

From the time she was a child my mother was taken to the opera: my grandparents would carry her with them, knowing that she would be quiet. Mother often told me that she could not remember when she learned the arias, for she was humming them without words before she could talk. Music was a second language in the Hall family. Grandfather Ernest Hall sang baritone, Uncle Tyley Hancock, Mother's uncle, was a tenor, and my grandmother a soprano who gave concerts in the Chicago area. What they needed to round them out was a contralto, and little Grace Hall remedied this deficiency. Friends of my grandparents told me that my mother was able to harmonize in the family quartet when she was just a baby tied in a high chair. Ernest Hall never missed an opera if he could help it, and his little daughter went frequently enough so that my grandmother noted in a diary, "Baby Grace slept through *Aïda* again tonight."

When my mother was about seven she had scarlet fever, and the illness left her completely blind. The doctor gave the family little hope that she would ever recover her sight. During the months of her blindness, Gracie learned to play the parlor organ by ear. Later her parents bought her a piano.

One day when all the family was at church, the little girl sat playing the piano. Her hands were straying over the keys finding harmonies here and there, when suddenly she thought she could see the outline of the fingers of her right hand. At first she couldn't believe it, then she stretched out her left hand toward the lower end of the keyboard to make sure. She thought she could see those fingers too. In telling me about it years later she said that after the first feeling of seeing, she rubbed her eyes and closed them tight for a minute and prayed very hard that God would give her back her sight. Then she opened her eyes again and put her hands straight out in front of her on the keys. She *could* see her fingers! Little Grace was so excited that she jumped from the piano stool and ran toward the stairs, shouting the news, but not even the servant heard her cries. She returned to the piano and played again.

During the half hour or so before her parents returned from church, Gracie's sight became clearer and clearer. By the time her father and mother walked in the door, the little girl ran to them shouting hysterically, "I can see, Mama and Papa! I can *see!*"

My mother told me that she would never forget the hug of joy her mother gave her and the feeling of her mother's happy tears on her own face.

Though her eyesight returned, my mother's eyes had lost some of their normal ability to adjust to light. Bright lights hurt them. Sunlight on the water was unbearably painful to her, and she usually wore dark glasses when she went outdoors on a bright day. Even electric lights in an auditorium were painful to her, and she often carried a fan to shade her eyes or would hold the program to her forehead in a concert hall or in church.

Because light hurt Mother's eyes so much, she tended to apply her feelings about it to her children, and consequently we rarely had enough light in our house. Often when we children were reading we had to strain to see. If we asked for brighter bulbs or more light Mother would say, "Oh, my dear child, I must protect your eyes. I couldn't have the light hurting you the way it hurts me." She really thought she was helping our eyes by keeping the lights dim.

Mother hated her glasses. She felt that they were particularly damaging to a woman's looks, and it was her desire in later years to keep her daughters as good-looking as possible. As a result, she fought as long as she could the idea of any of her daughters wearing glasses. I remember that when I was in grammar school, I had difficulty seeing the blackboard up in the front of the room. Almost every day I raised my hand to ask the teacher if I might walk forward from my seat in the rear, to see what was written on the board. When I told Mother of my difficulties, she suggested, "Why don't you ask the teacher for a front seat, dear?" But Daddy thought it was time for me to be checked for glasses. Even after I got them, Mother still urged me to leave them off as much as possible. She felt they were "so unfeminine."

Daddy's eyes were so perfect that as a young man he had been given the name "Ne-tec-ta-la," which meant "Eagle Eye," by the Indians in the Smoky Mountains. Daddy had twenty-twenty vision and never needed glasses until he was past fifty, and then only for reading. But Mother wore glasses all the years that I can remember.

For a while after they left the Fulton Street house, Mother's family lived on Oakley Avenue, farther west in Chicago, in a white clapboard house surrounded by an apple orchard. While they lived in this home, my Uncle Leicester was given one of the fashionable new high-wheeled cycles. He rode it proudly and his sister Grace envied him. Bicycles were precarious devices in those days.

Only men and boys dared to ride these new contraptions. The front wheel measured higher than a man's head, and the lack of balance between this big front wheel and the tiny wheel behind made these vehicles extremely tippy and dangerous. Mother resented the conventional restrictions that were considered necessary for the upbringing of a young lady of the 1880's. She longed for the freedom that the boys had. One day when she was about twelve years old, Grace Hall could stand it no longer. She put on a pair of her brother's trousers — a shocking thing for a girl to do in that Victorian period. She jumped on her brother Leicester's high cycle and rode around the block. People rushed to their windows, shopkeepers in their aprons stood in doorways gaping in wonder at the sight. To my mother's great delight she heard people calling to each other, "Come quick and look! It's a *girl* on a bicycle!"

Mother told me that men and boys, women, children and dogs followed her down the street. She was always proud that she had dared to be the first girl in Chicago to ride a boy's high bike. Later on, when lower-wheeled safety bicycles came into style, Grace Hall enjoyed her own and also riding tandem with the other young people.

Following her first year in West Division High School, Mother had another illness, chorea — then usually called St. Vitus's dance, which kept her in bed for six months and had a surprising result. In her early teens, she was almost as small in stature as her mother, who was only four feet eleven inches tall. Grace was five feet two when she became ill, but after six months in bed, she had grown six whole inches. Her tiny mother was overwhelmed. Not a single thing Grace owned would fit her. Even her shoes and stockings were too small, and her dresses, of course, were ludicrously short. Instead of being an average-sized girl, Grace now towered nine inches above her mother, and to her family she seemed a giantess.

That was the year the Halls moved to Oak Park, and it was at Oak Park High School during Mother's sophomore year that she and my father first met. Years later Mother told me that she didn't pay much attention to Daddy at that time. Clarence Edmonds Hemingway at fifteen, she told me, was tall, dark-haired and very thin. She remembered him as being somewhat awkward in his movements. He was interested in nature lore and animals and chemistry and scientific things, while she was drawn to music and the arts. Grace thought he was a nice boy, but she felt rather sorry for him because his clothes were outgrown and obviously mended. She told me that Ed, as his family called him, seemed to her to have very large wrists and ankles because his coat sleeves were too short and his long trousers stopped too far above his shoe tops.

Mother was a pretty girl with pink cheeks, blue eyes and light brown hair, which she kept curled. She had lots of pretty clothes and lots of young men paying her attention. She wasn't good at mathematics or Latin, and she had no interest in any of the sciences. She loved literature and enjoyed French and history, but music was the main interest in her life. Even before she was of high school age, all her training had been toward an operatic career. At home my efficient Grandmother Hall practically forbade her the kitchen, saying:

"Run along, dear. Don't soil your hands with cooking. I can do it more easily alone. You tend to your practicing. There is no use any woman getting into the kitchen if she can help it."

So it was natural that my mother, with her good memory and her beautiful voice, should concentrate on music,

in which she excelled. Mother had always had a remarkable memory. Years later, when I knew her, she could go
to a concert, hear a completely new oratorio or opera,
and carry it in her mind so accurately that she could come
home and play the whole number or several numbers
through, in detail, including all the harmonies of the music
she had just heard. Even in her girlhood she composed
music. She sang in church choirs and her parents continually took her to concerts and the theater, as well as the
opera, in preparation for the life of an opera singer which
they planned for her.

Mother often chuckled when she told me that she was
sure she never would have graduated from Oak Park High
School, since she could not have passed her courses in
mathematics and was very poor in Latin, if it had not been
that the principal needed a soloist for the graduation exercises. Only her voice, she would insist, had obtained her
diploma that June of 1890.

After graduation Mother really concentrated on music.
Though her eyesight was still very bad, and she was often
bothered with headaches because of bright lights, she studied voice and languages, sang in concerts, and taught pupils. She never lost sight of her goal — the opera in New
York.

It was not until 1894, when her mother was very ill
with cancer, that Grace Hall and Clarence Hemingway
became close friends. Though he had lived across the street
from her for several years, since high school graduation
young Hemingway had been away at Oberlin College in
Ohio, then at medical school in Chicago and briefly in
Europe. But when Mrs. Hall was ill, young Dr. Hemingway, as Dr. William R. Lewis's new assistant, came in often
to see her and became a sympathetic friend of my mother.

Their friendship grew into love as Mother came to lean

on him in the last tragic stages of my Grandmother Hall's illness. She died on September 5, 1895.

Often Grace and young Dr. Hemingway took rides in his buggy. I remember hearing the story of how they became engaged while jogging along behind the horse on a country road north of Oak Park. It seems my father had been trying to get up his courage to ask the fatal question, and had just managed to do so, when the horse stopped of his own accord in front of a building. The young people, abruptly shaken out of their daze, looked up to see the words *Justice of the Peace. Marriages performed*. Mother told me she said "Yes" to her young man immediately and they both dissolved in laughter at the appropriateness of the spot where the horse had stopped. They always said Old Prince must have had better ears than they gave him credit for.

That fall of 1895, Grace Hall went to New York for the long delayed season of study with Madame Louisa Cappianni, the well-known opera coach. Mother took a feminine version of her father's name, Ernestine, for her professional middle name. She lived at the Art Students League that winter and had a lesson every day with Madame Cappianni, working on voice production in Madame's famous diaphragm control method as well as coaching for the contralto roles of many of the operas she was preparing. Grace Ernestine Hall met stars of the Metropolitan who were also preparing their own operatic roles with the same famous teacher. Madame Marcella Sembrich and Jean and Edouard de Reszke were others who were studying for their current opera roles at the same time with Madame Cappianni. To be escorted around New York by such glamorous people was enough to turn the head of any young lady from the Middle West.

Grace Hall met young singers, dancers and painters that

winter, and she had her portrait painted by a fellow student at the Art Students League. In the picture she is wearing a pink satin evening gown, its huge round puffed sleeves and low neck trimmed with lace. It was a dress she had worn for concerts in Chicago the year before her mother died. This graceful portrait, showing Grace Hall posed before a potted plant, still hangs on a wall of my home.

Whenever my mother wanted to settle her payments for lessons with Madame Cappianni that year, her teacher protested that Miss Hall should not mention the subject of money until she could earn the total fee for all her lessons in one singing engagement. Mother could not believe it was possible that her voice would be able to command such a fee. Toward the end of her period of study in New York, she owed Madame a thousand dollars. It worried my mother that she had not settled her bill, but Madame was nonchalant about it.

"You have a great voice, my little one," she said. "I am in no hurry for your money. One encounters a voice like yours perhaps once in a generation. I am so sure of your success that I wish to wait until you earn the whole amount in one night."

That season Madame arranged for her talented pupil to be heard by some of the heads of the Metropolitan Opera. So impressed were they that she was offered a contract by that famous organization. That season, too, Grace Hall sang in the old Madison Square Garden, but she dreaded the footlights because of her eye trouble. She did receive one thousand dollars for that concert, which she promptly paid to her teacher. But Madame was not eager to have her promising pupil pay in full. She preferred to have her continue in her plans for an operatic career. Madame Cappianni urged my mother to accept a contract for opera the next year and to remain in New York to continue coaching for the roles she would sing. Madame used every argument at her command to encourage Grace Hall to postpone her return to Chicago. My mother was flattered and tempted, but she put off deciding.

The enthusiastic teacher felt she had found a really great voice. She was sure my mother could fill the place as leading contralto of the opera, for Madame Sofia Scalchi was retiring. But Madame Cappianni had not reckoned with the persuasive powers of young Dr. Hemingway. His letters and his pleading that my mother return to Oak Park and marry him the next fall were pulling Grace Hall away from her influence. Also my Grandfather Hall's wish that his daughter go to Europe with him one more time that summer of 1896 influenced Mother to decide in favor of marriage and against the operatic career she had trained for all her life. Telling about it years later, she said:

"You know, dear, Schumann-Heink is now taking the place I might have had in opera. But I have you children. And besides, my eyes would never have stood it, all those bright lights on stage would have been too much."

Dr. Edward Buzzard, a British relative of Mother's and Queen Victoria's personal physician, begged her to let him arrange for her presentation at Court during her summer trip to Europe. But Mother thought that it would be silly to spend weeks in getting together the expensive outfit — the three ostrich feathers worn in the hair by debutantes, the special shoes which must be acquired only through the Court bootmaker, the special gown with a train of designated length, and all the other rigidly prescribed details of presentation garb — for a few minutes at Court; it was not nearly as important to her as buying her own trousseau for her coming marriage to my father.

Grace Hall did agree that she would be delighted to

sing for the Queen if she were so commanded, and a date was arranged for this musical presentation at Court. But due to some circumstances which have been lost in the retelling — either the Queen was not well on the day Mother was to sing or some other circumstances intervened — Grace Hall's appearance before Her Majesty was postponed to a date past the time of the sailing of the ship on which Grace and her father had reservations for the trip back to New York. Regretfully Mother felt she must then refuse the honor. Getting back to Chicago and her Clarence was more important to her.

While in Paris on their way home, Mother bought many beautiful gowns and hats and a large supply of French kid gloves, most of them of shoulder and elbow length, to match the gowns she bought for her concert appearances. At that time (she told me this years later of course), our government charged duty on three dozen pairs of gloves, but not on a lesser number. So Grace Hall cannily brought in thirty-five pairs, including a pair of long red suède gloves, several pairs of shoulder-length white kid gloves with tiny pearl button closings, beautifully made short peach-colored ones, and light yellow and light blue kid pairs which I wore to dress up in years later.

Grace Hall and her father got home late in August, and invitations were sent out; the wedding was small in deference to the death of her mother the year before.

My mother and father were married in the First Congregational Church of Oak Park on October 1, 1896. Mother's wedding gown had ninety yards of white organdie in the puffed sleeves and the many layers of floor-length gown with its double train.

At the time my parents were married, Mother had over fifty voice pupils in the west side area of Chicago, and she was earning as much as a thousand dollars a month with her music. She sang in concerts and was a soloist in a church choir. With this substantial income she convinced my father that they could manage very well if they lived with my Grandfather Hall in his large six-bedroom home, even though my young doctor-father was only just getting started in his profession. Dr. Hemingway's income at the time of their marriage was sometimes as little as fifty dollars a month. But it soon increased as he became known and as he continued to work as Dr. Lewis's assistant.

I never smell lilies of the valley without thinking of my mother. Mother always smelled nice. Often she used a talcum powder with a violet scent, but her favorite was a perfume from France, made from lilies of the valley. I remember that it came in a handsome wood-grained box, rounded at the top. Inside the box was a much smaller vial holding the strong fragrance. The perfume was so potent that just one drop of it on a pile of her handkerchiefs permeated the whole top drawer of her bird's-eye maple dresser.

Mother, with her five feet eight inches of height and her good carriage, looked well in proportion to my father's six feet. As a little girl I remember Mama with light brown hair — mousy brown she called it, and with her deep blue eyes usually wrinkled at the corners from smiling. Her generous mouth took its cupid's bow shape from her father's. Her complexion was typically English, pink and white; her rosy cheeks and red lips needed no artificial accentuation. Usually she used a light liquid powder to tone down the pinkness, as she put it.

Mother's speaking voice was low and rich, much like her singing voice. As a young girl she had been very slim, but she gained weight following the birth of each child, and by the time the third child, my sister Ursula, was born when I was four, Mother had a rather buxom figure.

I remember Mother coming into Ernest's and my nursery bedroom at Grandfather Hall's house and leaning over our twin white cribs to kiss us goodnight before she and Daddy left our house all dressed up for an evening party. I remember the feeling of Mother's soft powdered cheek and the light tickling wisps of the curls of her hair touching my face. Earlier I had watched her curl it as she held a wooden-handled curling iron over the chimney of a lighted lamp. I admired the neatly boned white net collar of the guimpe she wore inside her evening dress and the soft white lace hanging down from her sleeves. Sometimes when she leaned over to kiss me, I noticed she was wearing a green chiffon bow — or an orchid one or now and then a pink one — at the back of her collar. I used to plan that when I grew up I too would have a collection of chiffon bows of all the colors of the rainbow to keep in my dresser, just as Mother kept hers in a flowered cretonne box on the marble-topped table in her room beside the cut-glass jar full of dried rose leaves.

Mother often told me she had always wanted twins, and that though I was a little over a year older than Ernest (he was born July 21, 1899), she was determined to have us be as much like twins as possible. When we were little, Ernest and I were dressed alike in various outfits, in Oak Park in gingham dresses and in little fluffy lace-tucked dresses with picture hats, and in overalls at the summer cottage on Walloon Lake. Later, we had a sort of compromise boy-girl costume: a high-necked type of "Russian tunic," a belted blouse worn over bloomers. I remember one set was made of gray flannel bloomers with gray plaid blouses to match. We wore our hair exactly alike in bangs, in a square-cut Dutch bob. Ernest, in kindergarten, still had blond hair, while mine was always dark brown like my father's. Ernest even had blue eyes for a while when he was small. Later his eyes as well as his hair turned brown. Our much younger brother, Leicester, and our sister Sunny were the only blue-eyed blonds in our family. They took after Mother's side, the Hall family, she told us. Most of the Hemingways, I think, except Grandfather Hemingway, were brunettes.

Mother admired blonds and people with all shades of red hair — she always hoped one of her children would be born with auburn hair, though there was no history of it in our family. But many of us grew up admiring red hair because Mother always pointed it out to us as the most beautiful hair in the world. Ernest's first wife, Hadley, had hair that color.

Mother continued with her plan of making us into twins even into our school life. I had an extra year of kindergarten while waiting for Ernest to be old enough so we could start first grade together when he became six. After kindergarten we played with small china tea sets just alike; we had dolls alike; and when Ernest was given a little air rifle, I had one too — Mother was doing her best to make us feel like twins by having everything alike. She encouraged us to play together, and to fish, hike and take trips to Horton Bay together in the summers as we were growing up. We were congenial and enjoyed doing things together, but being older and a girl, I matured faster than Ernest, and there were times, especially in school, when I would have liked to go ahead by myself.

All my childhood I remember one great difference between my father and mother — my father loved nature so much that the small annoyances of bugs and flies and spiders didn't bother him at all, but my mother had such a horror of "creeping, crawling things," as she phrased it, that the thought of walking on a sidewalk after a rain, when she might have to step on a slippery angleworm, was horrifying to her. I remember many times Mother calling to the maid and sometimes to me to sweep off our front walk lest there be any worms on it before she would walk down it to get into Daddy's buggy. Spiders terrified her, even tiny ones. I remember her carrying a broom upside down around the house, dabbing at cobwebs. It wasn't that she was such a perfect housekeeper; it was her desire to remove the nesting places of spiders.

During the summers Mother spent at the lake cottage she longed to have fewer trees and a green lawn planted so that there would be less possibility of mosquitoes and spiders near the house. Daddy, on the other hand, wanted our summer home to be left in its natural setting. He liked piles of leaves on the ground and a woodsy feeling about the place.

Although Mother had a great aversion to insects and a feeling of squeamishness about spiders, bugs and worms that made her seem to be a timid woman, she really wasn't. She had tremendous courage about other things. She never hesitated to try something new and she was not afraid of being laughed at.

In 1906 when a gymnasium class for women was organized at the Oak Park Y.M.C.A., Mother was one of the first to join. There had never been a gym class for women in our town up to that time. Mother was delighted with the new outfit she and the other ladies wore for their exercises. The navy blue flannel blouse had a sailor collar and full, pleated bloomers. The short sleeves of the blouse were trimmed in white braid and came almost to the elbows. With this uniform she wore black cotton stockings and black tennis shoes. Mother attended the class regularly and proudly demonstrated her new accomplishments at home.

One day she told us she would show us how she could kick higher than her own head. We could hardly believe it.

"Lily," said Mother to our nurse-girl, "get a sofa pillow and stand up on a chair and I'll show you what I can do." We were all in the kitchen at the time. Ernest and I had just come in from our first grade classes at the Lowell School. Lily stood on a wooden kitchen chair, held a soft cushion at the height of Mother's head, and Mother put her hands on her hips and kicked it easily.

"Hold it higher, Lily," said Mother. "Keep raising it until I can't kick it any more."

Sure enough, Mother's toes could still touch the pillow when Lily held it a full thirteen inches above her head.

"Now I'll *really* show you something!" Mother announced in her gay, enthusiastic voice. "I'm going to turn on the gas jet in the ceiling *with my foot!* Have the lighter ready if I make it."

This was unbelievable! Lily hurried to fit the long white paraffin taper into the handle of the dark metal lighter we used in igniting the ceiling gas burner. Lily stood ready. Mother took a deep breath, ran forward three or four steps and kicked into the air at the fixture. The odor of gas poured out. She had achieved the impossible, I saw it myself!

Mother had four children and weighed about a hundred and eighty-five pounds at the time of her gas-lighting kick. During that season she lost several pounds, as she had hoped to do when she signed up for the class. Though I don't recall her doing any other special exercises, I do remember that she loved to walk. In the following years Mother and I walked two or three and sometimes even five miles at a time along the country roads north of Oak Park. Mother often said you could walk twice as far on springy ground as on cement sidewalks, and not feel half as tired.

All the years of our growing up, Mother was singing in public, composing songs, both words and music, many of which were published by Summy & Company of Chicago, and giving vocal lessons to her regular pupils and to other young people who could not afford to pay but who she thought had special promise. Mother loved to do things for young people which, as she said, "opened new windows to them."

Often I would wake up in the night, sometimes long after midnight, hearing the piano. I knew it was Mother working on some composition which had come to her in her sleep. She told us that if she dreamed a melody and got right up and played it out on the piano immediately, she could remember it the next morning, to write it down. But if she did not actually finger it out on the piano keys at the time, no matter how distinct the melody seemed to be, it was gone when she awoke in the morning.

Though most of Mother's pupils were girls and women, she did have men students as well. Mother charged high fees for those days, eight dollars an hour, but her pupils paid gladly.

Many times Mother gave vocal lessons to our cooks. Sometimes she encouraged girls who wanted to study with her to live in our house and do housework to pay for their lessons. At other times she offered to give lessons to young women already installed by Daddy.

At various times we had girls working for us who proved to have remarkable voices. I remember Marguerite, a girl of German descent from Petoskey, Michigan — the town nearest our summer cottage at Walloon Lake — who had a perfectly gorgeous voice. She trained with

Mother while she worked in our kitchen. Later she sang in the movies. Mother believed that Marguerite's beautiful contralto voice was big enough for opera.

Another young woman who worked in our home, named Emma, had a delightfully clear soprano voice. Emma was very much a lady. Mother gave her voice lessons too and later presented her in several song recitals, including some which Emma did charmingly in costume. She had real dramatic ability. Mother was proud of these young women and of many others who helped in our home and who studied voice with her.

Our house was never quiet. Between Mother teaching her pupils in the music room through the day, the sound of the piano when she composed at night, the round, full tones of the maids practicing their scales in the kitchen, and all of us children squeezing in our half hours of piano practice before and after school, our house might easily have been mistaken for a conservatory. Even Daddy, who had difficulty keeping on key, practiced his cornet in the basement.

It was quite amazing how many good voices Mother developed in people whom others did not think of as having talent in any way. I have records and printed programs of recitals that were given by some of these people Mother had taught, quite aside from her regular large classes of paid pupils. She gave formal recital programs for her "special people" with the same gracious hospitality she offered to the invited guests of her other pupils. Recital nights were exciting. As many as three hundred guests came to sit on the folding chairs in the big music room Mother designed for the home we lived in after 1906.

During the years between 1909 and 1915 Mother conducted two vested choirs of youngsters between nine and sixteen years old at the Third Congregational Church in

Oak Park. She organized an orchestra of a dozen children, who played for the church services robed in black and white vestments like the choirs. Mother held three rehearsals a week at our home, and a final one at the church for the orchestra (in which Ernest and I played), the boys' choir, and the girls' choir, in which Ursula and Sunny sang. About seventy-five youngsters came weekly to our home, as well as the soloists, who were coached separately. Mother contributed all this work and her services to the church.

Mother was much beloved by her pupils and she had many many friends. She liked to make people think well of themselves and they usually responded by giving her their affection. I once asked her how she had time for all these professional things, when other mothers were so busy with housework, and she replied:

"Well, you see, dear, I do these things because I can, but I pay out of what I earn in my professional life for the cook and the laundress and the nursemaid who do the work that other girls' mothers have to do."

4

Walloon Lake

SOME of the happiest times of our childhood were spent at our cottage, Windemere, at Walloon Lake, Michigan. Daddy and Mother's first trip north was in August, 1898; they took me with them (I was about seven months old) with my nurse, Sophie, and we stayed in a cottage borrowed from Mother's favorite cousin, Madelaine Randall Board. The trip, an arduous one, began on the lake steamer *State of Ohio*, which took us from Chicago to Harbor Springs. Here my parents carried their luggage aboard the local train bound for Petoskey; in Petoskey they again unloaded and changed cars for the train to the village of Walloon Lake, where for the last time they tugged out their luggage and transferred it to the little steamer which took them up the lake. This was to be our itinerary for many summers to come.

They enjoyed their first visit to Walloon and spent much of their time exploring the lake in a rowboat. They loved the clear spring-fed waters and the surrounding birches and pines, and having decided that they wanted a place of their own, they spent two weeks looking over the shore lines for a possible site to build on. The place that attracted them both was a baylike area on the north shore almost opposite Wildwood Harbor, owned by Henry Bacon, a farmer and a former Canadian from Manitoba.

The beach my parents selected was sandy and wide; the lake here had a good hard clean bottom and no abrupt drop-off into deep water. White birches and cedars grew along the shore, and maples and beeches and hemlocks farther back from the water. The bay was protected from the northwest wind by a point of land with a dock, referred to by all the local people as Murphy's Point. Everything about the spot appealed to my parents. The fishing in Walloon was good. Their land was close enough to Bacon's farm to get fresh milk and eggs easily, and yet not close enough "to smell the pigs," as Mother said. The Hemingways closed the deal for four lots, amounting to an acre in all, before they left for Oak Park that September.

The cottage, as Mother planned it, consisted of a living room with window seats on each side of the huge brick fireplace, a small dining room, kitchen, and two bedrooms. There was a roofed-over porch with a railing, and a hooked, hinged double gate across the front steps, which led down to the lake. The outside was white clapboard and the interior white pine. No plumbing, of course. A well was dug to the right of the cottage in the front yard. Visiting and communication were by water. Wood-burning steamers — the *Tourist*, impressive with its two decks, its uniformed captain and engineer, and the *Outing*, a smaller steamboat — made regular trips around the lake four times a day and sometimes a moonlight excursion in the evening. When we needed something, we flagged boats in to our dock by displaying a white banner — it could be a piece of torn sheeting, or even a bath towel. If the helmsman didn't toot to show he saw us, we would wave our white flag wildly until his whistle sounded and the boat veered toward our dock. If all else failed to get the pilot's attention, Daddy would blow on his bugle. He also used the bugle to call us when we were out in the fields or on the water near Windemere, or he would blow on a ram's horn, like the one described in the Bible, which he had bought in Switzerland before he was married. Though there was no variation in the tone of this instrument, the sound of its one note had tremendous carrying power and could be heard for great distances across the lake.

The nearest town, Petoskey, was nine miles away, and the road to it was a mere sand track over many high hills. For a farmer like Henry Bacon to drive his horse and wagon to town and back for supplies was a long day's chore. Nobody went to town any oftener than necessary.

From my earliest memories, Daddy always spent all summer with us children and Mother at the cottage. He had a license to practice medicine in Michigan as well as in Illinois, and he took care of any illness or emergency cases that might occur in the lake camps or among the lumbermen, or among the Ottawa Indians, who were hired to peel the logs. We either brought two maids with us from Chicago or hired a cook or a nursemaid locally. Sometimes the Petoskey or Boyne City girls who joined our household for the summer would come back to Oak Park with us in the fall.

During his lifetime Grandfather Hall visited us for a short time every summer and took long walks on the beach. He loved climbing to the hill behind our cottage to see the sunsets. We used to go with him, and he often held us by the hand as we climbed the hill. I remember his lifting Ursula to the top of the rock pile to see the sunset. That was the summer she was three, the last time he visited us at the lake.

Abba Hall didn't like fishing, nor was his fastidious taste

able to adjust happily to our extremely informal life. True, he wore a cap instead of a hat, but he never appeared without his regular starched collar and tie and his suit coat. Mama used to say that it was very nice of Abba to pretend he liked eating outdoors on the porch on an oil-cloth-covered table. Really, he loathed it. He was much happier in his own well-run home, or eating at a good restaurant, like Henrici's in Chicago, where the napkins were heavy white damask, and the service impeccable.

Abba only came to Walloon out of love. Though our family lived according to his standards most of the year, he found it almost impossible to enjoy descending to our vacation informality.

Grandfather Hall disliked fishing and cottage life, but our Granduncle Tyley Hancock took to them with enthusiasm. His visits were long, and his pleasure in being on the water was infectious. He was an excellent fisherman and an enthusiastic swimmer, and his appetite, which in the city was often a finicky one, was perfect at Walloon. He relished everything we served him. Daddy used to say, "Uncle, you're a different person when you're up here. Even your color is better. I guess what you need is more Walloon Lake and less time in hotel rooms."

Uncle wore old shoes, and canvas leggings that came to his knees over baggy old trousers; his comfortable, wrinkled tan corduroy jacket had lots of pockets for his pipe and tobacco and fishhooks. Though he didn't feel he could be quite so unconventional as to go without a tie, and never did, his battered fishing hat, worn slightly cocked over one eye, gave him a sort of rakish, sporty look that was just right for Windemere.

Among Uncle's catches were some of the biggest fish ever caught in Walloon Lake. A picture taken in July, 1905, shows my father and great-uncle shaking hands over a string of pickerel and pike, all six of them from three to four feet long. Uncle had great patience. I can still see him puffing on his pipe as he rowed the boat. After we got to the fishing grounds, he feathered an oar with one hand, just enough to keep the boat from drifting toward shore, as he kept his eyes intent on his fishpole. He wasn't very conversational when he had a rod in his hand. When he did speak, it was through an almost closed mouth, his teeth gripping his pipe stem. "Don't wiggle, you'll scare the fish. Trim the boat, Marce," he'd say. "Sit over in the middle of the stern. If you're tired of fishing, I'll take you to shore, but if you want to stay out here with Uncle, you must learn to be patient. That's the secret of fishing."

We loved having Uncle visit us. He was fun. He and Mother often sang duets in the evening, and sometimes Uncle danced a gay little buck and wing step or a hornpipe while Mother played on the parlor organ.

When we first went to Walloon Lake, lumbering was still going on in the area. A sawmill stood on the Boyne City side of the lake, a mile or two west of Wildwood Harbor. The superintendent and other executives of the mill lived in cabins along the shore, and the millhands lived in long, rough board bunkhouses up the slope behind the mill. Huge booms of logs moved up the lake toward the mill, drawn by chugging steam tugs, and now and then a boom would get loose and float down the lake — a great danger to the regular summer boat traffic.

When a boom got loose, a tug would pursue it, and an agile lumberjack, canthook in hand, would leap onto one of the rolling logs and attach the chain from the tug to the outside circle, and back the boom would be dragged, like a runaway child.

Sometimes in a storm a few of the loose logs in the center would escape the boom and float off by themselves.

They were dangerous to hit, especially when we were rowing in the dark, and if they were not found soon enough they often became waterlogged on one end and floated just under the surface, a threat to fishermen and motorboats and even to swimmers. We called them deadheads.

As small children, Ernest and I were often taken to visit the mill. We watched the logs pulled up the ladderlike chain from the millpond toward the screaming saw above. The saw operator pressed the lever expertly, first to cut off the bark on four sides of the log, then to slice it into boards, and next to press another lever that took the clean boards on an endless chain out of the mill, where they landed on a platform ready for the millhands to put them in air-spaced piles in the sun to dry. They stacked the boards two one way and two the other, making a hollow square pile at least three times the height of a man. The smell of fresh sawdust from the hemlock logs was a perfume we looked forward to every summer as long as the mill remained at Walloon Lake.

Once in a while we were invited into the mill cookhouse, where the camp cook, a mild-mannered old fellow, an apron tied over his pants, apologetically wiped his damp fingers on his apron and said in a gentle, almost ladylike voice:

"Pardon me if my hands are wet. I've just been making biscuits and you know how hard it is to keep your hands clean in the kitchen."

Often he gave Ernie and me a doughnut or a sugar cookie. They were delicious.

The old man was a good cook and the men liked his grub. But the contrast between this neat, gentle, kindly soul and the rough, unshaven, tobacco-spitting lumberjacks was so great that it is no wonder they made fun of him behind his back. The millhands called him "the old lady" and "the maid of the moist palm."

Once in a while Daddy took Ernest and me along for a ride on the horse-drawn lumber train from the mill to Horton Bay. The two or three open flatcars rolled on regular iron railroad wheels, over wooden tracks laid through the woods uphill and down to the boat docks in Boyne City. We rode on top of the piled lumber in the first car, right behind the driver. We could watch him flick his long whip to the ears and backs of all four horses, two abreast, that drew the lumber train. It was exciting to sit so high in the air with nothing to hold on to but the edge of the jiggling pile of boards. The wood felt hot to our bare feet, and we had to sit very still, because it was easy to get a splinter in our toes if we moved about. Often we had to duck to keep the tree branches from hitting us in the face as we passed.

Daddy taught us how to swim at an early age. I remember being supported by his firm hand under my chest while he taught me how to dog paddle. When I was three, my parents had post cards made showing a picture of Ernest and me in the water beside our rowboat. We almost lived in the water. There was just one rule. We were not supposed to fall in the lake with our clothes on, and were punished if we did.

Mother, having fair skin, never tanned; she only freckled and blistered. My dark-haired, bearded young father loved the sun and tanned to mahogany. Mother liked to swim, but she hated to touch her feet to the bottom for fear she would hit something "slimy." Actually, there wasn't anything to touch but some sticks or a sunken log. Mother would swim out to Dad, who would station himself, treading water, in deep water well over his head. Mother would rest on his shoulder for a moment, then turn and swim back. That way her feet never touched bottom until she could see the good hard sand in the clear water near shore.

As we grew older, we had regular lifesaving drills. Mother watched but never took part in the drills. She would stand on shore, calling "Be careful!" Dad would take us out in the rowboat into deep water. He would say, "Now, when I tip the boat over, swim for shore!" Other times he would call out, "When I tip the boat over, climb on top of it as quickly as you can — and hang on!" Then he would deliberately rock the boat until it capsized. It was exciting. Later we learned to undress in water over our heads, and Dad would time us to see how quickly we could take off clothing and tennis shoes and get to shore. We were keen to compete in these races. Our aim was to do it in one minute.

We had no bathtub at the cottage, of course, and we were often in and out of the water three and four times a day. Sometimes, as a special treat, we would be allowed to go into the water without bathing suits in the evening. This we called "Secret Society." We felt so free as the water slid past our naked bodies. Even in our teens, our parents let us swim this way on hot nights.

Each summer Daddy raised a flock of ducks and we fed them cracked corn on the beach. They kept to our shore line, but we were lucky if we had the same size flock at the end of the season as Daddy had bought in June. Foxes were not as active then as now — farmers' dogs and the bounty hunters received for killing them kept them down. But occasionally we found a lot of white feathers, and we knew that a fox or a skunk or possibly a mink had been busy.

For several years Daddy bought tiny pink pigs to occupy a pen he built at the back of the boathouse. We named them and grew fond of them as we fed them the family scraps three times a day, and we could never bear it without weeping when, at the end of the season, our pigs, now fully grown, were taken away squealing to a fate we knew only too well would result in ham and bacon.

Not only did our pigs grow in the summer, but we did too. Often the traveling clothes we wore to come up north on the boat were almost pathetically small for us three months later when we put them on to go home. One year, I remember, when Ernie was about eight or nine, he took off his shoes when he got to the cottage in June. He ran barefoot all that summer. For the whole summer he gave up going to town or visiting family friends with us rather than put on his shoes. When the last day of vacation came and we were closing the cottage, Ernest was dressed, all but his shoes.

"Hurry up! Put on your shoes and stockings," Daddy ordered. "The boat will be here in a minute. I've got to lock the doors."

"I can't wear them, Dad," said Ernie. "They hurt."

"Hurt or not, I won't take you barefoot on the steamer," his father replied.

Reluctantly, Ernie drew on his long black stockings, and after much tugging he pulled on his black laced shoes. He complained all the way down the lake and on the train from "the Foot" (as we called the town of Walloon Lake) to Petoskey. Daddy wanted to get Ernie a new pair of shoes in Petoskey, but he was afraid there wasn't time before the next train left for Harbor Springs. Fryman's Shoe Store, where we usually bought our footwear, was several blocks from the station. He and Ernest started up the street toward Fryman's; then Daddy glanced at his watch and realized they couldn't make it there in time. Back they turned to the station, Daddy striding ahead.

Ernie followed slowly. A summer visitor looked at the
little boy limping along and said, "Here, boy, here's a dime.
It must be awful to be lame!"

Ernie took the dime and hurried to catch up. He was
laughing as he showed Dad the dime.

"Look what the man gave me! Did you know I was a
little lame boy?" he said. "Now you'll *have* to get me some
new shoes!"

They were both hooting with laughter by the time they
reached the rest of us, where we sat with a huge pile of
baggage, and two crates, one of pigeons, one of cats, waiting for the train to Harbor Springs.

We had two rowboats, the *Marcelline of Windemere*, and
later, the *Ursula of Windemere*. And it was an exciting day
when Dad bought our first motorboat, about 1910. It was
named *Sunny*, was eighteen feet long, and was driven by a
Gray Marine motor. What a time Daddy had cranking that
inboard engine! He'd prime it and crank, then prime and
crank. Sometimes it took half an hour to start it. Sometimes the motor would give a little chug and then stop for
the day. Dad wasn't mechanical, and starting that boat
almost wore out his patience.

Now, my father was very particular about anyone's use of
profanity or even ordinary slang swearwords like "Darn"
or "Gosh" in his presence. He limited himself to phrases
like "Hold your horses!" or "Oh, rats!" But the way that
motor misbehaved forced out his favorite expletives, "Oh,
rats!" or "Dad gum it!", with all the fervor and emphasis of
the most violent oaths I've ever heard. I remember hearing
him tell Mother, "That blankety-blank-blank engine will
kill me yet!"

Mechanical ability of any sort was not one of my
father's strong points. He could do anything with a gun or

a fishing rod, or a knife or a surgical instrument. He had performed seemingly miracles in early plastic surgery, but a motor was a devil of obstinacy to him. He treated it like a personal enemy, and it behaved like one to him. In later years, even our second motorboat, the *Carol*, a slower, easier boat to run, was troublesome to Daddy.

My father was among the last of the doctors in Oak Park to give up a horse and buggy for his professional calls—not because he loved horses so much, though he was very fond of them, but because, after all the trouble he had had with that motor on the *Sunny*, he distrusted all engines. The thought of having to take time to fight with a motor in a car when he had to rush to a sick patient was frightening to him. He said he would hate to depend on any automobile.

"Besides," he said to Mother, "it wouldn't have sense enough to find its way home like a horse." Daddy counted on his horse when he was tired, and nodded after he'd stayed up all night with a pneumonia or heart patient or bringing a new baby.

Later, my father enjoyed driving a car. He grew to be so at ease with his Model T Ford that he would take both hands off the wheel while he pointed out the scenery. We were sometimes nervous wrecks as he drove.

In 1917, the first time Dad had a car at the lake, it was a terrific achievement to get from the cottage over the sandhills, nine miles to Petoskey. The narrow, loose-sand trail over the hills to town had not yet been improved, and Daddy always carried an ax to cut branches to get himself a firm start on top of the deep sand at the bottom of each hill. Usually he carried a rope and a shovel too, the latter to use to dig the car out of the sand and the former in case the car became so badly stuck it had to be pulled out by a laughing farmer and his team. I say laughing, for the farmers with their horses felt very superior to the "silly resorters" in cars. "Get a horse," was still a shout we heard from local residents near Petoskey.

One summer Daddy ordered a steel trap and three barrels of clay pigeons sent up to the cottage from Montgomery Ward in Chicago. That was a memorable time for us. Daddy thought it just as important for us to learn to shoot as to swim.

We older children had all been taught to shoot a twenty-two as soon as we graduated from air rifles. We practiced shooting at targets before we were in high school. Daddy was as careful in teaching us techniques for using guns as he was about teaching water safety.

"Accidents don't happen to people who know how to handle guns," he told us over and over. "Treat a gun like a friend. Keep it clean. Oil it, clean it after every use, but always remember, it's an enemy if it's carelessly used."

Keeping the gun pointed to the ground, never toward anyone, even in fun, was a cardinal rule. We learned these rules early. Dad let us load and unload his twenty-twos and his Colt revolvers, but only he touched "Old Ed," the heavy rifle he had had since his college days. "Old Ed" was the gun he had used on his trip to the Smoky Mountains in the early Nineties. He never let us shoot over water.

Dad showed us how a rifle shell was put together, and he would let us taste the strong saltpeter in the cartridge. He told us how hunters used to use this form of salt on game, if caught without supplies in emergencies in the woods.

In Oak Park during the winters, Dad let us help him mold bullets in an old army bullet mold which had been his father's during the Civil War. The sputter of the hot lead melting in the small funnel-shaped dipper, with its long metal handle (very long to reach over a campfire, he told us), still stays in my memory. The lump of lead was dull and gray when he held it over the gas flame on the basement laundry stove, but when the liquid lead was poured into the bullet molds and the cooled bullets were turned out, they were silver bright.

"Oxygen's burned off in the heating," he'd say, "but they'll pick up more as they stand in the air."

The summer the clay pigeon trap arrived, we were using guns with regular shells, not bullets. Before it came I had visions of a clay pigeon trap looking like the bear and mink traps hanging on the walls of hunters' cabins in our part of Michigan. I was glad when I saw how different the clay pigeon trap looked when it arrived at the cottage. It was a gray painted steel device that stood flat on the ground. It had a movable arm with a spring in it and a flat slot into which we put the slightly cupped blue clay disks that looked more like deep saucers than anything resembling a bird.

My father and Uncle Tyley and various friends had great fun at the trap that summer, and Ernest and I joined them often. Mother and the younger girls, Sunny and Ursula, shot too, but the recoil of the shot hurt Mother's shoulder. It hurt mine, too, but not enough to keep me from shooting. Ernest and I teased and teased to be allowed to try one shot with Dad's own rifle, "Old Ed." Finally Daddy gave in. He let us each try it once.

"All right, but it will knock you backwards," he said. He held the heavy gun against my shoulder, and I sighted and pulled the trigger. Even with his help in holding the gun, the thump was terrific. He caught me as I fell backward against him.

One childish gesture Dad would not permit. He got

terribly angry if he saw it happen. "Don't you ever let me catch you closing your eyes as you shoot. A marksman can be a murderer in a split second if he's not in control of his weapon. It takes judgment to shoot. It takes kindness to kill cleanly, and it takes a wise man never to shoot more than he can use to eat."

In the summer of 1913, while Harold Sampson was with us, he and Ernie went on a hunting expedition and shot a porcupine, and in accordance with Daddy's strict injunction that we eat everything that we kill, the boys had to prepare themselves a meal of it.

I remember this as if it had happened yesterday [Harold Sampson wrote me years later], but do you remember that we had to eat it? We cooked the haunches for hours but they were still about as tender and tasty as a piece of shoe leather. We never killed another porcupine.

I also wonder if you remember why we killed this animal? Bacon's dog came home with a mouthful of quills and they brought it to your father, hoping he could get them out. The big problem was that the dog would not let anyone touch it. I do not know what magic words your father used, but after talking to it very quietly for several minutes, the dog seemed to sense that he was trying to help and from then on the dog was quiet. Porcupine quills, as you know, have a barb much like the barb on a fishhook, and each quill had to be cut out. There were at least a dozen quills, so it was a long and painful ordeal, but the dog did nothing more than whimper. The faculty your father had for calming people and animals was wonderful and I think it was God-given.

This was the porcupine we killed. We found it in the woods back of the Bacon farm where a lumbering crew were cutting timber. At the time we thought your father was being a little unfair in making us eat it.

Father had the greatest contempt for so-called sportsmen who killed ruthlessly for the fun of killing or to boast about the size of the bag. He was a great believer in conservation and an exponent of decency in sport.

Of course, he was humanly fallible too. His sense of honor didn't keep him from getting an occasional grouse or woodcock for the table, even though the game-law calendar and his appetite might not quite coincide. This happened with trout too.

I remember once having what I thought was fried chicken for breakfast and wondering why Dad insisted we finish it so quickly. When every scrap was gone, Dad burned the feathers in the stove, making a nasty odor, even before we left the table.

"Do you have to burn the feathers now? Couldn't you wait till we're through breakfast?" said Mother.

"Never can tell who might be nosing around with a badge on," Daddy replied.

"Now, Clarence, what will the children think?" teased Mother.

"They ate it, didn't they? Tasted good, didn't it? I pay taxes for this land all year round. Too bad a man can't fire a shot at a moving object on his own property once a year without permission," he sputtered. "How did I know it was going to be a grouse?" But his sheepish grin belied the belligerence of his words. Mother smiled too.

"You're incorrigible, dear," she said as she kissed him.

One time, to entertain some of our young guests, Daddy got out his gun and a box of the regular white candles we used for light, and inviting us out to the back yard, said, "How much would you like to bet that I can't shoot a candle through a one-inch board?"

Our guests mentioned various amounts, and one of them

who was very sure of himself, said, "I'll bet anything you like, Doctor, that a candle can't go through a board."

"Well, take a good look at the board," said Dad. "It's a full inch thick, isn't it?"

Our friends agreed.

"All right," said the doctor. "Now, watch." He emptied the shot out of a shell, leaving only the powder for propulsion, cut the white candle in half and stuck it in the top of the shell where the shot had been. He loaded it in the gun, and taking careful aim, he pulled the trigger. There, exactly the size of the candle, was a perfect round hole in the board.

"Well now, boys," he said, "you've seen it done. Anybody else like to try it?"

Of course we all wanted to take a turn. The boy who was the most skeptical was the most enthusiastic.

"Wait till I get home," he shouted. "Will I make money taking bets on that!"

"Now I didn't collect from you," said my father, "and you said you'd bet me anything I wanted. So now I put it up to you. Have fun with the trick, but don't use it for gambling. There is one little secret I haven't told you kids. It's better to stick your candles in the icebox before you begin. If the wax is warm, all you'll get is a grease spot on the board."

In 1902, when Ursula was born, the enlarging of the cottage began; a kitchen wing was built and in time the cottage grew to have six bedrooms, three of them in a separate annex. Yet even with these extra rooms, Ernest and his boy friends usually preferred to sleep in a tent pitched in the back yard some distance from both the cottage and the annex, while Ursula and Sunny used

Ernest's room. Ernie liked to read at night, just as I did, but he had to drape a mosquito netting over his cot, because his lantern attracted the flying creatures that edged in around the tent flap. We often used candles to augment our kerosene lamps, but they were not allowed in the tent.

Daddy and Mother's idea of a summer cottage was a place where there was as much free time and as little work to do as possible. When we were small, in warm weather we wore overalls and blouses and went barefoot. Still, in those days of many petticoats and starched ruffles it was hard to keep laundry to a minimum, and after Ursula and Sunny were born, we four children, our parents, Uncle Tyley and the maids contributed a big load of clothing, sheets, pillow cases, bath towels and napkins to be done every week. Daddy acquired a formula for a washing solution to be added to the water in the boilers that was supposed to make soaping and rubbing unnecessary — I think he got it from Aunty Beth (Mrs. James Dilworth of Horton Bay), or possibly from Mrs. A. B. Nickey on Eagle Island. At any rate he bought various chemicals in town and made up a huge quantity of the mixture in some white enamel eight-quart pails. He let me wear one of his surgical rubber gloves to hold the tin funnel while he poured the solution into bottles; then he corked them with whittled-out wooden stoppers and stored them in the woodshed.

On washday half a bottle of this mixture was used in each of the two big metal boilers filled with water in which the laundry was boiled, one boiler at a time, for half an hour on our kitchen wood stove. It took a long time for the clothes to come to a boil, and the boiler then had to cool a little before it was safe for Daddy and one or two others to lift it off the stove. They had to keep perfect

Marcelline and Ernest as "twins,"
Oak Park, 1902.

Ernest Hall, our grandfather,
with Ernest, Ursula and Marcelline, Walloon Lake, 1904.

The house where we were born, No. 439
(now 339) North Oak Park Avenue, Oak Park, Illinois.

Mother's music room at 600 North Kenilworth Avenue.

Clarence and Grace Hall Hemingway,
Petoskey, Michigan, 1908.

Dr. and Mrs. C. E. Hemingway with Ursula, Ernest and Marcelline, 1903.

Ernest on Marcelline's lap,
taken at Grandfather Hall's home, 1903.

Mother's big fish,
a seven-and-one-half-pound pike she caught in Walloon Lake;
with Ernest, Ursula and Marcelline, 1904.

Family group. Standing, left to right, Grandfather A. T. Hemingway, Aunt Grace (Livingston), Aunt Arabell White Hemingway and baby Franklin. Seated, my father and mother and Grandmother Hemingway. In front, Marcelline, Ursula and Ernest. October 1, 1904.

My parents' sixteenth wedding anniversary, October, 1912. Left to right, standing, Ernest, Madelaine (Sunny), Marcelline, Ursula. Seated, Father, with Carol on his lap, and Mother.

Grace Hall Hemingway, singer and lecturer.

Ernest in Robin Hood costume
for seventh grade play
at Holmes School, 1912.

Ernest and Harold Sampson at Walloon Lake,
1913, with porcupine they shot.

Ernest with woodchuck, Walloon Lake, 1913.

Ernest at fifteen, Walloon Lake.

step as they strained to carry the painfully heavy, hot, steaming boiler out the back door, around the kitchen wing and down the slanted path, about fifty yards to the lake, where all of us children in bathing suits were waiting. We stood waist-deep in the water ready to rinse the clothes Daddy brought us. That was fun! Clothes were made of sturdy material in those days, and we used to play games with the big bath towels and Mama's long white nightgowns that ballooned up full of air, throwing them back and forth to each other, or two of us swimming out with a sheet between us, flipping it over as we paddled around. We had to be careful that somebody watched the small pieces near the shore or a handkerchief or a bib would float off down the lake while we were rinsing the big pieces, and unless one of the children was on guard to shout "There it goes!" various pieces of laundry seemed almost humanly possessed to escape.

By the time the second boiler of clothes came down to be rinsed, we were often rather bored by our duties, but on the second load Daddy got into his suit and joined us, especially to help wring out the bigger pieces. All the damp clothes were piled into big round galvanized washtubs and carried back up past the kitchen, behind the woodshed, to the clothesline stretched in the sunny part of the yard away from the trees. I can still hear the pistol-like flaps made by the sheets on a windy day. Nothing ever smelled so fresh as our clothes when they came in from the line.

The napkins and handkerchiefs and Daddy's shirts, and Mother's shirtwaists too, were ironed with flatirons heated on the stove. We found that we slept just as well on rough-dry sheets as on ironed ones.

But it wasn't all work and training at Walloon Lake. There were lots of parties and entertaining — not the kind we had in the city, but parties where we made our own fun. One of the first social events I remember was a barn-raising at Henry Bacon's farm. I wasn't yet five, but I still remember the thrill of being allowed to go along with my parents that day when Daddy helped the other men put up the framework of a big barn, while all the women and some of us youngsters kept at a safe distance and listened to the shouts as the main beams and braces were put in place. A barn-raising was a community activity in those days.

To feed the crowd, trestle tables were set up beside the Bacons' log cabin, with long boards supported by chunks of wood for seats on each side of the white-paper-covered table. Even the sawhorses that supported the table boards were homemade, and the nubby knots showed along the sawhorse legs. The man called the "master builder," who had no whiskers on his upper lip, but a squared-off beard and an almost bald head, was the one who told the other men what to do. Everyone treated him with respect.

The mass of food on the table that noon was exciting to me. I remember there were four kinds of cake — white-topped, chocolate, fruit, and a pink one with high layers; three kinds of pie — apple, mince, and blackberry; as well as big dishes of meat and potato salad and vegetables and cut-up cucumbers with onions in a big white china bowl. People took turns sitting down at the table, and I can remember Mother saying that Mrs. Bacon and all her girls must have cooked for a week to serve over a hundred people for supper that night. A big cheer went up when the top timber was put in place, and my father helped put it there.

We were always having picnics, marshmallow roasts, corn roasts around a fire on the beach. I remember one special Fourth of July picnic when Daddy dug a big pit and roasted half a lamb over coals, barbecue fashion. He had to make the fire hours ahead so the deep bed of coals would be just right to cook the lamb but not burn it. That same day a whole little pig, an apple in its mouth, was roasted in the oven in the kitchen, while dishpans — one filled with potato salad and one with popcorn — and big pails of lemonade were prepared for the crowd of guests who came from Boyne City and from other areas around the lake. The Shaws and Whites and von Platens were there.

The prettiest part of the Fourth was the evening, when Daddy set off rockets and flares at the water side. Sometimes he bought balloons — ingenious Japanese-made contrivances in which a lighted candle was placed, and when the wind was right he sent them across the water toward Wildwood Harbor. We could follow them with our eyes, almost the whole distance across the lake. Our friends on the opposite shore reciprocated when the wind was in their favor, and both groups took turns in an informal way, shooting off colorful fireworks so that we could both enjoy each other's celebrations. Often Daddy let us children hold the Roman candles and fire them over the water, or light the pinwheels he nailed to the flagpole. But the big skyrockets he handled himself.

Early in 1905 an old farm in Charlevoix County, on the opposite side of the lake from Windemere, was about to be sold for taxes. Friends in Boyne City told my parents about it. There were forty acres in the piece, with an old house, a barn and some sheds on it and a sizeable patch of virgin timber at the rear. It was available at a very reasonable figure, and Daddy and Mother decided to buy it — they had visions of living there perhaps in their old age. Mother named the farm Longfield.

Daddy installed at Longfield a tenant farmer and his

family, the Washburns, who were to run the farm on shares. My father was to pay all expenses and receive a third of the crops. Daddy put in several hundred fruit trees—cherry, apple, plum and peach—on one of the barren slopes, and he and Mother planted birch trees, hemlocks and maples on top of the central grassy hill, which they named Red Top Mountain because of the reddish tint of the grass growing there. Later my parents added twenty adjoining acres of wooded land on the east along the shore toward Wildwood. There was a bubbling spring of cold water on this new land and an old, neglected log cabin Daddy thought might be fun to keep for picnic headquarters.

Mother determined that someday she would build a house up there on Red Top where she could see for miles in all directions. Daddy thought it an extremely impractical place to build, because not only was it a long steep climb up the hill, but there was no water up there and no road to the top. But Mother knew what she wanted. She bided her time.

While the Washburns were running the farm, we had all the fresh vegetables and milk we could use. That was when Mother tried a recipe for Devonshire cream from her mother's old cookbook.

Mother could never have made it in Oak Park, for the recipe called for a gallon of fresh whole milk, with the cream allowed to rise in a flat pan over night. In the morning the whole pan, the cream undisturbed, was gently placed on top of the stove. There it warmed slowly until bubbles began to form around the edges of the cream. Removed from the stove, it was allowed to cool; then the thickened, partly cooked cream was skimmed from the milk with a ladle and put into a serving dish, usually a glass one, to cool further in the refrigerator. This was our

Devonshire cream, and it made a delicious accompaniment to gooseberry tarts or apple pie or nutmeg-flavored peach turnovers. Mother loved it so much that she could eat it plain.

Mother was proud of this recipe. Daddy actually was the better cook and got all the praise in our family, so Mother yearned to have one or two things she could make supremely well. She had never made a cookie or a cake in her life. Big boxes of cookies and cardboard barrels of gingersnaps were part of our huge order of canned goods and groceries sent up regularly by freight from Montgomery Ward every summer.

Mother showed my Grandmother Hall's English tea-cake recipe to Mrs. Dilworth. Though the directions were vague in the manner of the Eighties, Mrs. Dilworth worked out the exact proportions for this tasty yeast-based hot bread, and taught my mother how to make it. Mother practiced at the Dilworths', and when she had the secret she came home to make it for us. Seldom have I seen such joy on anyone's face as on Mother's when she baked her first highly successful English teacakes all by herself in the kitchen at Windemere. Ernest and I were in high school by the time this cooking debut of Mother's took place; Sunny and Ursula were of grammar school age, and Baby Carol was in her high chair. Daddy had just come in from fishing and rushed to wash his hands at the pump as Mother, flushed and excited, finished buttering the hot raisin-filled teacakes and sliced wedge-shaped pieces for each of us to taste.

"Delicious! Gracie, delicious!" Daddy gave his verdict with his mouth full. "You got any more in the kitchen? Where have you been hiding this talent all these years?"

"It *is* good, isn't it?" said Mother modestly. We all joined in extravagant praise. But the teacake was worthy of every adjective. From then on Mother served *her* tea-cake for every social occasion. She even looked up people she hadn't seen for years and invited them for tea. Later she proudly presented her recipe to the 1921 edition of the Oak Park Third Congregational Church Cook Book, and to this day, though she never baked but one other thing — a yeast roll recipe Mrs. Dilworth taught her — people still remember her as a "wonderful cook" and mention that delicious teacake.

Once I suggested that she learn to make a layer cake, a baking powder recipe.

"No, dear," said Mother. "I proved I could cook with my teacake, and I'm not going to take a chance of spoiling my reputation by trying anything else." And with few exceptions, she stuck to her word.

Fishing was excellent in Walloon Lake during our first years at the cottage, and pictures which were taken of Mother holding a seven-and-a-half-pound pike she had caught, as well as others of Uncle Tyley and Bobbie (Mother's helper, who was part of our family) and Daddy with their various big catches, proved it.

About 1907, Daddy and Uncle Tyley went to Brevoort Lake in the Upper Peninsula, where the muskellunge fishing was said to be really sporting. An old guide at whose cabin they stayed outfitted the party. Daddy brought home three hundred pounds of fish caught in three days! The muskellunge and northern pike were gigantic to my eyes. Daddy was busy all the first day back, giving away fish to the neighbors. He kept our supply in the wooden icebox under the trees, and for the next week we ate fish baked and broiled and fried. The pike was especially good baked with bread stuffing flavored with sage and onion, and the stories Daddy told of his adventures in acquiring his catch added to the zest of our fish dinners.

The next year Ernest was keen to go on the Brevoort Lake trip.

"I don't now about that," said Daddy. "You're supposed to spend your time learning your multiplication tables this summer. Your teacher said you couldn't pass to the next grade in September unless you memorized them. Besides, you don't like canned beans, and we live on canned beans at Brevoort Lake."

"I can learn to like beans," said Ernie eagerly. "I can learn the multiplication tables. Please let me go with you!"

"Well, then, prove it," said Dad. "I'll give you a can of beans, and you eat some of them every day for a week, and if you can learn your multiplication tables between now and next week, you can go. But there's to be no fooling about this. I'll try you on your tables a week from today, and if you miss a single one, you'll stay home. Is that understood?"

Ernie agreed, and Daddy came to me quietly a little while later and said, "Marce, you help Ernie learn his tables. He can do it if you just keep him at it."

We started in. We sat on the front porch, Ernie in the hammock and I on a chair beside him with the arithmetic book in my hand. We went over two times two is four up to twelve times twelve, over and over and over again. The sevens and the eights were hardest for Ernie. Every day, when he thought he had a group all memorized, I would skip around the tables, and he would miss some combinations. Ernie didn't think that was fair. If I would just ask for them in order, he knew he had them straight. But I knew Daddy wouldn't question him in any such orderly sequence.

Several times Ernie almost lost interest. He would pick up a magazine and start to read. Then I would remind him there were just three days before Daddy would test him, and he would reluctantly lay down the magazine and go on repeating the tables. Ernie gave up his morning swimming time. With a sigh, he would plunk himself down in the hammock after breakfast and go over and over the multiplication tables with me. I was as sick of them as he was by the end of the week, but the day before Daddy was to leave for Brevoort, Ernie passed his examination, and with a yell of delight ran off to pack his things. He had stuck to his promise to eat some canned beans daily, as I recall, and had earned his right to go on the trip. I don't know who was prouder, Ernie or I, when our menfolk started off for the Upper Peninsula. In afteryears, Ernie used to say, "You know, I love canned beans." I often wondered if he remembered how he came to like them.

The summer of 1911 at the lake was quite different from all the others. A new baby was expected, and I, who was thirteen, was old enough to be treated as a real confidante by Mother. The baby was expected in July, Mama told me, and rather than keep us all home in Oak Park in hot weather, Daddy and Mother planned that their fifth child would arrive at Walloon Lake. Long before we left for the cottage early in June, Mother talked over plans for the baby's birth with me and explained that a trained nurse, Miss Daubey, a graduate of Daddy's classes in obstetrics at Oak Park Hospital, would be with us at the lake, as well as our nurse and cook. Mother felt quite sure the baby would be born before the Fourth of July.

If it was a boy, as my parents hoped, he was to be called Forrest, and in anticipation I embroidered an Old English *F* in blue silk on a baby pillow. If it was a girl,

Mother told me, she would be called Carol, a shortening of my Grandmother Hall's name, Caroline.

Mother showed me all the little baby clothes and the piles of fresh new birds-eye diapers she had packed away in her room, and she let me help her fix the bassinet made of a clothes basket padded with cotton and covered in pink and white. The nurse arrived, and Daddy, who was going to perform this delivery himself, had everything in readiness. Mother had never been to a hospital in her life and insisted that she wanted this baby born at home just like all the others.

The days passed, and the first week of July came and went, but there was no sign of the baby. Every morning at breakfast Daddy would look inquiringly at Mother, and Mother would shake her head as though to say, "Not yet."

We were having breakfast on July 19, when suddenly Mother said, "Oh, dear!" It wasn't the words, but the tone of voice in which she said it. There were relief and fear combined. Daddy jumped from the table.

"Finish your breakfast quickly, kids," he said, "and make yourselves scarce."

Things began to happen fast after that. Each of us children had a place to go.

I was banished with a picnic lunch and told I could spend the day at Murphy's Point, a quarter of a mile away. I took along a sketch pad, writing paper, and a book. Bobbie took the younger children to Bacon's farm for the day. Ernest went fishing.

I resented being sent off, and I said to Daddy, "Please let me stay. I can help the nurse or Mother."

"No!" my father said excitedly. "Just leave us alone. We'll call you when the baby's here."

It was one of the longest days of my life. I waded in the cool water along the shore. I collected shells. I dug for crayfish. I gathered clams—they weren't good to eat like the salt-water clams I had eaten at Nantucket, but it was amusing to get a lot of clams together near the shore and then watch them slowly edge out along the bottom sand to deep water again. You really could not *see* them move, but if you took your eyes off them for a moment a wavy trail they had made in the sand was visible, so you knew they had moved.

The long afternoon dragged on. The sun was getting lower in the sky. I began to worry about Mother and the baby. What if something had happened to Mother? What if there wasn't going to be a baby? I made myself wait for what I thought was about an hour more. I could hear Bacon's cows mooing as they were being driven back for milking, so I knew it was almost five o'clock. I could stand the suspense no longer. I gathered up my things and slowly walked back toward the cottage. Miss Daubey, the nurse, saw me first, as I came into the yard.

"How's Mother?" I called.

"All right, but pretty tired," she said.

"Can I see her, please?" I begged.

"Not now. I'd let her rest awhile," said the nurse curtly. Not a word about the baby.

"And the baby?" I asked.

"Oh, she's a little darling," said Miss Daubey.

Then tension went out of me. I was happy again. My baby sister Carol was here and Mother was all right. It was a wonderful world, I thought, as I went out to the kitchen to see if the cook needed any help setting the table. I began to sing.

Later, I saw my new sister in her pink bassinet. Carol was tiny and dark-haired, with perfect features, the most adorable little creature I had ever seen. I loved her from that moment and have never stopped feeling that way. Carol was the most beautiful member of our family.

Ernest was very fond of Carol, too. He said she was almost his birthday present. Ernie didn't get much of a celebration on July 21 that year. But every July from Carol's second birthday on, they celebrated their birthdays together with a birthday tree. The day before Carol's birthday, Dad and Ernie would cut a small pine tree in the woods nearby, and Carol would ride back to the cottage on top of it as they carried it between their shoulders like a Yule log in pictures of early English celebrations. After that, the tree was set in a homemade stand on the dining porch, and the boughs were festooned with our decorations.

After Carol was born that summer, Daddy and Mother made ready for a special family reunion. Much sawing and hammering went on while a new wing was added to the screened-porch dining room. When it was finished, there was plenty of room for thirty people to be seated at the two long tables. The reason for the celebration was that Uncle Will and Aunt Mary Hemingway were coming home from China. Uncle Will was Daddy's cheerful, missionary doctor brother, and he and his charming little wife, Aunt Mary, who had been born in China, were especially close to me. I had been a flower girl at their wedding.

They had gone to the Orient right after the Boxer uprising, and since we were a family of inveterate letter writers and photographers, we had all kept in close touch. Uncle Will was a sort of hero to us children, and we had been brought up on tales of his courage. The story of how he accidentally cut off his finger in the corn sheller when he was a boy, and then had grown up to become a competent surgeon, even without the use of his right index finger, amazed us.

Ernie and I had often heard from Father the story of how Uncle Will, when he was a medical student, watched his own appendectomy in mirrors hung over the operating table. He just had to know how it felt from the patient's point of view.

We had read letters about Uncle Will's impulsive trip to visit the Dalai Lama in 1910, on the occasion of that god-king's traveling through Mongolia. Since the forbidden kingdom of Tibet was at that time completely closed to foreigners, on pain of death, Dr. Will Hemingway and his associate Dr. Francis Tucker decided to approach the camp of the royal personage while he was on neutral soil.

We chuckled when we learned that the gifts Uncle Will and his friend had offered to the Dalai Lama by way of his guards — huge men with drawn swords — were a jar of raspberry jam, a collapsible tin cup, a many-bladed knife and a kerosene lantern. These were all they had handy when they decided to ride over to the Lama's encampment. Luckily the gifts were acceptable. In return the Dalai Lama (later called "The Great Thirteenth") gave Uncle Will and Dr. Tucker some lengths of narrow dark-red wool cloth and some scarves of thin blue silk which Aunt Mary still has. The Dalai Lama told Uncle Will and his friend that they were the first Americans he had ever received.

When Uncle Will and Aunt Mary came home that August of 1911, they brought their two little girls to America for the first time. Adelaide, not quite six, spoke both Chinese and English, but little Isabel, we'd been warned, spoke only Chinese. We were filled with excitement as we waited to greet them.

The reunion was a big moment for our Hemingway

grandparents, too — the first time the whole family, four sons and two daughters, had been together since before Uncle Will's wedding in 1903. While Mother nursed month-old Carol and supervised the preparations, we twelve cousins romped in the water in our bathing suits, played in our tree houses, and had marshmallow roasts on the beach. Little Isabel learned English quickly, while we picked up a few words of Chinese from her.

We had a big beach picnic one night, I remember, and sang songs around the fire as the sun went down, while Mother accompanied us on the small autoharp she held in her lap.

Best of all were the stories Uncle Will and Aunt Mary told us. Kindly Aunt Mary, with her wonderful smile and gentle sense of humor, had the Welsh gift for storytelling, and one of the tales that stayed with us longest was the story of the finding of the abandoned orphan child Peach, our little "sister," whom Daddy and Mother supported in the mission school.

There were wild strawberries on the open slopes behind Echo Beach Inn and big patches of wild blackberries and raspberries growing along the road to town and even more luscious ones across the lake on Longfield Farm. The Indians from the bark peelers' camp charged fifteen cents a quart for their berries, so Daddy agreed to pay us the same. It was slow work picking the fragrant, juicy fruit in the hot sunshine, and hard to keep the tiny, soft, fragrant, strawberries intact; their fragile skins punctured at a touch, and it seemed to take hundreds and hundreds of them to fill a quart pail. Each stop we made at a patch on our kneeling, sitting journey around the pastures seemed better than the last one. Always the berries seemed bigger farther ahead.

Cries of "Oh, here's a grand bunch!", "No, they're thicker here!" "Mother, look at these, they're as big as thimbles!" would echo across the field, and all the while the wasps and those annoying flies — we called them "sweat flies" — would be hovering over us while we picked. We all ducked and swatted at them and spattered red juice on our faces and overalls as we slapped and ate and filled our pails.

Actually, the fun was in getting lots of berries for the shortcake Bobbie would make for supper that night.

The shortcakes were huge. Rich baking powder biscuit crust was baked in an oblong metal pan, at least sixteen inches long and about ten inches wide. The whole thing was popped into an oven made very hot by thin pieces of split cedarwood added at the last minute to the hardwood "holding fire" in the old iron stove.

When the shortcake was done (it baked while we ate our main course), Bobbie and Mother split the biscuit cake into two layers, slathered great gobs of golden butter on the bottom crust, spread the thick mixture of strawberries and sugar on it, laid the top layer of crust over it, and delicately piled the rest of the gleaming, fragrant, rosy fruit on top.

That quiet wait for the shortcake had the dramatic quality of the wait for a first-night curtain, as we listened to the pan and spoon sounds in the kitchen. Usually there was a pitcher of thick yellow cream ready to pour over it. At last Mother appeared, flushed and delighted, and she and Bobbie acknowledged our gasps of delight.

"It's beautiful, Bobbie! It's the best one yet!" we called.

Mother or Dad served generous squares to each of us. It was eaten to the last crumb.

"I can't resist it," Dad said. "I'll be sick afterward. Even if they don't agree with me, I love strawberries. What's a little rash compared to this glorious concoction?" We agreed with him. Two or three quarts of wild strawberries, a whole hot afternoon's picking, was gone at a swoop. But it was worth it.

Other times, when we found a few wild strawberries, just a pint or so, I'd make jam. It had to be cooked quickly and used very soon, as the subtle fragrance of the wild berries, so different from the cultivated ones, disappeared after a few days, no matter how well it was paraffined in jelly glasses. Nothing was added to the glistening berries but sugar, no pectin or apple bits to make it thicker — just the thin, heavenly flavor of the wild berries, sugar and sunshine. We served the jam on fresh toast or hot biscuits. This was no dish for squirrelish hoarding, to be saved as our other preserves were, for winter. Wild strawberry jam was a mouth-watering, nose-tickling delight to be eaten at once in grasshopper-like summer abandon.

Years later, in 1928, when I was studying sculpturing in Paris, and saw *gâteau avec fraises des bois* on the menu, my mind and tongue pictured our Michigan wild berries on biscuit shortcake. Sad was my disillusionment to find that the French, who know how to make such ordinary dull vegetables as peas and spinach into works of gastronomic art, were satisfied and even proud to sprinkle a few wild strawberries in neat, geometrical designs on top of a piece of *cake*, gooed up with thin layers of whipped cream or frosting, and then had the audacity to call it wild strawberry cake. I felt sorry for all the cooks of France who had never tasted our crusty, luscious, scarlet miracle as served at Walloon Lake.

We used to get a lot of reading done in the summer. There was one summer when Ernest couldn't get enough of Horatio Alger, and *St. Nicholas* used to be forwarded to us. We loved the Ralph Henry Barbour stories in it. And I can still remember the time in 1913 when Harold Sampson was visiting Ernest and we had started to read *Dracula* aloud in front of the fireplace one evening. Dad sent us to bed at nine-thirty, but Ernest couldn't wait to go on with the story, so he and Harold, who were sleeping in a tent behind the house, read further ahead before they blew out their lantern that night. About one in the morning there was a shriek from the back yard and Ernie's voice cried:

"Help! Help! It's got me!"

Daddy ran to the tent and the rest of us threw on robes and dashed for the back yard. The tent was dark.

"What's the matter, Ernie?" Daddy shouted. "Are you all right, boys?"

"Is that you, Daddy?" mumbled Ernie. "What do you want?"

"I don't know what it is," said Harold. "I thought he was really hurt."

By this time the lantern was lighted and Daddy glanced down and saw the book where it had dropped beside Ernie's bed. He picked it up and left the tent in disgust.

"It's all right, just a nightmare," Daddy called. "It's no wonder, reading that stuff about Dracula sucking somebody's blood. Why can't these kids read some nice wholesome stuff about cowboys and Indians?"

The household settled down to sleep.

That was the year Ernie and Sunny went fishing at the far end of the West Arm. Ernie took his gun along. Dad was away, or he would never have dared take a gun on the water. When a rare blue heron suddenly flew up near them, Ernie shot it. He told us later he wanted it for the school museum. Unfortunately for Ernie, the game warden's house was near that end of the lake. The warden was away, but the warden's son, just a little older than Ernest, yelled at the children and told them his father would arrest them. He came out in a rowboat, threatening and scolding; Ernest and Sunny were now thoroughly scared and started back to our cottage, several miles away, as fast as they could.

The first thing we knew about it was when they landed, out of breath, and Ernie gasped out the news that the game warden was on his trail and might be following him any minute.

"Quick, cover up the name of the boat!" he shouted. "That dumb kid wrote down *Ursula of Windemere,* but when he spelled it, he called it *Yous-U-La of Wall Dee Mire.*" We all laughed at that, in spite of our fear for Ernie.

"I've got to get out of here before the warden comes!" Ernie gasped.

"Aren't you going to eat first?" I asked.

"No time," said Ernie, as he shoved off in the *Ursula* and turned it toward Longfield Farm across the lake.

"Where will you be?" I called.

"First I'll go to Horton's. I'll ask Wesley or Uncle Jim what to do."

"When will you be back?" I shouted to the retreating boat.

"When you see me!" he yelled. "Maybe a week, maybe two weeks."

"I'll bring you some clothes to Horton's!" I shouted.

"OK," came Ernie's voice, as he bucked the waves outside the point.

He had about a half-hour start on me. I followed him across in the other boat and I never slipped and climbed those three miles of hot loose sandhills to Horton Bay any faster. When I got to the Dilworth house, I was worn out from running. It was a very hot day, and I remember sticking my head into the doorway of the cool dark summer kitchen and saying, "Where is he?"

"Why, Marcelline, how nice to see you," said Aunty Beth Dilworth. "Where is who?"

"Ernie. I've got his clothes." It seemed the most important thing in the world to me. I didn't see why she didn't understand.

"Oh," said Aunty Beth. "Wesley gave him a ride into Boyne City. Wesley called up Judge Stroud in town, and he and your Uncle Jim told him about Ernest's shooting the bird."

"But the warden!" I said. "He's after Ernest. He's going to put him in jail."

"Don't worry about that," soothed Aunty Beth calmly. "It's all arranged. Wesley will take Ernest to the judge. Ernest will confess that he has broken the law. The judge will give him the minimum fine. When he's paid it and has a receipt, nobody can arrest him again for shooting that bird."

When I got home from Horton Bay that evening, the warden and his son had been there and gone again, both of them vowing to catch Ernest if they had to come back every day.

When Ernie got home a day or two later, he proudly showed his receipt for his fine to Dad.

"I'd like to see the warden's face when he sees this," said Ernie, feeling very cocky about the whole thing.

"It's cheaper to obey the game laws," said Daddy.

Ernie said, "But *you* don't always keep the game laws, Daddy."

My father tried to look stern, but he had a little grin at the corner of his mouth. "But I don't get caught," Dad replied.

5

The New House

I N APRIL, 1905, Abba Hall came back from his annual
trip to California a very sick man. When he reached
home, he was spent and nearly unconscious with Bright's
disease. For weeks he lay ill in the front bedroom at
"439," his bed facing the fireplace. Sometimes we were
allowed to peek in to say good morning to him, but most
of the time we were kept away and cautioned to be quiet.
Late in May, Grandfather Hall died.

That summer Mother sold the house Abba had left to
her and all of us went up to our cottage at Walloon Lake
as usual. When we came back in the fall we lived tempo-
rarily in a rented house on Grove Avenue while our new
home at the corner of Kenilworth Avenue and Iowa Street
was being built. Long before Grandfather Hall died,
Mother had been making sketches on paper for a "dream
house" she wanted to build herself. Though she had never
studied architecture in a formal way, she had read exten-
sively on the subject. Now, watching the new house take
shape on Kenilworth Avenue was the one way she could
take her mind from her grief at Abba's death.

The foundation for the house was started early in the
fall of 1905, and on a cold windy day in April we gathered
in the shell for the placing of the cornerstone in the fire-

place. The wind whistled through the cracks in the lathing as we sat on upturned nail kegs around the cold, empty fireplace while the Reverend Mr. Armstrong, pastor of the nearby Third Congregational Church, conducted a simple service. The architect, Mr. Fiedelke, was present, as were our Hemingway grandparents and all of us children. A corner of the hearth gaped open, awaiting the covered tin box Dad had prepared. In it were family mementos, a brief history of our family in old Oak Park, and a copy of the front page of the current *Chicago Tribune* as well as a clipping from the local *Oak Leaves* mentioning the Hemingway family.

A mason stood by the fireplace while Mr. Armstrong said a prayer. My father placed the box in the hearth. The mason slapped concrete over it and smoothed it with his trowel, and while it was still soft Mr. Fiedelke inscribed the date, 1906, in his neat printing on the fast hardening surface. Spontaneously Mother began to sing "Blest Be the Tie That Binds," and we all joined with her.

Then the real fun began. Uncle Tyley and Daddy, with Ernest helping them, piled curly wood shavings and a few larger pieces of wood on the new brick floor of the fireplace; then Daddy brought out the black iron kettle filled with water to hook on to the crane set in the fireplace wall. By this time we were all moving around to keep from shivering, hardly able to wait until the fire was lighted. At last it flared up. Daddy added coffee to the water in the black pot while we slapped our arms across our chests and jumped up and down to keep circulation going until the coffee was made and refreshments were served. Mother brought out tin cups and a quart of milk. Nothing ever tasted so good as the three-layer chocolate cake, the first food to be served in our new home.

Our family by this time was a large one, and we needed

all eight bedrooms in the new house. There were Ernest and myself, Ursula, three years younger than Ernest, and the baby Madelaine, called Sunny, born the fall before Grandfather Hall died. Granduncle Tyley continued to live with us when he was in town between trips. The cook and nursemaid also lived in, making a household of nine.

The new house was built to fill all our family needs. It was large, oblong in shape, and covered in gray stucco with white wood trim. A covered porch ran across the front facing Kenilworth Avenue, but both the main and side entrances were on Iowa Street. A large plate-glass center window also faced on Iowa, rather like the picture windows of today. At the rear of the living room a severely modern red brick fireplace stretched square to the ceiling, and to the left of the fireplace stained-glass double doors with a red tulip pattern opened into the cheery dining room with its five large windows facing on the back yard. A glass door, leading down to the garden, added to the sunny effect of this happy room.

Mother had a frieze of Grandmother Hall's oil landscapes built around three sides of the dining room, scenes our Grandmother had sketched along the Des Plaines River or at lakes in Wisconsin or Colorado where Mother and her parents had spent the summers. In the center stood the round golden-oak dining table, and drawn up to it were a dozen armchairs with cane seats. Mother said she saw no reason why the head of the house should be the only one to have a comfortable dining chair with arms.

In planning the kitchen Mother had had the advice of a friend, Mr. Thaddeus Philander Giddings, the bachelor head of the Music Department in the Oak Park schools. Mr. Giddings had no use for the old-fashioned kitchen with a pantry attached.

"You should be able to sit on a revolving piano stool in

the middle of any kitchen," he said, "and reach every item in the room. Women walk miles a day from stove to sink, to icebox, to pantry, and more miles carrying dishes and food back and forth into a dining room. Why shouldn't all the food and equipment be stored in the walls of a small kitchen, where the housewife can work on built-in table space all around the room?" This was a new idea in 1905.

So we had built-in cupboards on three sides of the room, with hard-maple counters under each and with closed cupboards or banks of drawers beneath the counters. When the plumber remonstrated at the height Mother had selected for the sink, saying, "*Nobody* has 'em that high!", Mother was firm. We were a family of tall people, and our sink was the first comfortably placed one I had ever known.

"I want something to take smoke and cooking odors out of the kitchen," my mother told Mr. Giddings. "See if you can help me work that out." Together they planned a skylight over the stove, worked by a steel handle hanging down from the ceiling. It was cumbersome, but it did carry off the bacon and cabbage odors and cooled the small kitchen in hot weather.

Mother's music studio was actually a separate small building attached to the north side of the living room. Her great desire had been to design a room which would be acoustically perfect. The science of acoustics was still in its infancy, and many expensive public buildings had such echoes in them that they were unfit for concerts or lectures. One day while reading at the public library, Mother had come across an article describing a formula for an acoustically perfect room. Following its directions she sketched out a room which was exactly square, with the height equal to half the length of a side, and with a balcony half-way up one wall. The studio was built following these simple rules, thirty feet square and fifteen feet high, and it did indeed prove to be free of echoes. One walked down two steps to enter the music room through a double oak door, then down two more steps to the floor. There was no basement beneath this part of the house. Large radiators painted bronze stood in each corner of the room, and from them hung galvanized containers of water — Mother had heard that a sufficient amount of water evaporating would keep her Steinway grand in tune. The piano stood opposite the door at the left, next to a rug-draped platform about two feet high on which her pupils stood when they gave recitals. A lifesize portrait of our great-great-grandfather William Edward Miller hung on the north wall at the place where Mother hoped someday to have a pipe organ installed. The old melodeon found its place in here, and a carved black ebony music case that also had belonged to my Grandmother Hall. It was in this room that Ernest practiced his cello and I my violin. There was a practice piano in the dining room for the other children to use.

My father, of course, had an office in the new house, and the library doubled as his waiting room. To entertain his patients while they waited, Dr. Hemingway arranged his collection of stuffed owls, squirrels, chipmunks and a small raccoon on top of the built-in oak bookcases that lined two sides of the library. Volumes of natural history filled with colored plates of birds, animals and flowers were ranged beside the current novels and sets of the classics in the bookcases, but the works of Jack London were conspicuously absent. My parents disapproved of the violence and coarseness of his writing. They liked *John Halifax, Gentleman,* much better. Ursula had been named for the heroine of this novel.

In my father's office glass-fronted cases of instruments stood against the walls. More bookcases housed his medical library, and the stuffed head of a deer was mounted on the wall where it could gaze down on the black leather examining chair (it could be stretched out like a couch) which stood near his large, cluttered rolltop desk. An old typewriter stood beside a locked cabinet filled with the medicines, drugs, and pills he dispensed to his patients. In the smaller rear room a Bunsen burner stood on a glass shelf over the washbowl, and other shelves held bottles and jars filled with various colored liquids and — what always fascinated us — a preserved appendix and the tiny fetus of a baby, looking more like a miniature monkey than a human. In the closet Daddy kept an articulated skeleton which he took out to show us how the bones were connected and which sometimes haunted our dreams. He called it "Susie Bone-a-part."

Separating this professional area from the living room of our new house was a large glass-topped door in which our family crest was set. This crest was not one inherited from our English ancestors; the design was one my father and mother had worked out together, and it meant much to them as a symbol of family unity. It was a large light blue H, with the center bar of the H formed by two clasped hands standing for the union of Hall and Hemingway. Over it was placed a golden sun with rays extending outward, symbolizing warmth and love, and under the clasped hands was a white lily for peace and purity. My parents had stationery engraved with this symbol, and a few pieces of it remain in some of the memory books my mother kept for each one of her children.

In the fall of 1905 Ernest and I entered the first grade at the old Lowell School on Lake Street, where Miss Margaret Pumphrey was our teacher. Mother had held me back in kindergarten waiting for Ernest to become six so we could enter first grade together. We learned to read by the "sounding out" method, and we learned quickly. Our rented house stood right next to the public library, called the Scoville Institute, and by Christmastime we were both able to read books in the children's room of the library. When school was over, we would sit at the low tables in our small chairs devouring the simple stories available to us until the librarian sent us home at suppertime. Usually we took books home to read at night before we went to bed.

When we moved into the new house in the fall of 1906, Ernest and I transferred to the Oliver Wendell Holmes School. One sad thing happened to me in the second grade there that made me very glad to leave that room. During that previous summer, Mother, still wanting Ernest and me to look alike, had had my hair cut boy-fashion. When I came home that fall I was embarrassed about my partially grown out hair; I looked so different from all my classmates. One of the older girls in the neighborhood came upstairs to my pretty new bedroom after school one day, and while we were talking we stood in front of the mirror. Georgia looked at me.

"Look at yourself," she said. "How can you stand having your hair hang down in those funny wisps in front of your ears?"

"I don't like it a bit," I said, "but it's growing out from a boy's hair cut I had last summer."

Georgia picked up the manicure scissors on my dresser. "Here, let me even it for you a little," she urged.

"I don't know," I said. "Mother might be mad."

"Oh, this won't show," said Georgia, "and your hair won't look nearly so queer as it does now."

Georgia snipped a little first on one side, then on the other. But it still didn't look just right to her, so she went on trying to even it up. Georgia was older than I; I was the new girl in the neighborhood, eager for friends and much impressed by her assurance. She had turned me away from the mirror, and a few minutes later, when she said, "There, that looks a lot better," I turned and was horrified to see my hair cut almost to the top of my ears. I knew Mother would be disappointed in me and angry too. The growing-out period was so long and so ugly anyway, and she was as eager as I to have me look neat and girlish again after the experiment.

I began to weep. "I can't show this to my mother," I said. "I don't know what I'm going to do. I'm afraid to go downstairs. Oh, Georgia, why did you have to cut it *so short?*"

Georgia laid the scissors on my dresser. "I don't see why you're so excited about it. You don't look any worse than you did before. Anyway, I have to go now," and she skipped downstairs and out of our house, leaving me to face the family alone.

Everything that I feared was said that night at supper, and more too. Daddy said I should be spanked. Mother thought I should be kept in my room for a week, but Daddy reminded her that there was school, so she compromised.

"I want you to remember this as long as you live," she said. "You can't be seen like this. I am going to get you one of Sunny's baby bonnets." She came back with a white lawn bonnet covered with tucks and lace, with long white strings. She put it on me and tied it under my chin. The tears were running down my face.

"No," I said, "I can't wear a baby thing like this!"

"Now," said Mother, and she turned to Daddy as she said it, "your shameful appearance is decently covered, and I want you to wear this bonnet until your hair grows out."

"But what about school?" I said. "Do I have to wear a baby bonnet all through school? The other children will just tease me to death."

Daddy spoke up. "You should have thought of that before you cut your hair," he said.

It was an agonizing two weeks. Finally, somehow, the second grade teacher got up courage and urged Mother to relent on the punishment. A week after the bonnet was removed, I was promoted to the third grade, where my new classmates knew little about my humiliating experience, and I was on my own. From that time on until our last year in grammar school Ernest and I were in separate grades. By the eighth grade, however, he had caught up and we were again in the same classroom. This was the result of my parents' plan that I should stay out of school for a year between the seventh and eighth grades and devote the time to piano, violin and voice lessons, as well as classes in gymnastic dancing, which Daddy called "good exercise." Mother and Daddy had strong-minded theories about bringing up children, and one of them was that girls ought not to be kept in school and rushed through strenuous routines during the difficult maturing time of the early teens. That year gave Mother and me the chance to spend many hours together attending concerts and plays, taking long companionable walks out North Avenue toward the river, and working on my vocal training. Yet I hated leaving my classmates and missing all the school and social activities. Ernest went to school every day, and so did Ursula and Sunny. I resented having to stay home, but my protests did no good. My sisters felt much the same way when their turns came, but they had to stay out just as I had. Of course neither Ernest nor our younger brother Leicester was kept out.

After Mother had paid for the new house and the furnishings, and Ernest and I were established in school, there was still a little of Mother's money left from her father's estate. Daddy had been wanting to step up professionally from general practitioner to specialist, and Mother (she was generous with her earnings) made it possible for him to have a four months' course in obstetrics at the New York Lying-In Hospital in the summer and fall of 1908. Daddy's appreciative letters to his "Darling Gracie" are full of excited words about his work as house physician (he had, near the end of his time there, "delivered personally 73 babies in the past 21 days"), his joy in visiting his father's relatives in Thomaston, Connecticut, and his gratitude to my mother for making it possible for him to take a ship home from New York by way of the Gulf to New Orleans, which he had always hoped to visit. He received his postgraduate degree in 1908 in New York and sailed on the S. S. *Comus* of the Southern Pacific Lines, getting back to us all in Oak Park in November after a trip up the Mississippi by river steamer. From then on my father was a specialist in obstetrics and was later head of that department when the new Oak Park Hospital, built by the Order of the Sisters of Misericorde, was opened.

The summer I was eleven, Mother and I spent a month together at Nantucket Island. Mother felt that in a family as big as ours she could hardly know her children as individuals unless she could have them alone for a while, one at a time. In her childhood she had spent many happy summers with her family and cousins on Nantucket, and so she planned to take each one of us there with her in the summer of our eleventh year. As I recall, Sunny was the only one of us who did not go on this trip with Mother.

The trip to Nantucket by way of Boston was a delight. We saw the Old North Church and climbed about inside it, and Mother took me to Paul Revere's home. Bunker Hill seemed too small to call a hill, but Concord and Lexington gave me a thrill as Mother told me about my Hancock ancestry and we saw the home of the first signer of the Declaration of Independence, John Hancock. Mother reminded me that he was descended from the same Hancock ancestry in England as my grandmother, Caroline Hancock Hall. But the English Hancocks had been ashamed of John, Mother had been told, for to them he was a traitor to the king.

On Nantucket we lived in a shingle house on Pearl Street belonging to Miss Annie Ayers. It was over a hundred years old, and the ceilings were just six feet high. Mother used to hit the ceiling regularly on the upward strokes of her brush as she dressed her long hair every morning. Several times Mother and I attended meetings for the promotion of women's rights which were held in Miss Ayers's parlor, where I listened with astonishment to news of what a Mrs. Emmeline Pankhurst was daring to do in England. These respectable hatted and gloved ladies at the meeting all approved and murmured praise of Mrs. Pankhurst's courage in setting fire to mailboxes in order to get the vote for women. My eleven-year-old mind found it hard to understand how burning up somebody's letters was admirable.

Girls my age that summer were wearing middy blouses over pleated skirts. Sandals were just coming into style, and I longed for a middy and sandals, but Mother disapproved of middy blouses as being too nearly like the clothing professional sailors wore. She thought them "common." But to my delight Mother did buy me a pair of beautiful tan leather sandals. My toes, freed of their high black button shoes, felt wonderful in open sandals as we walked across the black-tarred island streets.

Bathing costumes were very formal at Nantucket in those days of 1909. Mother and I always wore long black stockings and black canvas bathing shoes into the water, and our decorous bathing suits had sleeves to the elbows and skirts over knee-length bloomers. Our bathing caps were floppy cotton ones with wide ruffles around the brim. They were not intended to keep our hair dry. Salt-water swimming was a wonderful surprise to me, so buoyant after the fresh water at Walloon Lake. But there was one great disappointment that month: I could never go sailing. Mother was firm. There were many invitations to go on sailing picnics to nearby islands, but Mother explained that four young people, two of them her first cousins, had been drowned at Nantucket years before when their sailboat overturned.

We met artists, musicians and writers that month, and I posed for an artist, Miss Achsah Barlow, who promised me anything I wanted in return for the sittings. I chose to use her tubes of oil paints, her palette, brushes and a new canvas. It looked so easy when she painted. I will never forget how surprised and disappointed I was when I tried to paint a sailboat on the waves and found the paints wouldn't do what I wanted them to.

In a letter from Daddy received at Pearl Street that June there was a note from Ernest.

> *Dear Marc,*
> *Our room won in the field day against Miss Koontz room.*
> *Al Bersham knocked two of Chandlers teeth out in a scrap and your dear gentle Miss Hood*

had Mr. Smith hold him while she lickt him with
a raw hide strap.

Lovingly,
Ernest

I liked Miss Mary L. Hood, the principal. Obviously
Ernie did not.

Ernest had his month at Nantucket with Mother the
summer of 1910. A picture taken of him on the day they
started from Walloon Lake for Massachusetts shows Ernest neatly dressed in a gray tweed Norfolk suit. His
knickers buckled below the knee over black-stockinged
legs, and he was wearing high black laced shoes and a pork-
pie hat. In the photograph he looked pleased but a bit
self-conscious in his city clothes as he stood beside Mother
waiting for the steamboat, the *Tourist*, to take them on
the first leg of their journey to the East.

Perhaps the reason why so much remains in my mind
about my mother's family is because of the visit to Nantucket, where there was time to walk and talk and become
friends without the pressures and interruptions inevitable
in a big household like ours.

Whether the winters of my childhood were really colder
than winters are now, I have no idea. Certainly they
seemed colder and snow seemed ever-present in those days,
from Christmastime on. After our first big snow my
father changed from his doctor's buggy to an open red
cutter with a thick fur lap robe, and sleighbells were part
of the harness. Christmas itself and the day after, called
Boxing Day in England, were big events in our family.
Christmas Day was always spent with the Hemingway
family. Dinner was served at the home of my Uncle
George and Aunt Anna, or at Grandfather Hemingway's,

or at our house. When we all got together there were at least fifteen of us; the adults were seated in the dining room with the best white cloth and silver on the table, and the children in an adjoining room, enjoying their freedom from supervision. We always had place cards at Christmas and at Thanksgiving, and often, as the oldest grandchild, I was asked to make them out with my water colors.

Weeks ahead of the great day, Daddy had begun the preparation of the Christmas beef and the "hockies" he made from boiled, highly spiced pork hocks.

Mince pies by the dozen were made by the cook, and put out on the music room porch steps to freeze. They stood, stacked in piles, with plates between each tin, and the white enameled bowls of jellied "hockies," a china plate over each bowl, stood in a pagoda-like tower beside the stacked pies in the snow on the open porch. It took weeks to make the Christmas beef. Daddy bought a huge roast, often ten or twelve pounds of meat, and cured it slowly over a period of weeks in the basement fruit room. Each day he rubbed a mixture of two-thirds salt and one-third saltpeter into the meat. When the curing process was completed the beef was roasted in a slow oven for several hours. Daddy carved it so thin the slices curled. It was delicious, hot or cold.

To make "hockies" my father boiled cleaned pig hocks in salted water until the meat fell from the bones. Discarding the bones and skin, he let the kettle of meat and liquid stand until all the fat formed in a heavy white layer on top. After removing the fat, he added salt and lots of pepper, freshly ground; then finely crumbled sage leaves, chopped celery and onions were added and the mixture cooked down until the liquid and the meat formed a sort of soft stew. Poured into bowls and frozen, the "hockies" were so solid even when defrosted that they could be easily sliced.

Boxing Day we celebrated with the Hall and Hancock relatives of my mother's family. That was a gay and happy occasion too. When it was our turn to entertain we had special food, lots of music and something going on every minute. The Hancock relatives were such fun.

The Boxing Day menu called for one other traditional Old Country dish, English teacake, served hot, dripping with butter. Usually cut-glass dishes of my father's crisp homemade pickles were served with this Boxing Day lunch.

After the meal was over, one of the cousins might start a song and the whole crowd would join in, harmonizing in four parts, trying always to achieve a new modulation better than the last. They sang folksongs, bits from opera, and lots of Gilbert and Sullivan. The only thing I can compare it to nowadays would be a spontaneous jazz session where each individual musician tries to achieve a more harmonious and original arrangement of the tune all are playing.

Uncle Tyley Hancock and his sister Annie Hancock Roome were in their element at these parties. My mother's Roome and Kester cousins and the families of her other cousins, Will, Fred, Albert and Frank Hall, enjoyed music to the full. Usually some in the group played a joke on the others, dressing up in funny hats or acting out charades in hastily improvised costumes. The house was filled with laughter. Uncle Tyley would bring his violin downstairs and join the singing group, playing an obbligato he made up as he went along. The whole day was full of spontaneous fun and we hated to have it end when our cheery relatives went home to Berwyn and Evanston, Illinois.

In winter Mr. Orth, our milkman, delivered his daily quarts to our house on Kenilworth Avenue from a square, low, open wooden bobsled, and we children took delight in getting "hitches" behind him on our small sleds or taking "flops" behind other sleighs or the faster wagons on runners, the ones that delivered groceries and laundry in the neighborhood.

Oak Park was on level ground, and our only slope was the slight hill in Scoville Place. A few of the very well-to-do families built wooden toboggan slides in their yards, but they were unexciting compared to taking a hitch on a wagon or sleigh. The trick was to steer with one foot and not be tipped over or entangled in the ropes or runners of the other sleds. Sometimes as many as six sleds clung by ropes, like a group of chicks behind a hen, to the back of a horse-drawn wagon. Our woolen mittens became soaked and caked with lumps of ice clinging to the wool as we lay belly-flopped on our sleds. I still remember the unpleasant fuzzy mouthfuls of ice and wool we tasted as we tried to pull the hard lumps of ice from our mittens with our teeth.

There was skating, too, quite near our house. Ernie and I often carried our skates up to the slough, a marshy area of prairie land north of Augusta Street, where we would sit on the hard, cold ground, take off our rubbers to put on our clamped steel skates, and then hang desperately to each other for balance as we tried to keep ourselves upright while sliding across the lumpy frozen surfaces. Frequently we jumped quickly, just in time to miss the occasional patches of swamp grass and earth frozen in lumps in the ice between smooth skating places.

The slough was a makeshift spot, however. Real skating was best on the wide frozen surface of the Des Plaines River, two miles or so west of our house. There we could skate up and down the open length of frozen water for a mile or more in either direction.

Though my naturally weak ankles pained excruciatingly at the beginning of the skating season, by February I could almost forget them and enjoy it all enough to make the four-mile round trip worthwhile. Ernest and I usually went together. Ernest enjoyed skating. His ankles were strong, and often he helped me by crossing hands with me as we skated in rhythm. Sometimes he would put a brotherly arm around my shoulder when I faltered. But usually we skated off alone or with others of our friends.

Daddy did many outdoor things with us children. Enthusiastically, he would suggest trips to us on weekends. Would we like to go to the Field Museum? Or perhaps we'd like to drive down to Riverside or the Lincoln Park Zoo? Once he even took us all the way to Joliet, Illinois, where the state prison was. He impressed upon us that if we obeyed our parents we would never end up inside those forbidding walls. We saw a great deal more of our father both winters and summers than most children do nowadays. He was, of course, away at his calls and at the hospital certain hours a day, but his office hours were kept after lunch in the office in our own house, and again in the early evening. Daddy was always home for lunch, and he liked to have one of us, and sometimes two at a time, ride along with him in his buggy when he made his afternoon calls. Sometimes he would tell us details of his cases, more to talk them out loud for his own sake than to inform us of any medical problems.

From our youngest days on, Daddy took us to the Ringling Brothers Circus at the Coliseum in Chicago every spring. Ernest and I saw our first circus in May, 1902, when I was four and Ernest not yet three. I vaguely remember that first thrilling experience. I was so excited by the noise, the animal smells, the popcorn and peanuts that I was sick afterward, and Mother noted in her memory book: "Too much circus. Marcelline lost her lunch from sheer excitement."

We all of us looked forward to the thrill of the circus every spring. We always wanted to see the wonders of the side show people first, so we got there very early, long before performance time. I used to rush past the fat lady — she was loathsome to me as she overflowed her chair. And I always felt sorry for the leopard boy, whose skin was mottled deep tan and white in spots. Daddy hastened to explain to us that the so-called African boy probably came from the southern United States, and looked the way he did through having his skin pigment grouped in clusters instead of spread evenly. We never for a moment believed that this quiet, sad-looking lad was related to the leopards of the jungle, as the ballyhoo man said.

I think the person in the freak show I liked best was the tiny girl midget, only eighteen or nineteen inches tall but perfectly proportioned in every way. Princess Tiny, they called her, as I remember. She remained with the circus for years. Every spring I wanted to stay longer near her than I was allowed to do. I liked to listen to her talk in her high, squeaky baby voice. I loved to watch this tiny human doll sell her photos and move her beringed hands daintily as she shifted and jingled her many miniature bracelets. In spite of her tiny size, she was a canny businesswoman. If you didn't buy her picture for fifty cents she wouldn't talk to you at all. She had no desire to be admired by a huge human child. Perhaps I embarrassed her by my size. She seemed to want only adults with full pocketbooks to surround her, and she was quite frank about it.

Ernest always hung back to watch the leopards and the lions pacing in their cages. I hated to think of anything being kept in cages, excepting perhaps the monkeys. They seemed to be enjoying themselves, swinging on their red-painted exercise bars in the circus wagons and grabbing for peanuts from the customers' offering hands. The big beasts all looked so sad in cages.

By the time there were four of us Daddy had a hard time keeping us together in a crowd. He used the family whistle (the bobwhite call) to bring us back when one of us, usually Ernest, would slip away. Once Ernest had strayed away to go back to feel the third leg of the three-legged man to make very sure it was real. I guess the third leg was an actual part of the man, for he kicked a football with each of his legs in turn, but Ernest pinched the third leg and was not satisfied with the man's angry exclamation; Daddy caught Ernest asking this extra-footed gentleman to get up from his stool and let him see where the extra leg was attached. Daddy got to Ernest just in time and hurried us all into the main auditorium, where we edged our way to our reserved seats near the acrobats in the top balcony.

6

High School Years

THE DAY Ernest and I started high school in the fall of 1913, Daddy took a picture of us. No one seeing it would have guessed that we were fourteen and fifteen and a half. Ernest was almost five inches shorter than I, about five feet four. He came just above my shoulders. I had reached my full height of five feet eight and a half inches at fifteen, and I towered over him. I didn't like it; neither did he.

Ernest had a plump, round, little-boy face. His hair was parted at the side and brushed straight across his forehead. Most of the time it dropped into his eyes. The day of the picture he was wearing knickers, long black stockings, high shoes and a visored cap. The contrast in our heights was greater because I had on my new grown-up suit of plum-colored wool, ankle length, with a tight skirt slit up one side; I wore a plum-colored silk hat which I had made myself, and felt extremely well dressed and ready to face the new world of Oak Park High School. I don't know how sure Ernest felt of himself, but I do know that he resented being smaller.

Both Ernie and I had planned on going to college, and among the subjects he chose were Latin, algebra, English and the general science course. Mother had so disliked Latin when she took it in high school that she warned me against it, telling me it had been completely useless to her. She suggested I study a modern language instead, so I picked Spanish. Ernie at this time in a vague way was planning to be a doctor.

At home we had a family orchestra: Father on his cornet (his ear was never reliable), Ernie with his cello, I with my violin and Mother at the piano. Sunny also played the piano, and Uncle Tyley had his flute. We played hymns, Gilbert and Sullivan, and the simpler parts of the famous sonatas. With this background we both qualified for the high school orchestra, Ernie with his cello and I in the second violin section. There was a shortage of violas and so I volunteered to learn to play the viola, though I didn't know then what difficulties I was getting into. It wasn't only the fact that the viola is tuned one fifth lower than the violin, but I had to learn different note intervals for the fingering and, worst of all, transpose all the music at sight from either treble or bass clef to tenor clef, a third up or down from the regular clefs I knew. Yet in time I came to enjoy the rich mellow notes and lower key of the viola even more than I had liked playing the violin.

Ernest worked hard on his cello, but had great difficulty in tuning his strings and playing in key. Often Mother or I helped tune it for him. Though he wanted very much to be a good cellist, he was finding many other interests.

As he grew taller and more interested in athletics, he disliked the long hours of practicing the cello after school and longed to be with his friends. He never stayed out of school to study cello and gave it up by his senior year. Mother, who had paid for all of the music lessons, gave up when Ernie would not practice. Ernie always had other boys around, and usually a gang of them were at our house after school or in the early evening. At least once when he was practicing in the music room with the door closed, he set the metronome going and bowed back and forth on his cello with one hand while he held a book in the other; he read while he put in the required practice time playing all the time on one note. I saw him myself from the small door to the music room balcony.

Mother hoped we would enjoy music as much as she did, and to that end we were all given piano lessons. My sister Sunny was the only one of us who really enjoyed the piano enough to play it well. She used to sit in on Ursula's piano lessons and listen to the teacher's instructions. Sunny could play by ear, and even before she had lessons she could do the exercises and play the pieces which Ursula or any of the rest of us labored over. I still remember the secrecy with which I once slipped a piece of popular music to Sunny, for Mother disapproved violently of ragtime. Sunny practiced the piece surreptitiously and kept it hidden. When she could play it well, Daddy overheard her. "That's a nice jolly tune," he remarked. We were greatly relieved.

In her school days Sunny wanted to be a dancer; but Daddy would not permit her to study ballet, though we all felt that with her good coordination she had a natural aptitude for it. In later years she studied the harp with Joseph Vito of the Chicago Symphony and became a harpist with the Memphis Symphony Orchestra.

Mother had great hopes that I would be a singer, and from the time I was twelve she gave me the same vocal teaching that she gave her other pupils. I liked to sing and did take part in church choirs and in some amateur operas, but I had no ambition to be a soloist. I knew mine was not a great voice. Mother hoped one of her children would inherit her voice and become famous in the professional world of music, but none of us did.

She gave Ernest and me, and to some extent the younger children, a wonderful background in appreciation of music. I saw my first opera in Chicago in 1914, and Ernest and I had season tickets to the Columbia Opera Company in 1915. Naturally it was Mother who took us to symphony concerts and operas in Chicago, just as it was Mother who saw that we had music lessons all our growing-up years. I was started on the piano when I was five years old, and Ernest began the next year.

In my teens, Mother planned that I should have a different corsage of flowers to wear at each opera. "I hope the music and the perfume of these flowers will always remind you of each other," Mother told me. They did. Even today the odor of roses brings back the first time I heard *Romeo and Juliet* at the Chicago Opera House. The scent of mignonette and the music of *La Bohème* are forever tied together; so are *Faust* and the exciting tang of freesia a part of each other. Spicy pink carnations were worn to *Norma*, I recall, while the duet in the tomb of *Aïda* and that haunting, chanted cry of the priests in the temple above the dying lovers stays in my memory with the ephemeral sweetness of English violets worn on the dark fox collar of my winter coat.

"A girl should always have enough flowers and candy and love at home so she doesn't think she's in love with the first man who offers her these tributes," Mother said. "One should fall in love for reasons far more important than the flattery of a corsage." Daddy agreed, and during high school days all of us older girls and Mother often had fragrant corsages to wear to church. (The fact that Daddy had a patient who was a florist did not detract from the romance of these gifts.)

Sometimes Ernest and I were given tickets together to the opera for the evening. Mother went with me to Saturday matinees, usually. She was already teaching me arias from some of the operas we saw at that time.

I remember one evening, during our later years in high school, Ernie and I went to *Madame Butterfly* together. We had the libretto with us to read on the elevated train as we rode the forty-five minutes or more it took to go from Oak Park to the Chicago Opera House. But we had such fun talking as we rode that we were forced to read like mad in the theater before the curtain went up, and between acts as well. We even read aloud the translation to one another as the acts progressed, to the evident annoyance of our neighbors in adjoining seats. That night a Japanese soprano was singing the title role, and we both, I remember, were wet-eyed in sympathy with Butterfly at the end of the opera as Lieutenant Pinkerton walked off with his American wife.

We had weird and wonderful nicknames in our family. Some evolved naturally, but most of them, the ones that stuck the longest, were Ernest's creations. For instance, Sunny, whose christened name was Madelaine — she was named for Mother's cousin Madelaine Randall Board — had in infancy been nicknamed Sunny Jim because she had a blond wispy curl on top of her otherwise bald baby head. At that time, in 1904, there was a cereal called Force which showed a cover picture of a grinning bald man with one curly topknot, named Sunny Jim. I never heard her called Madelaine except when our parents were being very stern. During high school Ernie changed the nickname to

Sun-bones and then to None-bones — and eventually she became Nunny. Sometimes she was called James or Jimes.

Ursula was called Mrs. Giggs or just Giggs as a very little girl; then, during high school, Ernie called her Ura-legs for no particular reason, and Ura was the name that stuck. When our youngest sister Carol first tried to say "Me," in baby fashion she said, "Bee" instead. Ernie labeled her Bee-fish, and Beefie she remained. Strangers hearing this name applied to the beautiful, tall slender person she grew to be could never understand the connection. My younger brothers and sisters called me Mazaween or Maaz, but Ernie called me "the Great Iverian" from a character in a Latin play in high school. Naturally this was soon shorted to Ivory, and those not in on the joke assumed this referred to the status of my intelligence. One of my pet names for Ernie was "the Old Brute," which he invented for himself, and there were many times he deserved it literally. Daddy and Mother were about the only ones who escaped Ernie's rechristening. But there were times when Ernie referred to Dad with mock reverence as "the Great Physician."

When baby Les was born in 1915, Ernie made up the two-line verse:

Leicester Clarence
Pesters parents —

and for a while Pesters or "the Pest" was the name he lived up to. (We were always having to hush our voices and tip-toe around in the evening, and sometimes the baby's wails wakened us at night.) But he was a darling blond baby. I wheeled him for his airings after I came home from high school classes and I gave him his bottle when he went to bed before our dinner at night. I was old enough to be his mother. Ernie's other name for Les was Gaspipe. No wonder that years later when Les grew up and went away to school in Honolulu, he told everyone his name was Hank.

Ernie called himself Eoinbones and later Stein, a shortening of the name Hemingstein which he assumed as a sort of *nom de plume* when he wrote Ring Lardner takeoffs in the high school weekly paper.

Ernest had two particular pals, Ray Olson and Lloyd Golder, who had lockers next to his on the ground floor of the high school. Ernie drew three circles with yellow chalk on all three lockers, and the boys called this spot the Three Ball Joint. Then Ernie renamed himself and his pals in keeping with the pawnshop sign: Olsen became Cohen, Golder was changed to Goldberg, and Ernie, Hemingstein. Everybody at school wanted to know what the three balls meant. Ernie loved creating attention and arousing curiosity. He hoped people would ask that question.

"It means just what it says," he would reply. "We deal in funds. We don't lend. You lend to us. We promise to use any money anybody wants to contribute and we promise never to return it." Those three nicknames stuck for years.

Morris Musselman, whom we called Mussie, was another close friend of Ernest's who was often at our house, and so was Harold Sampson, called Sam. Lyman Worthington and George Medill (inevitably nicknamed Pickles) were others who were often around after school.

We often saw Morris Musselman's father, A.J., working in his garage on North Grove Avenue, and we knew that he was doing some experiments down in the basement, but it was a long time later that we learned that what he was working on turned out to be the first successful balloon tire. He held all the basic patents, and years later Morris wrote a book about him and his many inventions called *Wheels in His Head.*

Though our parents provided for us generously, we had very little spending money of our own. True, we knew we had birthday and Christmas goldpieces in separate green flannel bags, marked with our own names in Daddy's box in the vault of the Avenue Bank. Daddy took us in and showed them to us every year or so. But we did not have much spending money.

Dad felt we had small need for cash. Everything we needed was provided for us, he used to say. In grammar school and even into the first years of high school, each of us was given an allowance of one cent a week for each year of our age — five cents for the five-year-old and fifteen cents for the fifteen-year-old, and so on. If we wanted more we were expected to earn it. Out of this munificence we had to contribute to Sunday school as well as buying any candy or small items we wanted. We had to keep track of how we spent our allowances and show our account books to Daddy once a week. I remember overhearing Father say to Uncle Tyley: "B.T., Ernest's system is unique. He puts down five cents for Sunday school and all the rest under Miscellaneous."

My earnings took the form suggested by the Sunday school leaflet. These ads urged any ambitious young person to send for packets of sachet, sewing needles and the like, to sell at a profit. It sounded so easy. All the young salesman had to do, the ads said, was send for *twenty* packets. No money needed. He or she was to sell the first ten packages, at fifteen cents each, to friends and neighbors, return this money to the company, and then sell the *remaining* ten packets and *keep the money himself!*

What could be easier? But there was a joker in the offer. Ten households were, I found, the very limit of the number of interested adults who were willing to buy fifteen-cent packets of unknown scents of sachets or needles of the same type anybody could buy for ten cents at a local store. To sell the last ten packets meant going out of one's own neighborhood; it meant calling on numbers of strangers who slammed the door on a youngster like me who began her sales talk:

"Would you like to buy a nice sachet?"

"No, we don't want any," the housewife would interrupt before I could finish my first sentence.

I found that half the other children in our Sunday school who read the same advertisements were also trying to sell the identical merchandise. Our neighborhood was a saturated market.

I had made a little money, but I still had a big stock of lavender, rose and carnation sachets and gold-headed needles on hand when I ran out of customers. For a long time after my efforts at door-to-door salesmanship had ceased, the family was understandably suspicious of small wrapped packages as gifts from me.

"Not sachets *again!*" groaned my sisters frankly, upon opening any ribbon-tied gift of flat, square shape. So eventually even that outlet for my stock was gone.

I tried selling subscriptions to the *Youth's Companion* before Christmas several seasons, and that worked for a while. After that I learned to make doughnuts, and my sales of these eatables were more successful, for I had no nearby competitors in this field. Grandmother Hemingway loyally bought a dozen of my wares every week, even though Grandfather hinted that his digestion was delicate and fried foods were not his choice.

Ernest was smarter. He found lawn-mowing jobs and did snow shoveling in winter. He also had a regular income from his job delivering our local paper, the *Oak Leaves*. This weekly was published by Telfer MacArthur, brother of Charles, the Chicago newspaperman who later married a girl named Helen Brown, but more famous as Helen Hayes of Broadway.

Ernie carried his weekly papers in a cloth sack hung from his shoulder. His was a long route of many blocks, and it took him several hours after school and sometimes into the evening to finish his lengthy list of customers each weekend. Often he had to return to our house from a mile away to refill his bag and complete the deliveries.

The *Oak Leaves* wasn't a mere sheet; it was thick and bound like a magazine. Even in 1914, it was a heavy volume each week. Though our parents left us to our own initiative where jobs were concerned, on days when the rain poured down Dad would sometimes relent in his firm attitude toward us and help Ernie. I can recall his voice as he said, "Here, boy! Hop in." Then Dad would take Ernest and his bundles of *Oak Leaves* on the rounds in the black-curtained Model T Ford.

We always had company at home, it seemed. Mother and Dad said the big round table in the dining room could always squeeze in one more. It was not unusual for us to seat twelve at a meal. Father usually did the marketing while he was out on his calls, and as a rule he was the one who gave the cook directions about meals. Daddy enjoyed buying and planning our food, and quite often he would countermand Mother's orders when she had the menus arranged. He didn't intend to annoy her; he'd simply bring home something he saw that appealed to his palate, like smoked whitefish or steak or calves' liver and bacon, and announce to the cook, "It's for lunch." He liked to pretend he was saving Mother trouble and worry in the domestic field, but actually he enjoyed running things in the kitchen end.

He often bought food in large quantities. He loved an excuse to stop at Gotsch's Meat Market on Chicago

Avenue or Walter Whittelsey's grocery on Oak Park Avenue or at Tony's fruit stand on Lake Street. All these proprietors were Daddy's patients as well as his friends, and he liked nothing better than a chance to drop in and chat with them all between his sick calls.

Daddy was always willing, as was Mother, to let us have groups of our friends in for Sunday night supper. The maid went out after our noon dinner on Sundays, so our guests pitched in to help fix shrimp salad, cocoa or tea, and the muffins I often stirred up for supper. Usually the cook left a couple of frosted cakes for dessert. Ernie and I had good times being in charge of getting the meal and sharing it with our friends. Sometimes as many as eight or ten guests of our own age besides the family were present on Sunday nights. We didn't mind cleaning up afterward. Ernie was very particular that all the dishes should be rinsed off under the faucet before they were put in the pan of hot sudsy dishwater. With all our guests helping us, the dishes were dried and put away quickly.

One night, I remember, there was another kind of get-together at our house. It was a Saturday night and Ernest was very mysterious about who was coming over to see him. He had given us all instructions to keep *out* of the basement and away from his bedroom.

All evening long boys kept arriving, a few at a time, and Ernest let them in the back door. There were whisperings in the back hallway and thumping sounds of scurrying boys' feet running up and down the back stairway from the basement to the third floor. When I could not contain my curiosity any longer, I caught sight of Ernest on one of his trips to the basement, in the dark hallway, and whispered to him: "Hey, Ernie, what's going on tonight? What's all the mystery about?"

"Just keep that kitchen door closed! Keep out of this,

Sis," he hissed. "We're having an initiation for new members of the Boys' Rifle Club and the new guys will be here any minute. I don't want 'em to hear a voice or see a light."

I noticed that Ernest had an old dried porcupine skin in his hand, and a flashlight. I heard him say to the other boys who were waiting in the dark basement: "Hey guys! How about this for the final torture? We'll take off their shirts and rub this up and down their backs! That'll get 'em! Here, feel these quills!"

"Yowee!" somebody yelled.

I shut the kitchen door quickly and just in time. The side doorbell rang that minute, and Ernest, flashlight in hand, went to greet the initiates.

Later that evening, after a long time of unnatural silence, we heard wild shrieks from Ernest's room on the third floor. Daddy asked Mother if she knew what was going on up there. I kept very quiet while they speculated about it, but I knew the porcupine quills were proving effective.

Ernest and I did a lot of reading. Sets of the classics, Scott, Dickens, Thackeray, Stevenson and Shakespeare filled many of the shelves in our family library. I don't think we skipped any of them. Only the fact that I was out of school with mumps one spring and had run out of all other reading matter provided time for me to read all the tragedies of Shakespeare as well as rereading the comedies. Ernie's attack of mumps followed mine, and I know the same volumes were available to him. We both devoured Stevenson, especially one of his lesser-known volumes, *The Suicide Club,* as well as *Treasure Island.* Thackeray wasn't as easy reading as Kipling or Stevenson or Dickens, but the green cloth volume of *Vanity Fair* we read from cover to cover. We both read Horatio Alger books in third and fourth grade, and Ernest took them seriously.

The *Youth's Companion, St. Nicholas Magazine*, the *National Geographic, Scribner's*, the *Outlook*, the *Ladies' Home Journal, Harper's, World's Work*, the *Atlantic Monthly* and *Good Housekeeping* we grabbed the minute they arrived; we even paged through Dad's American Medical Association magazine. The truth is that we both were interested in medicine, of which we had heard so much from our father. When Ernest was a young boy, he signed a family guest book at one of the many family dinner parties *Ernest Hemingway, M.D.* — he was about nine at the time. Daddy laughed about it, but he was pleased that the boy planned to be a doctor. Daddy let Ernie help him in his office at times and watch while he dressed wounds, or when he treated the Ottawa Indians up at the lake. Once I remember it was a gunshot wound that Ernie watched being cleaned out, and another time Ernie helped while my father cleaned out a bad cut suffered by a young boy. In this case Ernie held the boy while Daddy probed into the wound for the splinters of wood which had been driven into the flesh. Later, Ernie watched an operation. Dressed in a white gown, he was permitted to stand at the top rear of the operating theater at the hospital where Daddy was on the staff as head of obstetrics. Ernie was interested, but he sat down when he felt faint and he did not go again.

Later, in our junior and senior years in high school, both Ernie and I attempted to write acceptable essays for the *Atlantic Monthly* Contributors' Club. Some of our classmates made that column, but I don't think either of us ever did. It would have been too big a thrill to have been forgotten.

In addition to all the reading at home, and in connection with our schoolwork, we both entered a Bible reading contest. Mr. Fred Sweeney, father of our friends Mildred and Chesley Sweeney, was the adult adviser of the Christian Endeavor Society in the Third Congregational Church. Mr. Sweeney kept the meetings of this group very lively. He offered a prize to the member who first completed reading every word of the King James version of the Bible. One of Ernie's friends, Harold Sampson, finished first. But though it took us longer to get through and we knew we'd missed the prize, both Ernie and I completed every word. I still remember plowing through the "begats" and wondering why all those family names were important. We passed a detailed test on the Bible reading and we both learned a lot.

Though I seem to be mentioning Ernest and myself rather constantly, it is not done to exclude the other children. Since Ursula and Sunny were nearly four and a half and almost seven years younger than I, and in grammar school, their activities were naturally different from Ernie's and mine in high school. They went to bed at seven-thirty, just as Ernest and I had when we were their ages, and though our parents preferred that we keep a ten o'clock bedtime on school days, we were often up much later completing our assigned homework. Little sister Carol, who was over thirteen years younger than I, and Leicester, who was born when I was seventeen, were almost like a second family to my parents. Ernie and I were very fond of these little ones. Ernie liked to pick up Carol and dandle her on his knee. There was no doubt that she was his favorite sister in those days.

Both Ernie and I entered into many other high school activities beside our memberships in orchestra and glee club. Ernie belonged to the Burke Club, a debating society for boys. We each belonged to a Rifle Club (the girls' Rifle Club had regular target practice), and in senior year Ernie was track team manager. I was in the Drama Club too. I still have a typical Ernest-type note my brother sent me when, as one of the twelve out of one hundred who had submitted a manuscript in the tryouts for the Story Club, I was lucky enough to be chosen for that group. Ernie's note, written on a page of tan paper headed *Memorandum*, was as follows:

> *Hey, how in the name of all things just and unjust did you get in the Story Club? If I couldn't write a better story than you, I'd consign myself to purgatory. Congratulations!*
> *Thine eternally,*
> *Ernestums*

It was dated May 5, 1915.

From his first year in high school, Ernie was eager to make the football team. At first he was too small, and though he could not make the heavyweight team under Coach Zuppke, Ernie was faithful in practicing with the lightweights, where he served as a substitute. As he grew and his weight went up, he became a bit too heavy for the lightweights, so he used to starve himself before weighing-in time for the Saturday games. Often toward the end of the week Ernest would stick to a diet of lettuce and a little water, just to keep his weight down. As a substitute he played in enough games to qualify for his letter as a member of the lightweights in his junior year. In his senior year, when he was almost six feet tall, he made the regular team, first as a substitute and finally as a regular, just before the end of the season.

Ernie practiced with the swimming team at the high school. He was good at plunging. He worked at it and had more success as a swimmer than in any other sport.

I think it was about 1916 that Ernie first went to a professional prize fight in Chicago, and through some connection he got a chance to see boxers training in a downtown gym. He did not take lessons, though he wanted to do so, but he watched others boxing on several occasions. From that time on, he and his pals practiced whacking each other with boxing gloves every chance they got. Usually the bouts took place in our music room. We girls watched them from the balcony and teased the fighters by throwing paper wads and sofa pillows down on top of them. They yelled at us to stop, but I think they liked the attention just the same.

Luckily, with all the punches Ernie and his gang threw at one another, nobody ever got really hurt. A nose bleed was the nearest the boys ever came to a casualty. The legend that Ernie broke his nose or hurt his eye badly is not true. I saw him every day as we went to school together.

During our four years of high school, Ernest and I enjoyed our English classes, and we both liked chemistry and ancient history. In other subjects we needed tutoring: Ernest in Latin during his first year, and I in math (only Miss Mary Payne's help after school got me through algebra and geometry). But we both did well in English. During our first years in high school we were together in the classes taught by the head of the English Department, Frank J. Platt; he taught in the oak-paneled English Club room, where his students sat in leather-seated arm chairs under the beamed ceiling. Mr. Platt was a dignified, rather quiet, unexpressive man himself, but he liked our efforts at originality, and his appreciation and high marks gave Ernest's and my egos a much needed boost. Once Mr. Platt assigned a story to be told by each of us, and I brought in an original tale. When he asked me to read mine, I sat on the floor to recite. Quite unshaken by this unusual behavior, our teacher permitted me to continue, but at the end he inquired mildly, "Was sitting on the floor necessary?"

"Of course," I replied, "I was telling the story around a campfire."

"Yes, now I understand," said kindly Mr. Platt.

Later Ernest worked with Miss Margaret Dixon, while I was in Miss Bell's and then Miss Wright's senior English class. But I think that the two subjects we enjoyed the most were the electives, English V and VI, taught by Miss Fanny Biggs. Miss Biggs, a plain, thin woman, was possessed of great charm. She wore thick spectacles and screwed her hair into an old-maidish knot on top of her head, but her warm smile made her beautiful. Her keen sense of humor and her enthusiasm for the subjects she taught inspired all her pupils.

English V was a course in the short story, while English VI was in journalism. In the short story class we studied various styles of writing, and I remember Ernest turning in tales of his own in the manner of Poe, Ring Lardner and O. Henry. I remember that I wrote one myself with a plot about cannibals catching and cooking a missionary. The O. Henry surprise ending was the shock to the cannibals when they bit into the missionary's leg. It was wooden.

Ernie used Walloon Lake backgrounds in his writing at this time: tales he had heard form some of the Indians at the bark peelers' camp not far form our cottage, and experiences old-timers had told him about the lumberjacks, the saloons in Boyne City, and the rough old days in the north woods, were picturesque source material which he had stored away.

One of his first stories, "Sepi Jingan," appeared in the November, 1916, issue of *Tabula*, our literary monthly

—I still have my copy. That narrative, with its abrupt, short sentences, its stylized repetition and natural, vivid dialogue is a forerunner of his later published books.

In English VI, Miss Biggs conducted the class as if it were a newspaper office. We each had daily assignments covering the various phases of a small-town sheet. We took turns being editor, special columnists, writing the advertising, doing features, straight news and sports. It was wonderful experience. One day we might have six advertisements to write, ones with "pull"; another day a news story and a feature story might be the assignment. We took turns doing "Society" and a personal column. "Tell your whole story in the first paragraph, then develop details in relation to their importance," Miss Biggs told us. "Leave the least important parts to the end. The editor may have to cut your stuff. Write so he can cut from the end and always retain the story if only the first paragraph is left." We also had exercises in expanding a one-sentence news item to fill up space in a column.

Miss Biggs insisted upon style in her students' work. She was strict, and our assignments had to be in exactly on time every day. She kept us on our toes. Her enthusiasm was contagious and her sarcastic disapproval could be stinging. She didn't mind how far we stretched our imaginations or how absurd the subjects we chose for our advertisements. I remember some of the items we promoted. One was an all-wicker bathtub. Another ad I wrote was for silent poker chips. I stressed their advantages for evening use in a household where the wife and children must not be kept awake by the click of the chips at the card table downstairs. Morris Musselman brought in one for a fur-lined coffee cup.

Naturally, members of the English VI class were eager to use their training on the staff of the school newspaper. Eight of us, including Ernest and myself, were chosen as the editorial board of the *Trapeze*, the school weekly. We took turns serving as editor-in-chief for a month at a time. The editor gave out assignments each week. I remember an issue when I was editor, in which I told Ernest what to write, and a few weeks later he was ordering me.

Ernie used to do some features for the *Trapeze* in the style of Ring Lardner. There would be a serious report on a football or baseball game played with a neighboring school, and after it Ernie would write a "Ring Lardner" feature on the same game in his own hilarious style, under the name of Hemingstein. It was always Hemingstein who scored the touchdowns or hit the home runs. I think I can truthfully say that the hours spent in our class in English VI, our after-school work on the paper with congenial friends, our headline writing and proofreading at the local printing office were some of the happiest hours of our schooling.

Our principal, Mr. Marion McDaniel, was an extremely dignified man, gray-haired, handsome, but almost completely lacking in humor. He represented law and order in our school, and he had little patience with Ernest or me. The independence which Miss Biggs encouraged in us, Mr. McDaniel frowned upon. So it delighted our souls when Miss Biggs, leaving the lunchroom one noon, lifted a piece of ice from her water glass and accidentally-on-purpose slipped it down the back of Mr. McDaniel's neck as he sat at the table in the school cafeteria. Miss Biggs was disappearing through the door when he felt the shock and let out a yell. News of this daring act spread like wildfire through the school, and when Fanny Biggs entered her journalism class that afternoon, the whole group rose and clapped.

Ernie and I didn't go to many parties our first year in high school, but in the spring of our freshman year, when I was sixteen and Ernest nearly fifteen, we were invited to a dance at the local Unitarian Church House. Frank Lloyd Wright, a neighbor of ours, had built this first Oak Park church of modern design on Lake Street at the corner of Kenilworth Avenue. It stood opposite the conventional steepled First Congregational Church and was a forbidding oblong building of gray stucco without steeple or windows, lighted by a glass skylight in the roof. Mother thought the Unitarians very daring and a little crazy to let anyone talk them into such an unchurchlike edifice.

Attached to the church on its south side was a smaller building which did have windows and good polished hardwood floors, and it was here that the dance was held. Our Congregational Church did not allow dancing even in the Sunday school room, but the Unitarians did.

As usual I went with Ernest to the party, since I had not yet been allowed to go out with other boys. Neither of us had ever been permitted to dance, and of course we had never had any instruction. I was wild with excitement when Mother said we could go. I remember the lovely lavender and cream silk of the new dress I wore that evening. Aunt Mary, the missionary in China, had sent the material to me from the Philippines. It was wonderful to be going to a dance at last.

When we got to the Church House we sat in chairs around the sides of the room. Boy after boy came up to ask me to dance, but after a few awkward turns around the floor, I struggling to follow the lead in the hesitation waltz, each partner would return me to my seat with a mumbled excuse. I couldn't dance. It looked easy but I just couldn't do it.

Ernest couldn't dance either, but he didn't care much. He

talked to his friends near the doorway and eventually disappeared outside for a while. I was left stranded. When the music stopped and it was time to go home, Ernie came back and together we walked the five blocks home, up Kenilworth Avenue in the darkness.

"I'm never going to a dance again unless I learn how," I said. "It's cruel to be the only one who never learned the steps." I was damp-eyed and still upset the next morning.

Mother's breakfast greeting, "Did you have a good time, dear? Your dress looked so nice!" brought on a flood of tears and recrimination. You *couldn't* have a good time at a dance if you didn't know *how* to dance was the gist of it. No matter how pretty the dress was, it didn't mean anything, I told her. It was horrible! I was through with such parties forever.

Much parental consultation must have gone on in the weeks following my humiliation. Even Grandmother Hemingway agreed with Mother, we learned later. Ernie and I never heard any of the arguments between our parents, but when Miss Marybelle Ingram's dancing classes started at the Colonial Club the next fall, Mother announced one night during dinner that she and Daddy had arranged for Ernest and me to take lessons in the evening class on Saturdays. Ernie wasn't too impressed. To him it meant dressing up, wearing a stiff starched collar and tie as all the older boys did, polishing his shoes and being nice to girls. Ernie didn't mind learning to dance, but he did hate wearing that high starched collar. Girls at that time were a bore.

The thought of finally going to dancing school delighted and panicked me at the same time. Surely the evening classes were for those who were experienced, the young people who already knew how to dance. I mentioned this.

"Don't worry," said Mother. Daddy kept unusually quiet, his eyes on his plate. "Miss Ingram understands. She says that with a little extra instruction you and Ernest and the others who are starting for the first time now will soon be up with the rest of the class."

"But how will we get way down to the Colonial Club?" I asked.

"Daddy will take you in the Ford, of course," Mother replied.

Daddy acquiesced in silence. He had not said a word. Although he still didn't approve of dancing, he had given up fighting the idea.

Daddy took us as Mother had promised, and he picked up Ruth Allan too, my pretty blond schoolmate who lived down our street a few blocks. Every Saturday evening that winter Dad would bring his car to the front door and honk the horn loudly, even if we were waiting right on the steps.

After we three were in the back seat, we girls carrying our cretonne slipper bags, Daddy drove us the two miles to dancing school. All the time he kept muttering:

"Leads to hell and damnation — don't know what the world is coming to — it's all your mother's idea," and phrases like "Don't blame me if this leads to . . ." and his voice would drop. What it would lead to we never found out. But he could see how happy we were. Toward the end of that year he'd often greet us at the ten-thirty closing with a cheery "Have a good time, kids?"

At Christmas a year later there was a small shiny mahogany Victrola under the Christmas tree, a present to Ursula. Records we played on it were squeaky and nasal, but we didn't care. Everybody in the family except Dad learned to dance that winter. Often our friends came in and we danced to records with them in the music room too.

I think Daddy was secretly pleased that we were learning to dance, as he had never had the chance to do. Before the year was out Ernie and I were both fairly proficient. Then, in his junior year, Ernie suddenly became interested in girls. He had been constantly surrounded by womankind, with four sisters, his mother, a nurse-girl and the cook living in the house, and my school friends in and out all the time, but none of these people had ever registered with Ernie as being actually female. I remember the whispers of excitement around our house when we learned that he had invited a pretty dark-haired girl named Dorothy to a basketball game. Mother was pleased too. We all thought it was about time Ernie had a date. From that time on Ernie enjoyed parties and dances. With him taking other girls, at last I had a chance to have dates of my own.

In November that year Mother said one day, "How would you and Ernest like to have an evening party for all your friends and we'll call it your debut? We'll have a tea in the afternoon for you to meet all my friends, soon after you're eighteen, but Daddy and I thought you and Ernest might like to have your first evening party on New Year's Eve." This was wonderful news.

Ernie and I began making lists, and Mother and Daddy had formal invitations printed on light blue stationery, with Old English lettering:

Six hundred, North Kenilworth Avenue

DR. and MRS. CLARENCE E. HEMINGWAY

request the pleasure of your company

at a party for their daughter

MARCELLINE

On Friday Evening, December 31, 1915

At eight o'clock

R.S.V.P.   "Salmagundi"

"Salmagundi" was the popular name for a varied program of entertainment. Daddy had some programs printed for us, with table and couple numbers at the top, the date and *New Year's Eve* in the middle, and at the bottom of the cover, again in Old English letters, *At the Hemingways.* Inside was the one word *Salmagundi,* with numbers from one to twenty to be filled in by the boys' names on the girls' programs and the girls' on the boys', just as dance cards were filled in in those days.

We started the evening with a stunt guaranteed to break the ice at any party. It was Mother's suggestion. She and Daddy had encountered this same sort of startling introduction at a party they had attended in another town. We chose two of our most dignified school friends and rehearsed them ahead of time as "Mr. and Mrs. Butterfly." "Mr. Butterfly" wore a tall silk hat and white gloves. "Mrs. Butterfly" wore a woman's hat with a plume and lace mitts, and next to them stood their daughter, "Miss Letterfly" who had in her hand, held behind her back, a damp washcloth. The stunt was to have these three people standing in a receiving line in our music room with the doors closed. As our friends from school were brought in one by one, Ernie or I would say, "Oh, I do want you to meet our guests of honor." Solemnly they shook hands with Mr. and Mrs. Butterfly. When the guest put out his hand to greet the third in line, Ernest or I would say, "And now, meet Miss Letterfly," and that was just what she did.

The sudden slap of the damp cloth to the cheek was such a shock to the guest that the first reaction was instant anger, followed immediately by a hoot of laughter as the victim realized it was all a joke and joined the crowd of those previously "introduced" to watch the fun of the next introduction. The stunt was a great hit, and instead of being self-conscious the boys were in a mood to give the girls a wonderful time.

There were conversations arranged for in various small rooms around the house, with a sign on the door suggesting a topic, and never were any couples left alone more than five minutes. There were square dances in between the fox trots; then the whole crowd entered into childhood games like London Bridge and blindman's buff, and at midnight, when the refreshments were served, Mother sat down at the Steinway grand in the music room and all of us joined in singing anything she could play.

7

Graduation and War

OUR SENIOR year was a crowded one. Ernie had his
work cut out as a member of the football team and a
regular on the swimming team, and both he and I took
part in community plays besides our social and church
activities. By the fall of 1915 our family had moved over
to the First Congregational Church from the smaller Third
Church. We joined our Hemingway grandparents and
their youngest daughter, our Aunt Grace Hemingway, a
professor at National Kindergarten College, ten years
younger than our father, and we all sat in the Hemingway pews. On Sundays, Grandmother and Grandfather
beamed with pleasure at having so many of their family
with them again.

Ernest and I were active in the young people's group
of the church — the Plymouth League — which met
about five o'clock Sunday afternoons; the refreshments
served after the meetings were quite an attraction for the
high school members. Ernest was by turns the program
chairman and the treasurer, and occasionally speaker at our
meetings. On a church leaflet dated 1915, Ernest's name is
given as the one in charge of the Sunday afternoon service.
He and I played in the church orchestra, and once all five
of us — Ernest, Ursula, Sunny, Carol and I — dressed in

Chinese and Japanese costumes and took part in a three-day missionary pageant downtown called *The World in Chicago*. Learning the Japanese national anthem, phonetically, was fun.

There were times when Ernest took himself, we thought, a little too seriously. Mother and I were reading Booth Tarkington's *Seventeen* in the late summer of 1916, and I remember her laughing when she thought she caught echoes of Ernie in that delightful novel. We both recognized things the hero of *Seventeen* did that explained much that troubled us about Ernest.

Dr. William E. Barton, father of Bruce Barton, the author and advertising man, was our minister. Dr. Barton had a brown mustache and Vandyke beard much like my father's, and though we respected and admired him and enjoyed his sermons, he was so dignified he rather overawed us. But Mrs. Marie Cole Hunter, the director of the young people's work, with her warm manner and charming smile was a close friend to us all. She made our church and all its charitable activities so attractive to us that any unpleasant feeling we retained from Daddy's earlier restrictive religious discipline practically evaporated. She had a good deal of influence on both Ernest and me. Since Dr. Barton did not approve of dancing, even though the Unitarian minister across the street did, Mrs. Hunter encouraged us in other social activities. With her help we gave amateur plays, entertainments of various kinds, picnics and socials and get-togethers which stimulated our age group in the church to the point that friends from other denominations joined us. The First Congregational Church House became our social center.

Our school senior play in 1917 was *Beau Brummell*, by Clyde Fitch. Morris Musselman had the lead, and most of our best friends were in the cast. I was an usher and a member of the orchestra, but Ernest was much more important. He played Richard Brinsley Sheridan, second lead in the show, and he was excellent.

Ernest was selected to give the class prophecy on June 13, 1917, and Edward Wagenknecht, a serious scholar, gave the valedictory; it was no surprise to us that he later went on to be a well-known teacher and critic. My speech at commencement was entitled "The New Girlhood"; it was full of high-flown idealism, and how I labored over it! But Ernie's class prophecy was so clever and so full of fun that for years afterward members of the class would remind each other of his witty sayings.

College educations for all of us were a hopeful part of my parents' plans; there was a college tradition in our family. Grandmother and Grandfather Hemingway had gone to Wheaton College in Illinois. Mother's brother, Leicester Hall, was a graduate of Amherst. My father and his brothers and sisters had all been educated at Oberlin, and it was taken for granted that Ernie and I would go there. Our interest in college was further stimulated by a visit at this time from our attractive cousin, Walter Edmonds Johnson, of Montclair, New Jersey, who was a Princeton man and accompanist of the Princeton Glee Club. Ernest, however, talked about going to Cornell, and the University of Illinois was also in his mind. This was quite natural, as Oak Park High School's football coach, the great Robert Zuppke, had recently gone from our school to the University of Illinois.

Mother took me to visit Oberlin in the spring vacation of our senior year, and I had such a good time that I gladly applied for admission as a Conservatory student the following fall.

But when June, 1917, arrived the boys in our class had the war even more than college on their minds — in April,

1917, President Wilson had given up neutrality. Ernest put off deciding and tried to line up some work for the vacation. Our uncle Alfred Tyler Hemingway, of Kansas City, was a friend of Colonel Nelson of the *Kansas City Star*, and Dad hoped he could help Ernest get a summer job on that fine paper. Uncle Tyler made inquiries, but there were no openings on the *Star* until September; the paper would take Ernest as a cub reporter at that time if he was willing to wait, our uncle told Dad. Ernie decided to wait.

Twice before this at the beginning of vacations, Ernest had walked up to Walloon Lake after taking the boat across from Chicago to the lower part of Michigan. Once Louis Clarahan went with him, and the other time, as I recall, Harold Sampson made the long hike — over three hundred miles — with him. The boys camped along the way, sleeping in pup tents, cooking their own meals, swimming or fishing as they pleased, and grateful for the few lifts they got from passing cars. Our parents admired Ernie's initiative, and perhaps it was his account of his adventures on the way to the cottage that inspired Dad and Mother to make the journey in an open car. With Ernest, and with baby Leicester on Mother's lap, they drove all the way to the cottage in Daddy's Ford touring-car — four hundred and eighty-seven miles from Oak Park to Walloon Lake, according to Dad's diary, which I have. This included various detours and is over one hundred miles more than the distance shown on a map. It took them over five days to make the trip over the dusty, rutted roads. Part of the way, especially the stretch near Traverse City, Dad told us, was only a sand track. On several occasions he had to use the shovel they carried along for emergencies. They finally arrived at Uncle George Hemingway's cottage near Charlevoix late on the fifth day, too exhausted to attempt the extra thirty miles which would have brought them to Windemere cottage that night.

Dad had a tent along for camping and some of the party slept in the car on their way north. He took pictures of Mother and Ernest frying eggs over a campfire as they all breakfasted along the route toward Petoskey. When our parents and their two boys finally got to Windemere, they were as proud as if they had discovered a new continent. Dad was right; it was an achievement in 1917 to drive so many miles with a two-year-old along. We girls went up on the S. S. *Manitou* from Chicago, and we were waiting when the car arrived.

All that summer Ernest worked with Dad on Longfield Farm across the lake from Windemere. With the help of a farmer, Warren Sumner, and Warren's mules, they moved off the old tenant farmhouse on a stone boat. They built a new icehouse under the apple trees which Warren promised to fill during the winter. He said he would cut the ice after Walloon froze over and store it between layers of sawdust until we were ready to use it the next season. Daddy and Ernest took care of a big vegetable garden on Longfield, and they both cut the hay on about twenty acres of hilly land on the farm. They also put in more fruit trees. It was not all hard labor: Ernie had some boys come up from Oak Park to visit him, and I had a quite special party.

My big thrill of the summer was being invited to visit the Trumbull Whites in Bay View, a mile from Petoskey. While staying with them — Mr. Trumbull White was the manager of the Bay View Chautauqua that year — I rehearsed and played with the Bay View Orchestra. I sat at the same stand with a violist from the Chicago Symphony Orchestra, one of the nucleus of professional musicians who made up the Bay View summer orchestra.

We amateurs added numbers, but probably not too much else to the total musical effect. The learned gentleman next to me — possibly tortured beyond endurance by my performance — offered to tutor me in the viola parts if I would stay after the regular rehearsals for an hour each day. I was grateful for his help. We put in several extra hours rehearsing together. On the night of the final concert that season, when we finished the last number, he patted me on the back.

"You kept right in time," he said kindly, "and I don't think you made more than half a dozen mistakes all the way through. It was wonderful!" That from a member of the Chicago Symphony was praise indeed.

I met a wonderful crowd of new friends in Bay View that summer, among them Sterling Sanford, a senior at the University of Michigan. Red-haired Frances Butterfield from Louisiana, the Grundy family — Bill, Lillian and Mary — of Louisville, Kentucky, and the Gregory girls, Ruth and Alice, also from Kentucky, joined with Owen White and his little brother Kenneth from New York and others in picnics at Menonaqua Beach, swimming parties, and trips to the roller rink. I hated having to leave all this fun at Bay View when it was time for me to go home. At Walloon that August, Mother agreed that I might return the Bay View hospitality by asking the whole crowd to a pot-luck picnic at our cottage.

Ernie was delighted they were coming. When we talked over plans for the party, Ernie offered to take our open launch down to the foot of the lake to meet those guests who would come by train from Petoskey. It was a windy day, the lake was very rough, and most of the guests Ernest transported were damp from the splashing by the time they landed at our dock. The rest of the Bay View group had crowded into Sterling Sanford's Buick. They drove the ten miles over the sandy hills and arrived in time for lunch.

Ernest enjoyed my new friends, and he showed the boys around and was pleasant to the girls as he acted as host in Daddy's absence. The Bay View crowd had brought sandwiches and potato salad with them, and I had fixed a huge hot meat and macaroni casserole and made two chocolate mahogany cakes. This special kind of chocolate cake is made with sour milk; in some way, the use of this ingredient turns the melted chocolate in the dough to an attractive reddish brown. It was a recipe I had found in our old Third Church cookbook. Between the three layers of the rich brown cake I had put thick white frosting — the boiled kind — and the cakes turned out to be not only attractive-looking, but tender and delicious. Years afterward, Sterling admitted to me that it was when he first tasted my mahogany cake that he decided he'd like to have the girl who made it occupy his home permanently. But he said nothing of this at the party that day, though he did eat two pieces of my cake!

Just as we were finishing dessert, another boat drew up at the dock, and Ernie and Sunny hurried down from the screened porch dining room to see who had arrived. To our delight, it was Dad, the busy doctor, back from delivering a baby in Chicago. He was whistling as he walked up the grassy slope from the dock to meet us.

"Just in time for dessert, I see!" said Daddy gaily. "My, but it's good to get back in God's country after the heat of the city. Feel that breeze! Does anybody care if I peel my coat off and roll up my sleeves?"

In less than a minute Daddy was chatting with our guests, and in less than an hour he was a friend of all of them. Daddy had a gift for friendship. When he was not in one of his stern moods, Daddy was a "real charmer," as Mother said.

"Let's get some pictures of this crowd," he called to us when he had finished the meal. "With nice people like these, Marce, I can see why you liked to stay in Bay View. I didn't think we'd ever get her back to Walloon," Dad remarked, turning to Fan Butterfield.

Sterling Sanford had brought his camera along, and he and my father took snapshots of the group. Later these pictures became especially valuable to us, as they were some of the last ones taken of Ernest with all of us before he went to Kansas City a few weeks later to start his first job as a reporter on the *Kansas City Star.* The legend has it that Ernie ran away from home, but this simply is not so. Daddy bought him his ticket and saw him off, and during his first weeks in Kansas City Ernest stayed with our uncle Alfred Tyler Hemingway. The pictures meant a lot to me for another reason, for Sterling Sanford went into the Army soon after that, and exchanging pictures of that picnic with him led to a correspondence and eventually to a love that has lasted all our lives.

That fall I entered Oberlin Conservatory, and besides my musical studies, I took dramatic reading and English composition and I audited a class in sociology. I got no credit for it, of course, but I found that I liked sociology even more than piano and violin, and I enjoyed my brief experience writing for the college paper.

While I was away at college, Ursula was starting high school, where she made excellent marks and never had to be tutored in anything. Sunny was in the sixth grade of the Holmes School, and little sister Carol entered kinder-garten that fall. Ernest was earning his own living for the first time in his life. So Mother and Daddy had only one baby left at home, little Lessie, who was then two and a half.

At first I was lonesome and a bit homesick at college. All the young men students who had given me such a pleasant rush when I had visited Oberlin with Mother the spring before were now away in the Army. Many of the girls I had met then had graduated. Excepting for my cousin Laura Hines, who was a senior, I knew no one.

Food rationing was in force, though it was mostly voluntary, and our college menus were drastically restricted. At Barrows House on South Professor Street, where I lived, the house mother used to keep us constantly stirred up by her appeals to our emotions. She made short speeches in the dining room before almost every meal. Typical of her remarks was:

"Now, let's see how much sugar we can save today. It's for the starving children in Belgium. I am not saying you *can't have* any sugar — you notice the sugar bowls are full — I just put it up to your consciences not to use it on your cereal. You lucky young people should be thinking about the starving children in Europe while you eat your nice breakfast this morning."

Often our whole midday meal that fall, for all the young men and women who ate at our house — and this included several members of the football team — was a casserole of creamed cabbage leaves with a few bread crumbs sprinkled on top. One casserole to each table of eight! One roll apiece of nonwheat bread mixture was also served, but the lady in charge frowned on jelly or butter. Hardly a satisfying diet for healthy young people, so we all went out and spent our allowance for extra food in the tearooms. After a few weeks of this semi-starvation some of the college faculty became aware of what was going on and the menu was revised.

Ernest liked Kansas City. His letters to me and to the family that fall told of his excitement at being a real reporter on a real newspaper at last. He covered, as he told us, fires, fights, and funerals, and anything else not important enough for the other more experienced reporters. Ernie was learning a lot; he told us about his new friends on the paper, many of them men years older than he. He met a movie star and he wrote me three pages of raves about her.

Although at first Ernest stayed with Uncle Tyler and Aunt Arabell White Hemingway in their house on Walnut Street, he soon found a room of his own nearer to the *Star* office downtown. He was feeling very grown-up to be so independent. My letters to him seemed kiddish in contrast, as all I could write him about were my activities at Oberlin. Instead of being older than he, I now felt younger, as Ernest's new experiences made him seem so much more a man of the world. Like our father, he had a rare talent for friendship. He had the ability to be congenial with people of all ages and from all backgrounds. He soaked up other people's experiences like a blotter, and later he sometimes gave them out as his own. This was true later when he wrote some of his Nick Adams stories, many based on the experiences of a fellow reporter on the *Kansas City Star*.

Underlying all Ernest's pleasures in his new experiences and his work on the paper was his great, compelling desire to get into the war. He had tried to enlist in all the services, he wrote me. He told me that the Army, the Navy, and the Marine Corps had all turned him down, not for being under age, since he was past eighteen, but because he could not pass the physicals due to his bad eye.

"We all have that bad eye like Mother's," I remember

he wrote in one note. "But I'll make it to Europe some way in spite of this optic. I can't let a show like this go on without getting in on it. There hasn't been a real war to go to since Grandfather Hemingway's shooting at the Battle of Bull Run." That Grandfather Hemingway served at Vicksburg and didn't happen to have been in the Battle of Bull Run did not affect Ernie's point at all. I sympathized.

Ernie wrote that he had decided not to go to college; he liked newspaper work. Then, early in 1918, came a letter from Ernest addressed to the whole family. It was full of jubilation. Ernest told us that he had been assigned to interview a group of Italian Red Cross officers who came to the United States to recruit volunteers for the American Red Cross Ambulance Corps in Italy. When he interviewed them for the *Star*, he learned that the Red Cross was only accepting men who were not eligible for the United States services and the draft. They took men in general good health who were unable to fulfill the physical requirements of our own country's armed services.

"Could a man with poor vision in one eye get in?" he asked them, he told us later. The Italians answered in the affirmative.

Ernest was delighted. At last he had found one service where his eyesight was no handicap. At last he had found a way to get to the war in Europe! Ernest signed up at once and was assigned to Ambulance Unit 4 for Italy, and he called several of his friends to tell them about the opportunity, men who had also been turned down by our Army or Navy for one defect or another.

Ernie's own enthusiasm was contagious. Theodore Brumback, son of a judge in Kansas City, was one of several who joined the Red Cross Ambulance Corps with Ernest. Charles Hopkins, city editor of the *Star* from Muskogee, Oklahoma, wanted to go with them too, but he was not exempt from the United States service.

Ernest wrote us in the spring of 1918 that everything was set for him and his buddies to come to Oak Park for one final fishing trip to the north woods. The American Red Cross, Ernest told us, would send a telegram to our house to notify the boys when to be in New York to sail for Italy. They were sure of at least three weeks' notice before sailing, they had been told, and Ernest assured our parents that the telegram would come in time to have a good seven days' notice of the actual sailing day on the S. S. *Conte Grande*. Dad and Mother and all of us were tremendously pleased that the boys were coming to Oak Park.

The group of five or six young men had a regular house party with our family, late that May. Daddy took lots of pictures of Ernie and his gang, and he was as thrilled as Ernest was that Ernie was finally getting to do what he had so longed for. My father would mention at this time how he himself had longed to serve in the Spanish-American War, but because he was married and the first baby had just arrived, he did not get a chance to be active in the Army Medical Corps as he had hoped. I think, however, that Daddy was secretly relieved that Ernest was to be in a noncombatant branch. Dad himself at this time was a medical examiner for the local draft board in Oak Park.

Ernie and his friends were impatient to get off on their fishing trip. The boys took old clothes, their fishpoles, knives and camping gear, as they headed for the spot Ernest knew of up north on the Canadian Soo Line. No town existed there, only a railroad station, an unfrequented spot where trains stopped only on signal. When they arrived at this railroad station they arranged with the lone occupant, the Canadian telegraph operator, to contact an Indian runner who could be alerted to go after them wherever they were fishing when the message came through from our house giving the date of sailing. My father had promised to relay the telegram when it arrived in Oak Park.

But when the message finally did come to our home, it had been delayed en route and the sailing date was only a few days away, as I recall. Daddy rushed off a wire to the telegraph operator in Canada; he knew the boys would barely have time to make the ship even if they got the news immediately. Later we learned that the Indian runner started at once from the railroad line to the boys' first camping place only to find that they had moved on. When the panting runner finally found them, the boys didn't wait for anything. They started running pell-mell for the railroad station. Bearded, filthy, they grabbed up their suitcases at the station and made the only train out of there that day by minutes. They arrived in New York just in time to board the ship. It turned out to be the French Line SS *Chicago*, which sailed May 28, taking them to Bordeaux. They reached Paris early in June. Two days later they were in Milan.

We learned most of this story later from Charles Hopkins, who went along with Ernest and the gang to New York and saw them off on the ship; then he told us all about the fishing adventure on his way back to Kansas City. Later Hopkins trained at Great Lakes Naval Station, only a few miles from Oak Park, so we saw him frequently while Ernest was in Italy.

I had returned from Oberlin at Christmastime following an attack of appendicitis. Then, when the question of my returning for the second semester came up, Daddy and

Mother announced that I was not going back: it had cost so much more than they had counted on for one semester. So, at the time Ernest and his friends visited Oak Park, I was nearby at school (the Congregational Training School) on Ashland Avenue in Chicago, and of course I was with the family in Oak Park every weekend. I was beginning to earn a little helping Dr. Barton and Mrs. Hunter.

When Ernest left for the Red Cross service in Italy, he expected to be behind the lines. But after he landed and had driven an ambulance for a few days, he and his pal Bill Horne found the place where they were stationed too safe and rather dull. They heard there was a chance to volunteer for a special branch, the Red Cross Rolling Canteen Service, which operated right up to the front lines. It was early July and Ernest was excited and happy when he wrote us that he and Bill had managed to work their way forward where things were going on. He had volunteered to be one of the bicycle riders who distributed mail, chocolate and tobacco to the soldiers in the trenches at the front.

In Italy the attack on the Piave had started, and the Austrians were shelling the Italians only about fifty yards away across the Piave River.

Dad and Mother lived for Ernest's letters. He wrote only once and briefly, as I remember, those first few days. Dad had always loved Ernest especially dearly, and he missed him and prayed for him daily. Mother prayed too. She felt sure Ernest would be protected from harm. Mother had a calm faith, but Daddy was very tense, worrying about Ernest's safety. All the while Dad continued his heavy schedule of medical calls, visits to his hospital patients and long hours of work as an examiner for the draft board.

One day, July 8, 1918, while Ernest was on his bicycle

at the front delivering mail and chocolate— it was just six days after he had transferred to the Rolling Canteen Service and less than ten days after he had gone to the active front in Italy—he was handing a cigarette and chocolate to an Italian soldier when a trench mortar shell hit and almost buried him. It knocked him unconscious and filled his body below the waist with over two hundred pieces of shrapnel. When he came to and went to the rescue of a wounded Italian, he was hit again, with a machine gun bullet in the right knee. Ted Brumback wrote us about it from Milan, and my father later gave his letter to the *Oak Leaves*, which printed it on October 5, 1918. This is what Ted told us:

> I have just come from seeing Ernest at the American Red Cross hospital here. He is fast on the road to recovery and will be out a whole man once again, so the doctor says, in a couple of weeks.
>
> Although some two hundred pieces of shell were lodged in him, none of them are above the hip joint. Only a few of these pieces were large enough to cut deep, the most serious of these being two in the knee and two in the right foot. The doctor says there will be no trouble about these wounds healing and that Ernest will regain entire use of both legs.
>
> Now that I have told you about his condition, I suppose you would like to know all the circumstances of the case. Let me say right here that you can be very proud of your son's actions. He is going to receive a silver medal of valor, which is a very high medal indeed and corresponds to the medaille militaire or Legion of Honor of France.
>
> At the time he was wounded Ernest was not in the regular ambulance service, but in charge of a Red Cross canteen at the front. Ernest, among several others in our section, which was in the mountains where there was not very much action, volunteered to go down on the Piave

and help out with the canteen work. This was at the time when the Italians were engaged in pushing the Austrians back over the river, so he got to see all the action he wanted.

Ernest was not satisfied with the regular canteen service behind the lines. He thought he could do more good and be of more service by going straight up to the trenches. He told the Italian commander about his desire.

A bicycle was given him which he used to ride to the trenches every day laden down with chocolate, cigars, cigarettes and post-cards. The Italians in the trenches got to know his smiling face and were always asking for their "giovane Americano."

Well, things went along fine for six days. But about midnight on the seventh day an enormous trench mortar bomb lit within a few feet of Ernest while he was giving out chocolate. The concussion of the explosion knocked him unconscious and buried him in earth. There was an Italian between Ernest and the shell. He was instantly killed, while another standing a few feet away, had both his legs blown off.

A third Italian was badly wounded and this one Ernest, after he had regained consciousness, picked up on his back and carried to the first aid dugout. He says he did not remember how he got there nor that he had carried a man, until the next day, when an Italian officer told him all about it and said that it had been voted to give him a valor medal for the act.

Naturally, being an American, Ernest received the best of medical attention. He had only to remain a day or so at a hospital at the front when he was sent to Milan to the Red Cross hospital. Here he is being showered with attention by American nurses, as he is one of the first patients in the hospital.

I have never seen a cleaner, neater and prettier place than that hospital. You can rest easy in your mind that he is receiving the best care in Europe. And you need have no fear for the future for Ernest tells me that he intends now to stick to regular ambulance work which, to use his own words, "is almost as safe as being at home."

Since writing the last lines I have seen Ernest again. He told me the doctor had just seen him and made another careful examination. The result showed that no bones were broken and the joints were unharmed, all the splinters making merely flesh wounds.

By the time this letter will reach you he will be back in the section. He has not written himself because one or two of the splinters lodged in his fingers. We have made a collection of shell fragments and bullets that were taken out of Ernie's leg, which will be made up into rings.

Ernie says he'll write very soon. He dictates love to "ye old Ivory," "Ura," "Nun-bones," "Nubbins," "ye young Brute."

Please include my love also, although I haven't had the pleasure of meeting the foregoing. Tell Mrs. Hemingway how sorry I was that I didn't get to see her in Chicago.

In a postscript Ernest himself added, whimsically:

> *Dear Folks:*
> *I am all O.K. and include much love to ye parents. I'm not near so much of a hell roarer as Brummy makes me out. Lots of love.*
> *Ernie*
> *Sh — Don't worry, Pop!*

It wasn't until Ernest was wounded and we began to read the names of other boys we knew personally in the casualty lists of the *Chicago Tribune* that most of us realized what war really meant.

But at the Congregational Training School we still lived a rather quiet life, protected from war's realities. Two afternoons a week I had a part-time job working for Dr. Barton at the home church. Very often he kept me busy pasting up the scrapbooks he kept about the men in service from our community. This work kept me in closer contact with news of the war than I might otherwise have been. But back at school, Marion Vose and I often sat on each other's cot beds and played ukuleles while we sang "There's a Long, Long Trail A-Winding," "K-K-K-Katy," "We Won't Come Back 'Till It's Over, Over There," and other popular war songs of 1918.

I was proud that I had a brother serving in Europe, and I tried to get into one of the women's services myself. But the regulations which then forbade a young woman to go to Europe with either the Red Cross or Y.M.C.A. Canteen Service (the only groups I knew about) if she had a husband, father or brother in the European theater effectively prevented me from joining up. So I went on with my training in social service work, though I spent almost every weekend being one of the hostesses for a servicemen's club — there were several of these hostess clubs downtown in Chicago with branches in Oak Park. With my sisters and mother I entertained a series of homesick boys in uniforms, most of them from Great Lakes. Each weekend the sailors, usually two or three of them, were sent out to our home from the service club in Chicago, where my parents had signed up offering to take the servicemen over Sunday. Dozens of other families like ours in the surrounding suburbs took in Army and Navy men too. Always the boys we entertained snapped pictures of my sisters and me, and of the "swell place" they had stayed for the weekend. Dozens of pictures of our family must have gone to waiting relatives in Chippewa Falls, Wisconsin, or Keokuk, Iowa, or Hibbing, Minnesota, enclosed in the men's letters home.

Because our house was large, with a room to dance in,

and we as a family felt a great need to do something for some other boys now that Ernest was away, our home usually seemed to be the center to which many of our friends brought *their* visiting soldiers and sailors on Sundays. I got so used to being told by our young men guests "You look *just* like my sister" — or cousin, or the girl back home — that I finally worked out an easy and rather flippant reply.

"Yes," I'd answer gaily, "it's a common model. They must have made a lot of copies!"

Daddy was patient and kind to all this influx of weekend guests. He often tried to talk to the young sailor boys about the war, or about Ernest, or his interest in hunting and fishing. Yearningly, he tried to find someone who'd give him a little man-talk. He missed Ernest terribly. A few of the boys responded to the doctor's fatherly kindness, but most of them just wanted girls and dancing. Usually some of the sailors were rather disappointed that there was no liquor in our house. Mother was hospitable to all the strange boys; she was eager to make them all feel at home. She and our cook fed them well, and Mother frequently said that she hoped someone in Italy was being kind to Ernest. Some of our sailor guests were not so homesick for good cooking as they were keen for a stolen squeeze in a corner. We girls grew quite adept in sizing up the nice ones and avoiding "parlor snakes," as a "wolf" was known in World War I.

But these too familiar young men were very much the exception. Most of our guests were courteous and fun to be with. Sometimes the boys came back to see us week after week, whenever they had a twenty-four-hour leave. Occasionally my Mother had grateful letters from some of their parents, which touched her very much.

Only once did Daddy get really upset by some sailor

guests. Two chaps from Great Lakes stayed with us one weekend, and when they left they walked off with some rather large framed photographs of my sisters and me. Dad was so indignant when he discovered the loss of the pictures (they were new and rather expensive ones) that he went right out to Great Lakes Training Center, got in touch with friends of his among the medical officers, found the boys, and got the pictures back. There was nothing hesitant about Daddy when he was aroused. He didn't report the boys to their officers, but he did get exactly what he went after.

It wasn't until late September, 1918, that Ernie wrote us at length about his narrow escape. This letter was also printed in *Oak Leaves* at my father's suggestion. The article in the paper was headed WOUNDED 227 TIMES, and the editor says:

Dr. C. E. Hemingway, whose son, Ernest M. Hemingway, was the hero of a fine Red Cross exploit in Italy, as told in a recent issue of Oak Leaves, has received a letter from North Winship, American Consul at Milan, Italy, praising the courage of the doctor's son and announcing his intention of keeping an eye on him. And from Ernest, in the hospital, comes the following letter:

Dear Folks: Gee, Family, but there must have been a great bubble about my getting shot up. Oak Leaves and the opposition came today and I have begun to think, Family, that maybe you didn't appreciate me when I used to reside in the bosom. It's the next best thing to getting killed and reading your own obituary.

You know they say there isn't anything funny about this war, and there isn't. I wouldn't say that it was hell, because that's been a bit overworked since General Sherman's time, but there have been about eight times when I would have welcomed hell, just on a chance that it couldn't come up to the phase of war I was experiencing.

For example, in the trenches, during an attack, when a shell makes a direct hit in a group where you're standing. Shells aren't bad except direct hits; you just take chances on the fragments of the bursts. But when there is a direct hit, your pals get spattered all over you; spattered is literal.

During the six days I was up in the front line trenches only fifty yards from the Austrians I got the "rep" of having a charmed life. The "rep" of having one doesn't mean much, but having one does. I hope I have one. That knocking sound is my knuckles striking the wooden bed-tray.

Well, I can now hold up my hand and say that I've been shelled by high explosives, shrapnel and gas; shot at by trench mortars, snipers and machine guns, and, as an added attraction, an aeroplane machine-gunning the line. I've never had a hand grenade thrown at me, but a rifle grenade struck rather close. Maybe I'll get a hand grenade later.

Now out of all that mess to only get struck by a trench mortar and a machine gun bullet while advancing toward the rear, as the Irish say, was fairly lucky. What, Family?

The 227 wounds I got from the trench mortar didn't hurt a bit at the time, only my feet felt like I had rubber boots full of water on (hot water), and my knee cap was acting queer. The machine gun bullet just felt like a sharp smack on the leg with an icy snowball. However it spilled me. But I got up again and got my wounded into the dugout. I kind of collapsed at the dugout.

The Italian I had with me had bled all over me and my coat and pants looked like someone had made currant jelly in them and then punched holes to let the pulp out. Well, my captain who was a great pal of mine (it was his dugout) said, 'Poor Hem, he'll be R.I.P. soon.' Rest in peace, that is.

You see, they thought I was shot thru my chest because

of my bloody coat. But I made them take my coat and shirt off (I wasn't wearing any undershirt) and the old torso was intact. Then they said that I would probably live. That cheered me up any amount.

I told them in Italian that I wanted to see my legs, tho I was afraid to look at them. So they took off my trousers and the old limbs were still there, but, gee, they were a mess. They couldn't figure out how I had walked a hundred and fifty yards with such a load, with both knees shot thru and my right shoe punctured in two big places; also over 200 flesh wounds.

"Oh," says I, in Italian, "my captain, it is of nothing. In America they all do it. It is thought well not to allow the enemy to perceive that they captured our goats." The goat speech required some masterful lingual ability, but I got it across and then went to sleep for a couple of minutes.

After I came to they carried me on a stretcher three kilometers back to a dressing station. The stretcher bearer had to go over lots, as the road was having the entrails shelled out of it. Whenever a big one would come, whe-e-ee-eeee-whoo-oosh — boom, they would lay me down and get flat.

My wounds were now hurting like 227 little devils driving nails into the raw. The dressing station had been evacuated during the attack, so I lay for two hours in a stable with its roof shot off waiting for an ambulance. When it came I ordered it down the road to get the soldiers that had been wounded first. It came back with a load and then they lifted me in.

The shelling was still pretty thick and our batteries were going off all the time 'way back of us, and the big 350's and 250's going overhead for Austria with a noise like a railway train. Then we'd hear the burst of the lines. Then, shriek would come a big Austrian shell and then the crack of the burst. But we were giving them more and bigger stuff than they sent.

Then a battery of field guns would go off just back of the shed — boom — boom! Boom — boom! and the 75's and 149's would go whimpering over to the Austrian lines. And the star shells going up all the time and the machine guns going like riveters — tat-a-tat-tat.

After a ride of a couple of kilometers in an Italian ambulance they unloaded me at a dressing station, where I had a lot of pals among the medical officers. They gave me a shot of morphine and anti-tetanus serum and shaved my legs and took twenty-eight shell fragments varying in size from (design) to about (design) in size out of my legs.

Then they did a fine job in bandaging and all shook hands with me and would have kissed me, but I kidded them along. Then I stayed five days at a field hospital and was evacuated to the base hospital here.

I sent you that cable so you wouldn't worry. I have been in the hospital a month and twelve days and hope to be out in another month. The Italian surgeon did a peach of an operation on my right knee joint and my right foot; took twenty-eight stitches, and assures me that I will be able to walk as well as ever. The wounds all healed up clean and there was no infection. He has my right leg in a plaster splint now, so that will be all right.

I have some snappy souvenirs that he took out at the last operation. I wouldn't really be comfortable now unless I had some pain. The surgeon is going to take the plaster off in a week now and will allow me on crutches in ten days. I will have to learn to walk again.

This is the longest letter I have ever written to anyone and it says the least. Give my love to everybody that asks about me. As Ma Pettingill says, "Leave us keep the home fires burning."

Ernest sent us a picture with this letter, and it shows him with his overseas cap on, propped up against pillows, a string from the light in the ceiling tied to the head of his bed and his lips pursed in an obvious whistle. Apparently his spirits were high even though it was taking his body a lot longer to recover than Brummy's optimistic guess of two weeks. His recovery was complicated by an attack of jaundice which kept him in the hospital until long after the Italian Armistice was signed.

When Ernie finally was up and able to get out occasionally in November, he sent us pictures of himself in a Red Cross ambulance driver's uniform with a nice-looking bearded older man and his family. They were the Conte Greppie, his daughter Bianca, and the "kid brother," Ernie wrote on the back of the snapshot. Ernest visited this family and others at Lake Como, and Ernie's letters about them made Italy and the Italians sound most attractive.

Though all of us Hemingways had been brought up on tales of bravery and heroism in the Civil War told to us by Grandfather Hemingway and his G.A.R. friends in the Borrowed Time Club (an Oak Park organization whose members had to be over three score years and ten), we now felt disillusioned. All Grandfather's stories had made us think war was something glamorous and exciting. Grandfather, in his Decoration Day addresses to the schools, always spoke of "our glorious Army", "our brave boys in blue," "our heroes," and all the while the gold braid sparkled on his neatly pressed Civil War officer's uniform, the one he always wore on those patriotic occasions. But Ernest's wounds made war seem cruel and disgusting.

Daddy, who was so devoted to Ernest, seemed greatly relieved when he knew he was safe in the hospital and having the best of care after his disastrous experience. Ernest wrote Dad in detail about the silver plate the

Italian surgeons had put in his knee cap, and he went into medical detail in later letters telling how the doctor removed the shrapnel pieces from his feet and legs. Ernest made light of his pain.

One night late that fall, Marion Vose, my classmate, and I decided to go to a movie near our school in Chicago. By accident, after the feature, we saw a newsreel about the work of the American Red Cross in Italy. The new Red Cross hospital in Milan was described and shown. Suddenly, in the silent film, Ernest appeared. He was in uniform, sitting in a wheelchair on the hospital porch, being pushed by a pretty nurse. Over his lap was spread a robe of knitted wool squares. He smiled at the camera and waved a crutch for a second. I was hysterical with excitement. At the end of the regular picture I waited for the newsreel to come on again. They didn't run it. Marion Vose and I went to the manager and asked if we could please see it again, and we told him why. He was kind, and said if we wanted to wait until the theater was empty he would run it once more, just for us. Later, the manager came over and sat with us as we saw Ernie smile once more. Then he gave us the name of the next theater where this same newsreel would be shown. Even though it was midnight, I stopped in at a drugstore to telephone the family in Oak Park to tell Daddy and Mother where they could see Ernest in the movie the next day. My parents went to that theater the following night and I joined them. We all wiped away tears of joy while we watched Ernest smiling as he sat in his wheelchair, wearing his military-looking cap and overcoat on the hospital terrace. This was the first time we had seen him since he left for the north woods before he sailed for Italy almost six months before. It was also the first time any member of our family had appeared on the screen!

Mother told me later that Daddy followed that newsreel all over Chicago. Mother saw it twice more herself, and I caught it another time at another neighborhood theater. No film ever did a family more good. It was as though Ernest had died in battle and we had mourned him, and now he had come to life again on celluloid. We wrote Ernest to ask if the nurse who wheeled him in the film was the same pretty one called Agnes he had told us about in his letters.

She was not, he wrote back.

"Ag is prettier than anybody you guys ever saw," he informed us. "Wait till you see her!"

8

Return from War

I HAVE several vivid memories about the fall and winter
of 1918, and one of them concerns Uncle Leicester
Hall, who was then flying with the American Air Corps
in England. He was well over the age to be a pilot, but
like Ernest, Uncle Les wanted to get into the war. Ernest
and Uncle Leicester were alike in wanting to be where the
excitement was going on.

Uncle Leicester had been a bachelor for years until, in
his forties, he married Nevada Butler, daughter of the
famous old miner Jim Butler, the discoverer of the To-
nopah (Nevada) goldfield. Our family was delighted and
very curious to meet her. After Uncle Leicester flew to
England, Aunt Vada wrote us that she could now come to
Chicago for a visit to meet her new family.

Aunt Vada was tall, dark-haired and strikingly beautiful. She had never lived anywhere but in the West, and
she was as thrilled to be in the "East," as she called Chicago, as we were to have her. Aunt Vada was quite unlike
her father. He was almost a legend, a former prospector
who had reputedly become a millionaire. We had heard
tales about Jim Butler for years. One of the stories told
about him all over the West was that he was never seen

without a huge black cigar in his mouth. It was rumored that he didn't remove it even to take a bath or go to bed. He was also famous for his extremely salty vocabulary.

His daughter Nevada, named for the state in which he had made his big strike, had been educated in a private finishing school in California. She was a charming person, with a gracious manner, an adorable smile, and a pleasant, low speaking voice. All of us loved her the minute we met her. The two weeks Aunt Vada Hall spent with us were probably our happiest time of that tragic war year.

Aunt Vada visited me at my Congregational Training School classes and went with me to my assignments in the slum districts of Chicago. I was partly earning my way through school, but I went to these areas as a volunteer helper at the outpatient clinic of Cook County Hospital.

With me as a guide, Aunt Vada also visited the settlement houses where some of us girls at the Training School assisted. She saw Hull House, where Jane Addams, by then white-haired, still headed that remarkable social center she had founded years before. We went to Firman House, another settlement, started by an Oak Park woman, a friend of my family, where underprivileged children attended after-school classes in sewing, cooking and crafts. Seeing this side of Chicago with me, even visiting the dusty Maxwell Street market area, where all the goods for sale were displayed right out on the sidewalks, was a novel experience to Nevada Hall and a contrast to her rather extravagant shopping expeditions to Marshall Field's store.

Aunt Vada loved the theater. We went to plays together several times during her visit and she urged me to go on with my dramatic training after I graduated from my religious-social-service courses. I told her I hoped to do that sometime, but of course I would have to get a regular paid job as soon as I graduated the following June.

Even before her coming there was news in the papers about the epidemic of Spanish influenza in Europe, and while Aunt Vada was with us that fall cases of influenza began to appear in Chicago. Aunt Vada decided she ought to return to California. The two weeks she had planned to be with us were past, and though Mother urged her to stay longer, she went back to California, there to await Uncle Leicester's return. That was the last time we saw her.

The flu was striking everywhere, and people were warned to avoid crowds and to travel as little as possible. I remember that my father was called so frequently to take care of flu patients that at one time he told me he had had no sleep in forty-eight hours. All the doctors were rushed and bone-weary in the same way. Though none of our family contracted the disease, as far as I remember, several of my classmates at the Congregational Training School were terribly ill with it. One of them died.

Marion Vose and I acted as volunteer helpers to Miss Wilson, a trained nurse who roomed in our school that winter. We tied on our masks and accompanied Miss Wilson to those homes where the mother, or both parents, were sick with influenza. As untrained helpers, all we could do was to change and bathe the babies, clean up the kitchens, and help feed the youngsters when the parents were too ill to do so. Real nurses were sometimes busier than the doctors, and harder to get, so even our help was needed.

As this siege was subsiding we heard that Aunt Vada Hall had died of the flu, pathetically alone at her home in Bishop, California. We never forgot her charm and her loving interest in us all. We grieved for Uncle Leicester, who was on a ship returning to this country. He did not hear the sad news of his wife's death until he landed.

It was in early January, 1919, that we finally received the long-awaited word that Ernest was about to sail home from Italy. Even before we knew the hour of his arrival in Chicago, Dad had heard about a newspaper interview with Ernest at the dockside in New York which was printed in the *Chicago Evening American* on January 21, 1919. The newspaper correspondent in New York told of the landing of the *Giuseppe Verdi* of the Transatlantic American Line; the ship had sailed from Genoa and Gibraltar bringing four hundred officers and men — the entire U. S. Naval Aviation Unit which had been stationed at Porto Corsini, Italy, on the Adriatic shore. On board as a cabin passenger, one of the sixty-eight in this class, came, "limping from his wounds," as the paper said, "the worst shot-up man that had come home from the war area, Ernest M. Hemingway, of 600 North Kenilworth Avenue, Oak Park, Illinois. . . . Hemingway," the article went on, "was the first American to be wounded on the Italian front and the King of Italy awarded him a silver medal for valor and the Italian Croce di Guerra."

Dad received a telegram from Ernest in New York saying his train would be in Chicago that night. (He had stopped overnight with his Ambulance Corps buddy Bill Horne in Yonkers.) Daddy picked me up at my school downtown and took me with him to the station. It was a cold, snowy January night, and when we got to the La Salle Street station Daddy asked me to stay up at the head of the stairs in the trainshed and wait for Ernest there, while he went down to the train platform. He wanted to meet Ernest alone. Mother, of course, was waiting at home in Oak Park with the other children. I could hardly bear the suspense as I stood there in the chilly air. I peered down the stairway toward the trains. I heard the puffing engines coming and going. Each time there was a new sound from below I felt sure it was Ernest's train.

Suddenly, Dad and Ernest were there! Ernie had on an overseas cap. He was wearing a British-type khaki-colored uniform, partly covered by a long black broadcloth cape flung over his shoulders. The cape was fastened at the neck with a double silver buckle. He was wearing knee-high brown leather boots, and he was limping a little and leaning on a cane. He climbed up the stairway slowly toward me, one step at a time. Dad was trying to get Ernest to hold on to him. At last Ernie was at the top of the stairs.

"Hello, Ivory! How's the old keed?" he said as he kissed me.

I dissolved in tears. Ernie was home again, looking older and more tired, but as pink-cheeked and as dimpled as ever. His thick brown hair gleamed under his overseas cap.

Dad was moving about nervously. He was excited and eager to help Ernest get out to the car.

"Here, boy! — Here, lean on me!" Dad urged, as we started out of the station down another long flight of steps toward the waiting Ford.

"Now, Dad," said Ernie, "I've managed all right by myself all the way over from Milano. I think I can make it OK now." Ernie gestured toward Dad. "You and Marce go ahead to the car. I'll follow down the steps at my own pace. I'm pretty good with this old stick." He was. But we both waited and walked slowly with him to the car.

Dad and Ernie dropped me off at my school on their way out to Oak Park and I didn't see Ernest again until I got home that weekend.

But Ernest wasn't the same old friend and playmate I had known. Though much less than a year had passed since he had gone to Europe — and only a year and a half since we had graduated from high school together — a lifetime of new experiences, war, death, agony, new people, a new language and love had crowded into Ernest's life.

Morning after morning Ernie lay in his big, green-painted iron bed in his third-floor room. He rarely stayed in bed all day, but it seemed to help his aching legs if he was not up and walking for more than half a day. I can vividly remember the sight of his brown hair, dark against the white pillows. Usually he had his Red Cross knitted cover spread over him on top of his other bedclothes — the same one we had seen in the newsreel, with its gay green, red, black, yellow and white squares. He didn't like to be without this cover somewhere around. When we asked him why, he said it kept him from being so homesick for Italy.

Ernie was remarkably uncomplaining about his suffering from the festered places in his skin. Tiny shrapnel bits kept working their way out of his legs and feet. He had visited Oak Park Hospital, where Daddy and his doctor colleagues examined Ernest carefully. Ernest didn't have to have any more actual operations, as I recall, but he needed constant medical care. He did go back to the hospital once, for treatment of an infection.

Once Ernie stuck one of his feet out from under his bedclothes and showed me how he could move his toes separately from one another, almost like fingers. The metal pieces had cut certain muscles apart and now his feet, though scarred, had more mobility — or rather his toes had — than ever before. Ernie seemed rather proud of the fact that he could even pick up something like a pencil with his newly agile toes.

"That's something good, anyway, I got out of this war," he told me.

Often Ernie was in real pain, but usually by the time he came downstairs he was quite cheerful. He wrote lots of letters to Italy, and he read for hours at a time in bed. He read everything around the house — all the books, all the magazines, even the A.M.A. *Journals* from Dad's office downstairs. Ernie also took out great numbers of books from the public library. Though Ernie rested most of the mornings when he first came home, by lunchtime he was usually dressed in his good-looking Red Cross uniform and his high, well-polished, brown cordovan boots. He was proud of these boots and shined them daily. After lunch with the family he would put on his overseas cap and, taking his cane, he would start out for a walk. Ernie tried looking up his old friends, but few of them were around town or free during the daytime as he was. Most of his pals now had jobs or had gone back to college after their demobilization. So Ernest began going to the high school in the afternoons; it was a place where he felt at home.

Ernie was soon in demand as a speaker — various organizations around town wanted him to speak on his war experiences. I remember one talk he gave at the high school in March, 1919. The headline in the *Trapeze* of March 21 refers to "Lieutenant Hemingway." ("That was a quick way to get promoted," he said to us afterward, and we all laughed.*) Ernie was introduced at the high

---

* As this book was going to press, I wrote to Bill Horne asking him to settle for me the question of Ernie's rank, and here, in part, is his reply:

school assembly by Caroline Bagley, a clever classmate of Ernie's and mine, who had also been a commencement speaker when we graduated in 1917. In Ernest's address to

Some people believe that Ernie ended the war as an officer in the Italian army; while you believe he did not.

To the best of my knowledge, he did not. In my opinion that is one of those myths that grow up about colorful and famous people.

When we arrived at Section IV (at Schio, Provinzia Veneto, at the rail-head north of Vicenza and at the mouth of the passes that come down from Mt. Pasubio), we were told that *all of us* ambulance drivers *rated* as *honorary second lieutenants in the Italian Army*. How true that was I don't know — but it makes good sense. That would allow us to mess (eat) at the officers' mess when we were "on post" at the line with Italian troops. We always did. It helped give our ambulances priority on the roads, which we had. It got us preferred treatment at the Army gasoline dumps. Certainly we always were welcome at the same restaurants, saloons and other pleasure spots where the *Italian officers went* and the *Italian soldiers did not go*. The Italians whom occasionally we entertained at our headquarters were always officers, sometimes majors and colonels yet!

When a number of us went down to the Piave for a short volunteer tour of duty setting up canteens at the front there, we messed with the officers of the infantry outfits. I was at San Pedro Novello, and my fellows were the officers of the Brigata Ancona — the 69th and 70th Infantry. Ernie was at Fossalta, the next whistle-stop. I don't know what regimental mess he attended, but they were certainly Italian infantry. Infantry is what there was on that part of the line.

That was early July; because I remember I was there over the 4th. A few days later I was returned to Section IV at Schio. Not until maybe 10 days later did I learn that Hem had been very badly wounded by a trench-mortar shell, evacuated to an Italian Army surgical post, discovered there by another Red Cross ambulance man, and taken to the American Red Cross hospital in Milan. I think it was probably July 6th that he was hit. He behaved most heroically, as you know — rescued an Italian infantryman at the risk of his life — stopped an Austrian machine gun slug with his knee. For his gallantry under fire, above and beyond the call of duty, he was later awarded the Silver Valor Medal. That's the highest military decoration Italy gave to living men. The fellows who get the Gold Valor were almost always dead.

I saw him at the R. C. Hospital in Milan in August (I was sent down there to get over a bad case of enteritis.) He was still a long way removed from being able to be up and about. To the best of my belief he was in that hospital until just before the Vittorio Veneto offensive got under way in late October.

I have a faint memory — and I'm not quite sure that it is a memory and not another fantasy — that he was allowed out; that we met somewhere down near Bassano where Section IV had been sent for the com-

The family at Walloon Lake, late July, 1915. Standing rear, left to right, Marcelline, Sunny, Ernest and Ursula. Seated, Dad with Carol, Mother holding baby Les.

Family swimming, 1916. Daddy holding Leicester, Ernest behind Carol, Marcelline (standing), Ursula and Sunny.

The summer that Dad drove to Walloon Lake for the first time —1917. Taken at Lake Charlevoix, Uncle George's cottage. Left to right, cousin Margaret, Aunt Anna Hemingway, my father and mother, cousin Virginia, Ernest and George, Jr. In front, Les.

Marcelline and Ernest, high school graduation day, June, 1917.

Ernest, waiting to hear about his job on the *Kansas City Star*, works with Warren Sumner on our farm across the lake, 1917.

Ernest Miller Hemingway, nineteen years old, Milan, Italy, November, 1918.

Ernest with Italian friends at Lake Maggiore, Italy, where he was recovering from wounds. Late November or December, 1918.

Ernest back from Italy at Walloon Lake, with sister Carol on Grace Cottage porch, 1919.

The first Italian party at our home in Oak Park, February 16, 1919,
in the music room. Ernest in the center, under the Italian flag.

July 6, 1919, at Walloon Lake. Ernest, Marcelline, Bill Smith
and Charles Hopkins.

At Ernest's wedding, Horton Bay, Michigan, September 3, 1921. Carol, Ursula,
Hadley, Ernest, Mother, Les and Dad.

the high school assembly, he talked particularly about the Arditi.

"These men," he said [this is the *Trapeze* account, which makes no allowance for exaggeration] "had been confined in the Italian penal institutions, having committed some mistake — such as — well — murder or arson, and were released on the condition that they would serve in this division which was used by the government for shock troops.

"Armed only with revolvers, hand grenades, and two-bladed swords, they attacked, frequently stripped to the waist. Their customary loss in an engagement was about two-thirds."

On the day of which Lieutenant Hemingway was speaking" [went on the *Trapeze* report], the Arditi came up in camions, the whole regiment singing a song which from any other body of men would have meant three months in jail. Hemingway sang the song for the audience

---

ing offensive; and that we spent that evening together watching the ceaseless lightning of the artillery preparation against his Mount Grappa position.

It must have been right then that the jaundice hit him, and I am quite certain that he was invalided back to the hospital in Milan. I don't remember much about that, because somewhere before dawn my partner and I drove our First ambulance #8 up the Grappa to an Advanced Surgical Post — about half a mile back of the line. There was real tough fighting up there for most of a week. Then the Austrians pulled out and ran for home. A tremendous rout. The war on the Italian front was over. That armistice was signed on November 4 . . .

If it comforts or pleases or gratifies any of those others who also love him to believe that he was an Italian officer — as well as a fine young American boy — then for gosh sake, let them believe it!

Remember Lincoln's words — ". . . beyond our poor power to add or detract"? What Ern was and what he did will live long years. What uniform he wore, or whose rolls bore his name those last few months signify nothing. He was, beyond those minor matters, a man. A fine man, who became an everlastingly great man.

That ought to be enough for all and any of us.

Yours with affection,

Bill

in Italian and then translated it. [When Ernie sang it to me, it sounded like this: "Oh Generale Cordorna escrita la Regina . . ."] Several hours after their initial engagement with the enemy, Lieutenant Hemingway saw a wounded captain being brought back to a field hospital in an ambulance. He had been shot in the chest but had plugged the holes with cigarettes and had gone on fighting. On his way to the hospital he amused himself by throwing hand grenades into the ditch just to see them go off. "This illustrates the spirit of these men," said Hemingway.

At the time he was wounded Lieutenant Hemingway was assigned to the 69th Regiment of Infantry. He was with several Italians in an advanced listening post. It was at night but the enemy had probably noticed them, for he dropped a trench mortar shell, which consisted of a gallon can filled with explosive and slugs, into the hole in which they were crouching.

"When the thing exploded," Lt. Hemingway said, "it seemed as if I was moving off somewhere in a sort of red din. I said to myself, 'Gee! Stein, you're dead!' and then I began to feel myself pulling back to earth. Then I woke up. The sand bags had caved in on my legs and at first I felt disappointed that I had not been wounded. The other soldiers had retreated leaving me and several others for dead. One of these soldiers who was left started crying. So I knew he was alive and told him to shut up. The Austrians seemed determined to wipe out this one outpost. They had star shells out and their trench searchlights were trying to locate us.

"I picked up the wounded man and started back toward the trenches. As I got up to walk my knee cap felt warm and sticky, so I knew I'd been touched. Just before we reached the trench their searchlight spotted us and they turned a machine gun on us. One got me in the thigh. It felt just like a snowball, so hard and coming with such force that it knocked me down. We started on, but just as we reached the trench and were about to jump in, another bullet hit me, this time in the foot. It tumbled me and my wounded man all in a heap in the trench and when I came to again, I was in a dugout. Two soldiers had just come to the conclusion that I was to 'pass out shortly.' By some arguing I was able to convince them that they were wrong."

Ernest also talked informally to the visitors who came to the house to greet him and to see his souvenirs. He had shipped home a trunkful of weapons and many types of uniforms. Some of the latter he had won in strip poker games, he told us. Among his souvenirs of the war were a captured Austrian automatic revolver, a gas mask, and his punctured trousers. The bloodstains were still visible on them, and Ernie took this garment with him to show audiences where he spoke. Ernie enjoyed showing his trophies, but actually it was Dad who invited most of the friends and neighbors to see Ernie shoot off his star shells in our back yard, brilliant signal lights my brother had managed to bring home with his other baggage. He did not suggest that he had been in any other service than the American Red Cross.

But in between these extrovert activities Ernie had quiet, almost depressed intervals when he retired to his room away from the well-wishers and curiosity seekers. It was during one of these quiet times of his (I think this was about a month after Ernie got home from Europe) that I remember I was very upset about something, a problem not connected with Ernie in any way. I remember I had climbed the third-floor stairs to Ernie's room to bring him some mail or magazines. Ernie was in bed. He noticed that something was wrong.

"What's the matter, Mazaween?" Ernie asked kindly. "Something got the old sistereen down?"

We talked for a few minutes, and I let off steam to Ernie just as we used to talk frankly to each other before he had gone to Kansas City.

Then Ernest said: "Here, take a nipper of this, Mazaween." He held out a bottle marked Kümmel. Hesitatingly I tasted the warm, sweet, anise-flavored drink. I rolled it on my tongue, but I didn't drink it.

"Don't be afraid," Ernie said. "Drink it up, Sis, it can't hurt you. There's great comfort in that little bottle," he told me, "not just for itself. But it relaxes you when the pain gets bad. Mazaween," he said, "don't be afraid to taste all the other things in life that aren't here in Oak Park. This life is all right, but there's a whole big world out there full of people who really feel things. They live and love and die with all their feelings. Taste everything, Sis," he went on. "Don't be afraid to try new things just because they *are new*. Sometimes I think we only half live over here. The Italians live all the way. What some of those guys I got to know in the hospital had been through! I could tell you stories, Maz —" I begged him to tell me. Ernie said he didn't want to shock me, but some of the stories came out, bits at a time.

Ernie told me that as he picked up more colloquial Italian and understood all the words, he'd heard some pretty raw tales. He told me a few of them, though I suppose they were well expurgated. In all the stories he told the family, Ernie was careful not to shock the sensitivities of our Victorian-trained parents. For Ernest it must have been something like being put in a box with the cover nailed down to come home to conventional, suburban Oak Park living, after his own vivid experiences. I wondered after that night if Ernie would ever again be happy living at home.

Naturally, Ernie saw his new Italian friends who lived nearby in Chicago. The Italian vice consul, "Nicki" Nerone, was a great friend of his. It was through the vice consul and the Italian-American organizations, whose members knew of Ernest's medal and honor, that a group of Italians organized a wonderful party which they gave for Ernest at our home.

A committee called on my parents to present their plan. At first Mother and Dad didn't understand. Why should all these people want to come out to our house and bring their own food? It didn't seem reasonable. But Ernest explained.

"Let 'em come, Dad. What they are saying is that they want to bring everything. They'll bring all the food and an orchestra and opera singers, drinks and the whole works."

"But the expense! We couldn't accept all that!" Daddy protested.

"They *like* to do it, Pop. You only hurt their feelings if you don't let 'em come. They love fiestas and they want to show that they love Americans too. Just relax, Dad, you'll enjoy it."

So it was arranged. We were to invite as many of our friends as we wished. The Italian hosts would bring their friends and all refreshments for at least fifty people. Our house could easily accommodate them all. That was the beginning of the fabulous Italian parties at our home.

True to their word on the appointed Sunday — it had to be Sunday, as most of the people in this group worked six days a week in their own jobs — out to Oak Park came cars full of voluble, laughing, black-haired people, carrying huge hampers packed with rich foods. When they unloaded their hampers and boxes the spaghetti and meat dishes were arranged in the center of our big dining room table. These were surrounded by more platters of roast chicken, strange, delicious fish salads, still more plates of small sweet pastries and other dishes of tasty tarts filled with highly seasoned ground meats and cheese. Near them stood frosted cakes, long loaves of crusty Italian bread and gallon jugs of red and white wines.

Three members of the chorus of the Chicago Grand Opera Company were part of the group. Several others, on week days chefs in some of the best restaurants in Chicago, put on their aprons and went right to work in our kitchen. They took charge of everything.

The musical members proceeded to give a concert of opera arias sung with all the volume and gestures they used on the stage. Two of the Italians had brought guitars, another had his violin, and still another played the mandolin. These musicians accompanied the singers with gusto. The concert took place in Mother's music room, of course.

Even Daddy, still rather dubious about the whole affair, especially since it was held on Sunday, finally entered into the spirit of the occasion. It was impossible to resist the friendliness of these generous people who had come to do honor to his son.

At last the Italian photographer, a professional, arranged the whole crowd, the chefs, the musicians and our family, in a group. We all stood just under the balcony in the music room. The photographer ducked behind his camera, put his black cloth over his head and sang out:

"Geeve a smile, please!"

We all grinned. The resulting picture showed us a very happy group.

We Hemingways loved every minute of the party, even when we understood only part of what was being said by our Italian host-guests. But we realized how sincerely they meant it when they told us how happy and proud they were to be able to celebrate Ernest's return from Italy with this fiesta at his own home.

One thing, however, seemed to disappoint them: we had not invited enough guests of our own to eat up all the food. The Italian group would come out soon again, they told us. Such a beautiful house, they said with feeling, should be filled with many friends.

Once more the friendly group chose a Sunday and brought all their delicious food and their musicians to our house again. By the time the second party was held the news of the Italians' unique hospitality had spread around Oak Park. Friends of Ernest's, Ursula's and mine were delighted to be included in the fiesta. I'm not sure, but I think that some young friends of Sunny's were with us too. Little Carol, who was seven years old, and three-year-old Les, the baby, were put to bed early.

After the second fiesta went on from noon to midnight and Ernest and I had finally said good-by to what we thought was the last of the noisy, shouting, singing crowd — this was about one o'clock in the morning — Daddy was distinctly annoyed. He was tired and he needed his sleep. Ernie and I were sorry he was tired and upset, but we loved the parties.

"You've let this sort of thing go too far," Dad told us. He said all the lusty vocalizing and the shouts of our jolly guests as they departed had become a neighborhood nuisance. Daddy said goodnight to us firmly and marched up to bed.

At last the front door was locked and the downstairs lights were switched off.

Ernie and I crept upstairs in the dark, hoping not to disturb the rest of the family. My room was on the second floor. But as Ernie reached for the light switch in his own, third-floor bedroom, he stumbled over something on the floor. He found it was one of the boys of our neighborhood, sound asleep.

On went the lights again. Ernie called me and together we made a thorough search of the whole house. One more friend was found behind the davenport in the music room, quite unconscious as he slept off the effects of Italy's vineyards. Reluctantly we agreed that Dad was probably right, the Italian celebrations had gone too far. That was the last fiesta at our house.

But the end of these gay parties didn't keep Ernest and me from going to some of the other Italian festivities downtown in Chicago. We danced the tarantella at the home of one of our fiesta hosts, and I remember that I went to the opera with some of that same friendly group that winter. Knowing these hospitable people opened a whole new view of Chicago to us.

For days Ernie had been watching the mails. He was irritable and on edge with the waiting. Then the letter came. After he read it he went to bed and was actually ill. We didn't know what was the matter with Ernie at first. He did not respond to medical treatment, and he ran a temperature. Dad was worried about him. I went up to Ernie's room to see if I could be of any help to him. Ernie thrust the letter toward me.

"Read it," he said from the depths of his grief. "No. I'll tell you." Then he turned to the wall. He was physically sick for several days but he did not mention the letter again.

Ag, Ernie told me, was not coming to America. She was going to marry an Italian major instead.

In time Ernest felt better. He got out among his friends again. I have thought many times since that day that the letter from Agnes may have been the most valuable one my brother ever received. Perhaps without that rankling memory, *A Farewell to Arms* might never have been written.

As time went on, that spring of 1919, Ernest grew impatient at his lack of physical activity. The silver knee cap the surgeons in Milan had put in place bothered him less, he said. Although bits of shrapnel continued to hurt and annoy him as they worked toward the surface of his legs and feet, he was determined to do something more active than merely walking with his cane. Ernie found he could dance almost as well as before he went to war. The sliding steps seemed easier for him than the abruptness of walking. Mother and Dad were worried about Ernest for several reasons. For one thing they knew he could not be happy without some athletic activity in his life. They were glad when Ernest decided to take up swimming at the Y.M.C.A. tank.

One night there was a swimming meet at the "Y." Ernie had been down to swim in the pool rather regularly, but we didn't see how he could swim in fast competition with that bad knee of his. We didn't mention our fears to him, of course.

The evening the swimming meet was held most of our family was gathered in the dining room after dinner was over. The dining room was smaller and cozier than the living room. The table had been cleared and, as we often did, my sisters and I stood leaning our backs against the big green enameled hot water radiator on the north side of the room. Mother, I remember, was seated at the black upright practice piano on the opposite side. Daddy, his suit coat hung over the back of his chair, was looking over some papers as he sat in his shirt sleeves at the empty white-covered dining table.

I remember that Ernie came into the house the back way. He walked into the dining room through the swinging door from the kitchen. Daddy turned toward Ernest.

"How'd it go, boy?" Daddy asked kindly.

"Swell," Ernie said.

"Which race did you swim in?" one of the sisters inquired.

"Listen, kid, I'm a plunger now, see. I don't go in for any other events. I got third."

Mother and I sighed with relief.

There were loud congratulations from everybody. Ernie beamed.

Finally somebody asked innocently, "How many were entered in the plunges?" For a minute Ernie didn't answer. He just looked at us without an expression on his face. We waited.

"Three," Ernie said. He turned and went upstairs to bed.

We all knew the sister who asked that question could have bitten her tongue out.

All these months Ernie continued to wear his Red Cross uniform. It was very becoming and he looked extremely handsome in it, but the main reason he wore it was because the high boots, which were part of the uniform, gave needed support to his wounded legs. He told me he didn't know how he could walk without those high, firm boots. He polished them daily. They were the nicest footgear any of us had ever seen. Ernie said he couldn't wear these good boots with civilian clothes, so he continued to dress in his uniform.

One Saturday that spring of 1919, I went to a matinee in a Chicago theater. In the row behind me I could hear two women talking. They seemed to be discussing a returned soldier.

"Why does that boy have to flaunt that fancy uniform

around the town all these months?" said a voice in my ear. "He's been home from war since last winter. Why doesn't he stop trying to be a hero and put on civilian clothes? I've got no patience with these kids that keep trying to show off."

"Maybe he hasn't got any civilian clothes left that fit him," said the other voice. "Don't be too hard on him."

"Oh that's not it," the first voice went on. "He just likes to get the girls crazy about him. Have you noticed how he hangs around the high school all the time? Wouldn't you think he'd find something else to do? Why doesn't he get a job? He likes having the girls moon over him! You know as well as I do that's why Ernest Hemingway wears his uniform."

I sat perfectly still for a minute. I was so shocked and angry I could hardly breathe. The women went on talking. I had to reply. When I could control myself I turned around in my seat to see that they were teachers from Oak Park High School.

"I beg your pardon," I said. "I couldn't help overhearing your remarks about my brother. Maybe it would interest you to know why he *has* to wear that uniform all this time. Pieces of metal keep coming out of his legs. Sometimes he has to wear dressings over the places that are festered. Do you know that those high leather boots give his sore legs support? He doesn't wear those boots for fun, he wears them because he has to. Most people don't know it, but Ernie has a lot of pain. He can't get a job yet, as you suggested, because he isn't able to stand on his feet more than a few hours at a time. I don't blame him for hanging around the high school. He just gets darn lonesome, and so would you if you were home and all your friends were away in college or had jobs during the daytime. I should think teachers like you would be more understanding instead of talking so mean about a boy who's going through all that Ernest has to bear!"

I was so angry I could feel I was beginning to cry. I was also so embarrassed after I had dared to say all this that I climbed out of my seat and went to the rest room until I calmed down. When I finally came back, the curtain was up and I watched the play, though to this day I couldn't tell you what it was about. I ignored the teachers. But at the first intermission, when the lights went up, they asked me to go out into the hallway with them, and they both apologized profusely. I said I was sorry I had been rude to them, but they insisted they were glad I had spoken up. One of them said she was sure that few people in Oak Park had any idea of Ernest's real situation. Though I was still upset, we parted as friends, and I watched the rest of the play. I was surprised at myself. Though I had often criticized Ernie personally, I had no idea I could become so angry when I heard someone else criticize him, particularly when, as in the case of the teachers, the criticism was so unkindly worded and unfair.

I remember that I told Mother about the incident when I got home that evening. Mother's reaction was typical of her.

"Good for you, Marce!" said Mother. "I'm glad you gave it to them! They deserved it!" But Mother warned me not to let Ernest know what the teachers had said. Mother and I both knew how sensitive Ernest was. We knew he would be deeply hurt if he thought others felt unkindly toward him. Ernest had enough to bear without any of us adding anything more.

Our parents worried very much about Ernest and his future. Ernest didn't seem to know what he wanted to do with his life. He wasn't doing any writing at this time.

He was still uninterested in going on with any formal education. He seemed to be at loose ends.

In June of 1919, I graduated from the Congregational Training School, which was later incorporated into the University of Chicago.

Both Ernie and I went to Walloon Lake with the family that summer, and with our friends we all pitched in to help Mother with the new cottage on Longfield Farm, our property across the lake from Windemere. The farm had stood vacant for some years, since the old arrangement with a tenant farmer to run the place on shares had proved unsatisfactory. Our only financial interest in it was the nut and fruit trees and the ice which was cut and stored in the icehouse. For several years before 1919 the farm had been used only as a vegetable patch and picnic grounds for our family.

There were times when my parents played with the idea of building a permanent home on Longfield for their retirement, but this idea didn't appeal to us children at all and Mother was persuaded to give up her notion. But she never gave up her hope of building at least a summer cottage at the summit of Red Top Mountain, the center hill on the farm.

She drew plans for the new house early in 1919, and in the summer of that year it was started. This was to be her own studio, where she could escape into privacy from her large, noisy family whenever she needed quiet.

"I shall do my composing there," she told us. If anyone asked her what else she would do, Mother said, "If I feel like it, I shall just rest. It's going to be wonderful!"

Mother designed a simple cottage of two big rooms, with a fireplace in the living room downstairs and a huge dormitory bedroom above it. It was her first idea that she would connect the two floors with a ladder, for she begrudged giving up any of the living room space to a stairway. But when we pointed out the inconveniences of carrying full water pitchers or bedding or mattresses, or anything else, up and down a ladder, Mother gave in and designed a narrow, steep stairway with a railing that took up little room. There was to be no plumbing, and since electric lines were unavailable, kerosene would be essential for the lamps and the small kitchen stove. There was a hand pump near where the old tenant house had stood at the bottom of the hill, but this source of supply was several hundred feet away from the location of the new cottage, and every pail of water had to be carried up the slippery, grassy hill on a hand-drawn cart.

When Daddy protested the idea of Mother's building a cottage at the top of the hill, saying that she would find it pretty hard to climb that hill every time she wanted to bring up groceries or water, her reply was characteristic:

"I want the view from the top of the hill. It's worth going without water and food to have peace and quiet and a place to be alone. I love you all, but I have to have a rest from you all now and then if I am to go on living."

Mother added a small separate bedroom behind the living room on the side away from the lake. This was for her private use. Her guests could climb to the second floor dormitory, but she intended to live on one floor. She also added a combination pantry and kitchen next to the bedroom, and a door from the kitchen to the living room. When we asked Mother why she had so little shelf and cupboard space in the kitchen, Mother said:

"I don't intend to do much cooking. I really can't cook and I loathe washing dishes. There is plenty of room here for me to make a cup of tea or cut bread for a sandwich.

If you think I'm going to waste my time stirring up or baking anything, you're very much mistaken. I expect to enjoy this cottage."

She did just that, often staying alone for a day or so, at times even longer, miles away from anyone. Sometimes she'd invite the rest of us over for a picnic meal. We enjoyed going.

We older children would take turns staying overnight in the second-floor dormitory, where the cot beds stood in a row. With the big shutters propped open on three sides, the moonlight streamed in and the night wind blew over us. As we fell asleep we felt as though we were drifting on top of the world.

Mother loved Grace Cottage. Its name came naturally. While it was still in the planning stage, Daddy referred to it as "Gracie's little house," and that's just what it was. When there was no wind and the lake was still, we could hear Mother's music drifting across the mile of water and we knew Grace Cottage was serving its intended purpose.

When Mother was ready to return to us, she would either row back to Windemere or, if she had no boat there, she would put up a piece of sheet or a Turkish bath towel to signal Daddy to come over and pick her up in the motorboat. He was delighted to have her back.

Though my parents frequently got on each other's nerves, they loved each other deeply. Mother always returned refreshed and happy from her quiet times alone. She knew her own needs. She was right, she needed time to be alone as much as she needed food and water.

The summer the cottage was being built, Ernie and I, Ursula and Sunny and several of our young friends around the lake took turns wielding a paintbrush, helping Mother stain Grace Cottage. She left the interior walls the natural wood color, but the outside clapboarding and porch were a warm shade of reddish brown. Even the little outhouse behind was painted the same color. The open porch, on two sides toward the lake, provided a superb view. In one direction Mother had an unhampered vista down the nearly five miles of open lake; the town of Walloon Lake dim in the distance looked like a gray dream city. On the other side one looked past Eagle Island, through the narrows far into the West Arm. Mother never tired of her hilltop contemplation of the lake, the surrounding farms and woodlands.

The furnishings of the new house were all of Mother's own making. She liked to try new things, and she started on this do-it-yourself job after a visit to the manual training class in Oak Park where the younger children were busy on woodwork.

"Could somebody like me learn to make things like this?" she asked the teacher.

The young man replied that he didn't see why not.

"Would you give me lessons?"

"I could," said the manual training teacher, "but I would have to charge you an awful lot if you were the only pupil."

"How many other people would you have to have in an evening class to make it worth your while?" asked Mother. The teacher thought quickly and decided that six adults would be enough.

Mother's enthusiasm was so great that within a week she had inspired, or coerced, enough friends and neighbors to fill the class. Mother had never so much as pounded a nail with accuracy, but she entered into the classwork, the sawing and hammering, with gusto. This was how she made all of the furniture for Grace Cottage.

Before the year was out, she finished an excellent living room table of bird's-eye maple with a nicely fitted drawer in one side of it. She made a small padded davenport with a straight back that could slide up over the top and form a table. Her prize piece was an almost professionally finished dressing table with four drawers that really slid back and forth easily. Next came a tea cart with a fitted tray for the top and a shelf below, the wheels for which she took from a discarded baby carriage. We watched her in amazement as she used a square, a level, and even a carpenter's plumb line to achieve perfection in her work. After she left the class, she built, on her own, a complete four-poster bed for her own room at Grace Cottage. It was somewhat crude in finish, of course, but it was extremely comfortable and had white dotted dimity curtains draped from the top and sides.

Then she braided rugs out of strips of old wornout sweaters, bits of old dresses, pieces of outgrown bathing suits — anything colorful. The rugs she made were circular or oval and very cheerful. She made all the bright cretonne curtains of pine cone design and upholstered cushions of the same material for the window seats.

Once I asked her why she had to be alone at her cottage, and this was her explanation: "People are made differently," she said. "Some women cling to their husbands and their children. They want to possess them. Some women feed their egos by touching and owning the members of their families. Others like to share their abilities and their interests, but they need solitude and communion with God — the source. I think I am one of these people. I must have quietness and peace to live. If I could wish for one great gift for each of my children, I think it would be that they each might find a mate who understands this need.

"Your father does not always understand this need for me to be alone occasionally. He is kind and willing for me to have this cottage, but he feels he is giving in to a woman's whim. There are times when I feel sure he thinks I *want* to be away from *him*, that my need for quietness is some personal slight to him. That's not true . . .

"I hope you'll remember this talk we've had someday, not just for yourself, but for the other children. Ernest is very like me. He will need to know these things, too. When Ernest gets through this period he's going through, of fighting himself and everybody else, and turns his energy toward something positive, he will be a fine man. I don't suppose you'll remember much of what I say. But anyway, I'm glad I had a chance to tell you," Mother said. And she kissed me.

Later that night in Windemere Cottage, I wrote down in my diary as much as I could of what Mother had told me. That's why I have it in such detail.

During the summer, while the cottage was being built and Ernie was at the lake, the family was increasingly worried about his lack of interest in going back to college or in getting a job. Mother talked to Sterling Sanford about it, and asked his advice as to what she or Dad might do to interest Ernie in going to college. Mother said, "You can't have a boy just fooling around all the rest of his life; he must get interested in something." Ernest, who would sleep in the mornings, was doing no writing, nor had he any plans at all, as far as we knew.

Toward the end of that summer, Ernie decided he would like to stay on at our cottage, Windemere, during the autumn. He said he could live there alone after the family went back to Oak Park. We had always talked about how nice it would be if the time ever came that we were free to stay on at Walloon and see the gorgeous autumn colors. His legs were well healed and he was capable of long walks.

In a letter of mine to Sterling from Oak Park, dated October 14, 1919, which he has kept, I wrote, "Ernie is with us again, but only for a week. He drove down with Bill Smith last Monday and expects to return to Horton Bay for the whole winter. Personally, I fear he will freeze, but he desires to write — to create immense quantities of literature — and I guess Horton Bay in the winter will be the quietest place on earth to do it."

But apparently Ernest found the cottage a better place to stay, for he did not go back to the Bay, but instead went to Petoskey later that fall when the fireplace proved inadequate to keep him warm.

That autumn of 1919 was the only long period Ernest ever spent in the town of Petoskey, as far as I know. During that fall Ernie got to know the townspeople far better than any of the rest of the family ever had; he had time that early winter to be a part of the town's activities. He also had a chance, living alone in a room in town, to start doing some writing, as he had said he wanted to do. But in no letter to the family nor in any word of his to any of us, that I remember, did Ernest ever mention doing any writing of his own during that fall and early winter he spent in Petoskey.

9

Leaving Home

FROM January to May, 1920, Ernest was in Toronto. The way he got there is rather interesting. While he was in Petoskey just before Christmas in 1919, he gave a talk on his war experiences, and at this one, as in those in Oak Park, he showed his souvenirs — various uniforms, his steel helmet, Arditi plumed hat, a star shell pistol, and other souvenirs from Italy. In the audience was Mrs. Ralph Connable of Toronto, a former Petoskey resident who happened to be back visiting her mother, Mrs. George Gridley. She was introduced to Ernest after the program, and finding that he had no particular plans for the rest of the winter, it occurred to her that he might be a helpful companion to her son, Ralph, Jr., who was one year younger than Ernest, at their Toronto home while the rest of the family went south that winter. Though our family had never met the Connables, my father and Mr. Connable had heard of each other. Ernest had written us delightedly of his invitation to go to Toronto and that his transportation was to be furnished by the Connables.

Ernest returned to Oak Park for Christmas. In January he became a part of the Connable household. He corresponded regularly with his hosts and their daughter, Dorothy, during their Florida sojourn, including a remarkable letter to Dorothy on how to win at roulette. After the Connables returned to Toronto, Ernest and Dorothy Connable and another friend, Ernest Smith, had great fun skating, attending the theater, and generally enjoying life. Mr. Connable was the busy head of the Woolworth stores of Canada, and it was Mrs. Connable who introduced Ernest to a friend on the staff of the *Toronto Star*. She told me it was this introduction that started Ernest doing occasional feature writing for the paper. Sometime afterward Ernie wrote Father about his first assignment. It seems he was sent by *The Star* to interview a man famous in the medical world. When the copy was finished, Ernest was complimented by the editor on getting all the correct technical facts and the exact medical phraseology. When Dad heard this he was pleased but not surprised: he said it showed Ernest's good training as a doctor's son. Ernest did occasional articles for *The Star* during the rest of his visit in Toronto, but he was not a regular employee that year.

I was delighted when Ernest came home to Oak Park from Toronto the last week of May, 1920. He was so gay and full of plans. When I asked him if he was going to write for the *Toronto Star*, he said, "Hell no, kid, I'm going to travel!" Then he explained that Brummie (Ted Brumback, who had been with him in the Red Cross Corps in Italy) was arriving from Kansas City, and Bill Smith, his St. Joseph, Missouri, pal who spent summers with his aunt Mrs. Charles in Horton Bay was driving up to our house too. They would take off for Walloon early in June.

Ernest seemed completely carefree. He was well and full of fun and more like a boy of sixteen than a man approaching his twenty-first birthday. He seemed to have none of the introspective thoughts he had expressed when he had first come home from Italy a year and a half before. He went to Ann Arbor and looked up Jack Pentecost, a high school classmate who was at the University of Michigan, who had his passport for the Orient, and together they made plans for some adventure for the following fall. Almost every evening he had groups of friends come in and I joined them on weekends, when I came home from my classes at the School of Speech at Northwestern and my work at the Kenilworth Church and Community Center.

The first weekend Ernie was home, he had three of his friends with him — Howell Jenkins, who had been in Italy with Ernie, John Baker and Ted Brumback. We had a moonlight dance and then Ernie suggested we all have something to eat together. The younger children were asleep, Daddy and Mother had gone to bed early, so the four boys and I raided the icebox and took our food with us, munching as we walked up Kenilworth Avenue toward a deserted subdivision, several blocks up our street. It was a real estate promotion area where elaborate stone walls and gates surrounded vacant lots, and cracked pavements encompassed garden spaces with carved stone benches and ornate jardinieres intended to hold geraniums, while water was supposed to have played in the empty, leaf-filled fountains nearby. Except for one house, which had been built by the subdividers, it was as quiet as a cemetery.

The moon shone brightly that night and the balmy air inspired us to song. "Let's make up an opera," Ernie said. "I feel like singing."

Somebody suggested Moses and the bulrushes as a good theme to base it on, and thus began one of the greatest unrecorded musical epics in the history of Oak Park. Since there was nobody around to hear us, we let our voices out in unrestrained bellows. One recitative was sung by Mir-

iam, Moses' sister, as she put the baby in the basket under
the bulrushes. Being the only girl present, I had to sing all
the female roles. The main phrase in Miriam's song was
"Stay here quiet, kid, don't yell, and hope the princess finds
you." Ernie added a chorus, "The crocodiles will get you
if you don't watch out." The four of us joined in a chorus
of bulrushes, these weeds voicing their complaint to the
tune of "There'll Be a Hot Time in the Old Town Tonight." The main theme of this number was something
like this: "There's a basket in the river, and they better
find it quick. There's a baby in the basket, you could hit
him with a stick,/We hate to hold the baby for it bends
our blossoms low./Come, oh come, my King Pharaoh."

Howell Jenkins sang the king's part — Ernie was Moses. There were other solos by the baby, to do with how
much *mal de mer* he felt in his insecure position on the
water, and by fishermen going by. I seem to remember I
reached heights as a soprano when, as Pharaoh's daughter,
I found the tiny child in the basket. But after each solo
came the chorus of bulrushes again, Ernie leading the singing as he made up words to several well-known tunes in
which the bulrushes commented on the story as it went
along. We were so inspired by our own verbosity and
vocal prowess that we might have gone on all night if a
light had not come on in the only house nearby. A second-
floor window went up with a crash and a masculine
voice shouted, "Why don't you damn kids shut up and
go home?" We were brought back to earth, and silently
we walked on.

In a letter to Mrs. Connable dated June 1, 1920, Ernest
confided his plans for three friends — Bill Smith, Jack
Pentecost and Brummie — joining on a trip to the Orient.
They evidently intended to work their way as seamen
or stokers, and Yokohama was to be their first stop. He

also told the Connables that his older sister was again his best pal and he expressed eagerness to have his parents meet the Connables. In late June the boys gathered in Oak Park and rode up together in Bill Smith's car to Walloon Lake to work out the details of their trip. The party broke up with their hopes still riding high, and Ernest spent the rest of his time that summer with friends in Horton Bay camping and hunting, and when there was no other target, shooting insulators off the electric poles. I saw little of him during this time, for I was working at the Community Center activities in Kenilworth and preparing to attend classes at Northwestern University that fall. But Ernest wrote to me often, as did Mother.

Mother, who had put up with a lot from Ernest and his lack of responsibility that summer, felt that eighteen months was too long for her twenty-one-year-old son to be without work or any plans for a job — except going out as a seaman to the Orient. She refused to give him money for a passport and the fare to San Francisco. She told him that it was time he got busy and earned his way.

So Ernie's dream of shipping out to the Orient never materialized. He had been home now for a year and a half; his wounds were completely healed, and had been for months; yet except for a few months of part-time employment in Toronto and the occasional pieces he had written for the *Toronto Star*, he had made no effort to get out on his own.

Ernest, who could be a most charming companion, could also be completely indifferent to other people's convenience or any responsibilities which did not appeal to him. Even though I was not present that summer, I knew that Mother was not in good health and that Dad was working hard in the heat in Chicago to help out the family finances, which were strained that year — largely because of Mother's being unable to carry on her usual strenuous teaching program. I also knew that Mother was economizing and as a result was employing less help than usual at the cottage, and that she and Dad were saving to send Ursula to college. Mother was also stuck nine miles from town without the car or Daddy to drive it and with no telephone; as usual, supplies were hard to get.

When he went north that summer, Ernest had promised Dad he would take care of the jobs Dad usually did. This included chopping wood, bringing ice across the lake from the farm, digging the deep holes in the ground for garbage disposal and other heavy jobs so necessary at a cottage. Ernest had planned to stay at Horton Bay and come to Walloon to help. Les was only five and had not yet gone to kindergarten. Carol was nine and my other sisters were in their teens. All the girls helped, but their big brother did not. Ernest simply didn't keep his word to help Mother. When he did drop in at the cottage, he came without warning at mealtime, bringing two or three husky friends also in their twenties. Though Mother implored Ernest's help and tried to talk to him about the family situation, he blithely ignored her appeals and managed to leave immediately after meals with his friends or go fishing when something needed to be done; he promised vaguely to help "some other time."

Finally, worried beyond endurance by Ernest's complete lack of adult responsibility, his rudeness and his willingness to let both Mrs. Charles, Bill Smith's aunt, and our family go on providing for him, Mother decided something drastic had to be done to wake him up. Following his twenty-first birthday, July 21, 1920, Mother wrote him a firmly worded letter in which she said that he would either have to get a job or get out; that it wasn't good for him to loaf any more. Ernie resented the ultimatum. The feeling between them that summer became quite tense and probably explains why Mother later went off by herself to Grace Cottage. Daddy was concerned, for he had no wish for an open break, but Dad agreed with Mother. The strong medicine had its effect, and at the end of the summer when the family returned to Oak Park, Ernie came to the house only long enough to pick up his clothes and move in to live with Y. Kenley Smith, Bill's older brother, and his wife in their commodious apartment in downtown Chicago. The job Ernie had found for himself after much looking was as an editorial assistant on the staff of *Cooperative Commonwealth*.

All the girls in our family had suddenly become conscious of their hair. "To bob or not to bob" — that was the question. It was Irene Castle who a couple of years earlier had started the fad for short hair. She shocked the country with her fluffy bob, but she looked so perfectly lovely as she danced with Vernon that we all wanted to copy her. It seems incredible now to remember what a storm was created by the American woman's desire to get rid of the buns and knots and side combs and masses of hairpins they had been wearing on their heads for years.

Daddy was furious at the idea; he said he would never tolerate any daughter of his cutting off her beautiful long hair. We girls listened to him, but we kept our own thoughts. I remember seeing headlines in the *Chicago Tribune* at this time about schoolteachers losing their jobs because they cut their hair. It seemed so silly.

At the dinner table one Saturday evening, our doctor father announced triumphantly that the hospital staff had agreed to fire any nurse who was found with bobbed hair. Daddy spoke of this decision in the same tone of voice an evangelist might use in defending the Bible. Now, *we* knew Sunny had cut off her hair at least a week before, but she wore her locks pinned closely to her head and Daddy had never noticed that her hair was cut. That evening Sunny smiled at Daddy and leaned toward him coquettishly. His face was still stern with the fervor of his crusade against bobbing. Sunny grinned at him. She opened her eyes wide and in a little girl voice said:

"Don't you love me any more, Daddy?"

"Why, of course I do," said Daddy in a matter-of-fact tone, seeing no connection with his previous remarks. "Why do you ask me?"

"Well, you said you'd throw out any of your daughters if we bobbed our hair," answered Sunny sweetly.

"*And I mean it!*" shouted Daddy.

"But why, Daddy? What's the difference whether hair is long or short?"

"Short hair is unwomanly and I won't have it in my house," said Dad sententiously.

Sunny grinned at him.

"I cut mine over a week ago, Daddy," she said in a soft voice, "and you never even noticed it, did you?"

Daddy tried to speak. He couldn't. He just sputtered. Actually there was nothing he could say. He got his mouth all ready to say something, and he closed it. He wanted to be angry, but he just couldn't. Ignoring Sunny, he glared around the table at the rest of us.

"Don't let me catch any of the rest of you cutting your hair," he said. We kept quiet.

The next weekend when I got back from my job and my classes at Northwestern, I saw Ursula had also cut her hair. I got up courage to cut mine shortly afterwards. But I didn't pin mine up or pretend at all. Daddy looked sternly at me as I sat down at the table one night that weekend. Before he could say a word, I asked him:

"How do I look, Daddy? Isn't it nice? I love my hair this way, it's so lightweight and easy to fix."

By that time Daddy was so used to shocks, he didn't even comment. But some time later, when Mother threatened to bob *her* hair, all of her daughters, emancipated females though they were, begged her not to do it. Mother looked so lovely with her long curled white hair piled high on her head that we implored her not to spoil her good looks by changing her hair style. Her creamy white hair, her blue eyes and her vivid rosy cheeks combined to create a uniquely artistic effect we all admired. None of us had any feeling against her bobbing her hair. We just hated to have her spoil the picture. She was so complimented she agreed not to cut it, to please us.

I was often invited to visit the Smiths (where Ernest was living) on Sunday afternoons when Kenley and his charming wife entertained a group of young people, including Bill Smith and Bill's sister Katherine (who sometime later was to marry the novelist John dos Passos). Bobby Rouse and Bill Horne, who had been with Ernie in Italy, came too. One of Kate's most attractive guests was a tall, auburn-haired girl from St. Louis who made a great impression on my brother. Her name was Elizabeth Hadley Richardson, but everyone called her Hadley and Ernie nicknamed her Hash Brown.

While Hadley was visiting in Chicago she hurt her ankle, and her foot swelled to such an extent that she couldn't wear a shoe. I remember Ernest telling me how much he admired her spunk when, instead of begging off, Hadley agreed to keep her date with him for a football game at the University of Chicago. Ernie thought she was wonderful to limp along so cheerfully with a red felt bedroom slipper on her bandaged foot.

"Anybody else would have been embarrassed," Ernie said. "I know you would have been, Marce. But Hadley paid no attention to her red slipper. She went along as though nothing had happened. That girl's a real sport."

It wasn't many months later that Ernest told us he and Hadley were going to be married. We liked her so much, we were all tremendously pleased. Mother and Dad offered to lend them Windemere Cottage when Ernest and Hadley told us of their plans for a summer wedding up north.

On the third of September, 1921, they were married in the little white Methodist Church next to the general store in Horton Bay. The informal reception for the families and the few close friends was held at Aunty Beth Dilworth's home across the road from the church.

Ernest and Bill Smith, Carl Edgar, Bill Horne, and the other friends who served as ushers wore blue coats and white flannel trousers. Hadley, of course, was dressed in white and wore a veil. Her parents were not living, but her brother-in-law and sister, Professor and Mrs. Roland G. Usher of Washington University, came on from St. Louis; the Connables, summering in Petoskey, were present; and of course, the Hemingway family.

The young couple spent their honeymoon that balmy September in our family cottage Windemere, which our parents and the younger children had vacated just before the wedding day.

That fall, Ernie and Hadley moved into an apartment in Chicago, where Ernest continued to write for the magazine. On October first, Mother and Daddy celebrated their twenty-fifth wedding anniversary, and they made the party an occasion for presenting young Mr. and Mrs. Ernest Hemingway to some four hundred of their friends and neighbors at a reception in our home in Oak Park. It was a beautiful party. Hadley looked radiant that night with her reddish gold hair glinting in the light. She wore her wedding gown, and Ernie stood proudly beside her, beaming at all the guests. I was so happy to have such a beautiful new sister. The evening stands out in my memory as one of the happiest times my mother and father ever experienced, for to them it was a time of hope for Ernest's future well-being. They loved Hadley and they felt sure that Ernest would stick to a job now that he had such a wonderful wife.

It was while Ernest was living at the Y. K. Smiths', before his marriage, that the first of his poems was published. I remember when he first showed me his poem in print. I was standing in the kitchen of our Kenilworth Avenue house when he breezed in, holding in his hand the thin, pale-green paper-covered volume.

"You wanta see something, Marce?" he asked me.

"Of course," I said. "Let me look."

Almost shyly he held out the copy toward me.

"Look at the table of contents, kid," he said. "Your old brother is a poet!"

I turned the pages until I came to Ernie's poem, and there it was in black type, *By Ernest M. Hemingway.*

"Neat, huh?" commented Ernie. I agreed that it was.

Ernest's verse was in one of the many small, short-lived magazines of that period. I am not positive, but I believe this poem was later included in a group published in 1923, in Paris.

He took the magazine into the other room to show it to Mother and Dad. They were suitably impressed at Ernie's first effort. Mother was pleased that he was writing something other than mere factual articles for the marketing cooperative. Both she and Dad encouraged Ernest in his desire to be a writer.

It was in the autumn of 1921 that the Italian Consulate

in Chicago informed Ernest that General Diaz was coming to the United States and would present Ernie with the Croce di Guerra Medal which he had won in Italy. Mother, Daddy, Hadley and I were invited to the banquet and the presentation ceremony in Chicago. The General was an impressive man, though short of stature, and our parents and Ernest and I were honored to meet him. The ceremony, of course, was very formal, and we were proud of Ernest as he showed becoming modesty when the General gave him the medal. Our friend Captain "Nick" Nerone, the vice consul, also received a decoration. That morning, his chest bristling with medals, he had proudly led the parade in Chicago honoring General Diaz.

Ernie's medal carried with it a pension of fifty lira a year for life. It also made him, the General said, "an honorary cousin of the King." In 1921 both fifty lira and the King were highly valued in Italy.

The thing I remember best about that exciting evening was the group of young officers, some of them connections of the royal family, who accompanied General Diaz to Chicago on his special Pullman car en route from New York to the West Coast. That evening I was the recipient of a gorgeous bouquet of pink roses and an invitation to join the group on the General's car for the rest of their journey. Needless to say, my father did not even consider accepting such an invitation for me — nor to be truthful did I. But it was great fun to be invited by a *real* cousin of the King. The graceful compliments of General Diaz's charming young officers added the perfect touch to a wonderful evening.

Just before Christmas in December, 1921, Ernest and Hadley left Chicago to sail to Paris. Hadley had a small trust fund and they had decided to skip abroad and stay for as long as they could. It was in Ernie's mind that he might send back some feature material for the *Toronto Star*. I went down to the railroad station to see them off, and I remember wondering what it must be like to start out for a completely new life in Europe as they were doing. The Smiths, Howell Jenkins, Bill Horne and others of the old gang joined us on the platform; it was a freezing morning, and as Hadley took hold of the iron railing of the Pullman steps, I noticed that her hands were bare.

"Do put on your gloves, Hadley," I called.

"Haven't got any, Marcelline," she said. "I don't need any. We'll soon be on the ship."

"Here, Hash, take mine," I said, stripping off my gray woolen gloves and tossing them to her as she stood on the rear platform of the train. She caught them and put them on, grinning at me.

"Thanks, Marce. That's a real going-away present!" Hadley called.

The train was beginning to move and Ernie stood with his arm around Hadley waving to us all. One of the boys, it might have been Jenks or Bill Horne, tore off his muffler, wadded it into a ball and threw it to Ernest.

"That's a going-away present for you, Ernie!" he shouted.

"Write to us from Paris!" somebody yelled as the train began to pick up speed.

Ernie and Hadley stood waving to us as long as we could see them while their train moved out of the station. Several of us were close to tears as they disappeared from sight.

IO

The Twenties

ERNIE was the first of us to leave home, and then in August, 1922, just about a year after his marriage, I became engaged to Sterling Sanford at Walloon Lake. That autumn I resigned as supervisor of the Kenilworth Community Center and left Northwestern University to prepare for our wedding, which was to take place on January 2. I felt badly that Ernest, who was still in Paris, could not be one of the wedding party. He wrote how sorry he was not to attend, and it consoled me that Bill Horne would serve in his place as one of Sterling's ushers. My sister Ursula, who was home from college for the Christmas vacation, was my maid of honor, and Sunny was one of the bridesmaids with Marion Vose, Polly Gerts, and my cousin, Margaret Hemingway; eleven-year-old Carol and her inseparable friend Dorothy Reed were the train bearers, and little Patsy Shedd Hemingway, Aunt Arabell's five-year-old adopted daughter, came from Kansas City to be the flower girl. My small brother Leicester, who was just two years older than Patsy, would have none of it. When he found that he had to polish his shoes and wear a stiff white Buster Brown collar and a necktie, Les said he'd rather stay home. But he was finally persuaded and took his place in the front pew with Mother, who was looking very beautiful in her new gray gown. Daddy in his tailcoat looked handsome as he escorted me down the aisle to meet Sterling, and the service was performed by our old minister, Dr. William E. Barton, who had baptized Ernest and Ursula.

We entered the church down a long aisle facing a group of trees made of yellow and orange calendula blossoms, rather a startling innovation for Oak Park. My dress was creamy white silk brocaded with a design of oak leaves and acorns; Lucille Dick Edwards, my matron of honor, wore white velvet; Ursula and the flower girl, Patsy, were in flame-colored taffeta; the bridesmaids, including Sunny, wore long apple-green Moyen Age gowns, and the two eleven-year-old train bearers, Carol and her friend Dorothy Reed, were in orchid.

Frail little Grandmother Hemingway, who had stayed in bed for almost two months because of her weak heart, came to the reception with Grandfather, and both of them — in their eighties — stood to greet our many guests in Mother's big music room. We had an orchestra for the occasion, Roy Bargee's, and Daddy had been determined to learn a few dance steps to please me. He wanted, as he said, "to be ready to dance with the bride," and it was a thrilling moment for me when he led me solemnly through the one-step.

Daddy had parked a car with a sign *Just Married* on it conveniently close to the house, and this fooled the young men who had planned to separate us on our way to the train. Sterling and I made our escape after the last kisses and the rice in the real getaway car, which took us from the reception to the Drake Hotel on our way to our train to New York. Ursula and Sunny had arranged to have the spark plugs disconnected in the cars of those who were to be our pursuers. After the honeymoon we began our life together in Detroit.

Through the spring of 1923 the family heard regularly from Ernest and Hadley, and I too got an occasional letter. The *Toronto Star* had made him a staff correspondent, and he was tremendously interested in the assignments which took him to the League of Nations in Geneva; he was interviewing diplomats and getting to know artists and writers, and there was no doubt that he was immensely happy in his work.

Ernie acquired another wound stripe when a skylight in their apartment in Paris slammed down on him, cutting a triangular wound in his forehead. It left a rather distinguished scar, and one which rumor later attributed to the war, to hunting, to boxing — anything but the skylight.

In the autumn of 1923 Ernest brought Hadley back to Toronto in anticipation of the arrival of their first child. He continued to work for the *Star* (he was put on the regular staff on September 8) while he was in Canada, and he was actually out on tour, covering Lloyd George's visit when John Hadley Nicanor Hemingway was born on October 13. Bumbie, as Ernest called him, was the first grandchild in the family, and my parents were elated about him.

Sterling and I came back to Oak Park to spend that Christmas with the family, and it was while I was there that Ernest gave me his first published book. He stopped by to see our parents during the holidays for only a few hours on his way home from an assignment. I remember that Daddy and Mother were upstairs and that Ernie, Sterling and I were sitting together on the big davenport in front of the living room fireplace. Ernest reached in his pocket and took out a dark-green paper-covered volume which he dropped into my lap. "Don't show this to the family,

Marce," he said. "It's just for you. Wait and read it after you leave here."

I glanced at the title, *Three Stories and Ten Poems*. I noticed it had been printed in Paris. I put the book in my suitcase and I didn't open it until Sterling and I were on the train returning to Detroit. Lying in my lower Pullman berth, I opened Ernie's book with eager anticipation. The first story was called "Up in Michigan." How nice, I thought. I read on a few pages. The two main characters of the story, a man and a woman, had the same first names as two of our close family friends, a couple of whom we were particularly fond. The descriptions of them in the tale, especially of the man, fitted our friends so accurately that as I read on and realized that Ernest had put these kindly people into this vulgar, sordid tale he had invented, my stomach turned over. It wasn't just the story that affected me, shocking as it was. It was Ernest's apparent lack of any decent consideration for the feelings of the people whose names and detailed descriptions he had used in the story that horrified me. Even though this little paper-covered book Ernest had handed me might never be seen by our Michigan friends, since the book would probably have only a limited circulation abroad, I wondered how my brother could be sure these people he had used would not run across this story sometime in the future and be humiliated and hurt beyond words.

I feel quite sure that my parents never saw the book; I never mentioned it to them and I doubt if anyone else ever did. I am certain that if they had read it there would have been an explosion from Daddy. My father's loyalty and devotion to his friends and his innate fastidiousness would not have permitted him to remain silent if he had ever read this shocking story of Ernest's. It was later incorporated into a collection of my brother's writing called the *Fifth Column and the First Forty-nine Stories*, published after Daddy died.

Ernest and Hadley left Toronto to return to Paris the following March, when Bumbie was five months old. What prompted the move was the news that Edward J. O'Brien was reprinting Ernie's story "My Old Man," which originally appeared in *Three Stories and Ten Poems*, in *The Best Short Stories of 1923* and that he was going to dedicate the column to Ernest. Ernie immediately broke his lease on the Toronto apartment, made arrangements with the *Star*, and then set out for Paris with his wife and baby, determined to spend as much time as possible on creative writing. To quote Dorothy Connable, "He was all lighted up when he learned the news." Dorothy said to him, "It is so wonderful, it seems as though something will go wrong. Maybe they'll misspell your name." They all laughed, but the strange part of it is that O'Brien did—the book was dedicated to "Ernest Hemenway," and with one exception his name was consistently misspelled throughout.

It was after they were resettled in Paris that the Hemingways in Oak Park and we in Detroit each received a notice from the Three Mountains Press in Paris enclosing an order blank for the first edition of Ernest's second book. It was to be a limited edition of *In Our Time*, and I looked with pride at the author's name, *Ernest Hemingway*. (Ernest had dropped the use of his middle initial by this time.) Daddy ordered half a dozen copies, and I sent in my order for two. Ernie's book was to be one of a series of six edited by Mr. Ezra Pound. Others in this series were *Indiscretions* by Ezra Pound, *Women and Men* by

Ford Madox Ford, *Elimus* by B. C. Windeler, *The Great American Novel* by William Carlos Williams, and *England* by B. M. G. Adams.

Whèn the package of books arrived from Paris some months later, I was surprised at the unusual design of the jacket. Both the front and back covers were made up of reprints of headlines and bits of articles and advertisements from various newspapers printed in red on a beige background. Some of them were from American papers, some from British, others from Spanish and Russian newspapers. The title of the book and author's name were printed in heavy black type over this colorful newspaper background. I think this was the first time I ever saw a title or a proper name printed in all small letters with no capitals whatever. The date on the title page of the book was 1924. Each copy was numbered individually, and the total number of copies was listed as one hundred and seventy in the front of my copy of *in our time*.

The stories were printed on a special handmade, deckle-edged paper, quite unlike normal book stock. Because an old friend, Sam Anderson, was so interested in Ernest's new publication, I proudly sent him one of my two copies. I tried to buy more copies later, but was informed by the publisher that only one hundred seventy had been printed. No wonder they are such rarities today. A year later an American edition was printed with capitals in the title.

I was not present when Daddy and Mother received their copies, but I came to visit them with my baby daughter Carol shortly afterward, and I sensed at once that something was wrong. Daddy went about his work with such a grim look. He was obviously furious about something, though his words and manner toward me were pleasant and welcoming. Mother, I noticed, showed signs of recent years. But it wasn't until I had been with my parents a day or two that Mother explained the reason behind all this suppressed emotion. I saw Daddy tying up a package in the kitchen on the day I arrived in Oak Park, but it didn't occur to me to connect that package and Daddy's grim manner. My father took the package to mail at the post office. Later, Mother told me that she and Daddy had read a copy of Ernest's new book. Both of them, very obviously, were shocked and horrified at some of the contents, especially Chapter X.

Daddy was so incensed that a son of his would so far forget his Christian training that he could use the subject matter and vulgar expressions this book contained that he wrapped and returned all six copies to the Three Mountains Press in Paris. He wrote to Ernest and told him that no gentleman spoke of venereal disease outside a doctor's office.

Mother had agreed with Dad in disapproving of some of the writing in the book, especially about Ag, but because it was Ernest's first book, as far as his parents knew, Mother wanted to keep just one copy for herself. Daddy refused. He said every one of the volumes must be sent back immediately. He would not tolerate such filth in his home, Dad declared.

I was startled but not shocked by Ernest's book. Of course, I had read the first one, which made this one seem mild. But I still wondered how Ernest dared to write as frankly as he did. It seemed a shame to me that Daddy had taken such a drastic step as sending the books back. It would be inevitable, I remember saying to Mother, that Ernest would learn of Dad's return of the books to the publisher and he would resent it bitterly, as he did. He simply stopped writing to the family for a time.

It was Hadley who kept us in touch with how things were going. Early in January, 1925, she wrote to the Connable family in Toronto from "our sawmill on Notre-Dame-des-Champs."

> *Bumbie [John] walking quite well. Talks in his own original language. Ernest is working hard on stories all the time, and Bertram Hartman is painting a lot, and I am playing on a funny little upright piano. Ernest has a book ready for selling in the States and several magazine articles. Ernest is getting more recognition all the time so that they will take anything he will write. Next summer we hope to go to Pamplona in Spain and then take Bumbie to some small seaside place. So much love to you all and Happy New Year.*

That was the year that Ernest accompanied Lincoln Steffens to the Geneva Conference. Hadley parked their two-year-old son with a nurse whose home in Paris was near their apartment, and then took the train to Switzerland. She had with her a hand valise containing Ernest's manuscripts and some of her personal things. At one of the stops she got off to walk up and down the platform for a little exercise, and when she returned to her seat the valise was gone. She called the conductor, and the train was searched, but in spite of their efforts the bag was never found. Hadley told me she had to borrow a comb and powder from the other correspondents' wives who were also en route to Geneva.

The manuscripts which disappeared were many of the Nick Adams stories, which Ernest was working on at the time. Hadley was deeply distressed when she reached Geneva and told Ernie of the loss. He took it calmly at first, confident that there were carbon copies back in the Paris apartment. But when she had to tell him that both the carbons and the originals were in the valise, he was "absolutely sick. It nearly killed him." He didn't blame her, she told me, but it was a crushing blow, for it meant so much rewriting at a time when he was on fire to do new things.

After my father's rejection of *In Our Time*, the family was sent no further announcements of Ernest's new work, but Daddy's attitude gradually altered, and I know that he took increasing pride in the fact that his son Ernest was an author. Shortly after *The Sun Also Rises* was published in 1926, Dad and my sister Carol were shopping together in the Chicago Loop district when they happened on a bookstore with a big display of Ernie's new novel in the window.

Pretending ignorance, Dad entered and inquired of the clerk, "Do you have a book here, called something like *The Sun Is Up* or *Sunrise* or something like that?"

"Oh, you mean *The Sun Also Rises* by Hemingway?" asked the salesman.

"That's the one," Dr. Hemingway agreed. "Is there much call for it?"

"Oh, yes," replied the clerk. "We have the window full of it; it's going very well." Daddy had Carol by the hand. She was jumping up and down with excitement. It was all Daddy could do to keep her quiet.

"Do most people like it?" my father inquired without a smile.

"I can't say as to that," he was told, "but they buy it. We just put in an order for more copies."

"I'll take a copy," said Ernest's father.

Proudly he brought the new book home and showed it to the family, including Sterling and me that evening in Oak

Park. Daddy said to us, "It was all I could do to keep my face straight this afternoon. I had to try hard to control myself, not to tell the man in the bookstore who I was."

"But you *did* tell him, Daddy!" little sister Carol spoke up quickly.

"Well, er, I guess I did," Dad confessed. He was only slightly embarrassed. "I wasn't going to let on, but yes, just as I left the bookstore I did say, 'My boy wrote that book,'" admitted Daddy with pride. It was a new sensation to be basking in the reflected glory of his son's success.

Mother had always said that when the time came that her voice deteriorated and lost its beauty, as it inevitably would, she hoped she would have sense enough to stop singing and take up something else. When she was fifty, she was prompted to do so in a rather amusing way. She had observed young Leicester's art work in the Saturday class he attended in the old Frank Lloyd Wright home on Chicago Avenue, and the more she saw of the children's painting the more interested in it she became herself. So she asked Leicester's teacher if she could join the class, and, somewhat surprised, the teacher permitted her to work along with the youngsters. Only a little later Grace Hall Hemingway registered as a student at the Art Institute of Chicago, where she studied for two years. As her work improved she became a private pupil of Pauline Palmer, a well-known Chicago artist, and during the summers she worked in an art class in Bay View. She signed her paintings Hall Hemingway.

Mother's very first paintings were not what she hoped they would be, but she took criticism, ignored laughter, and kept right on painting. At the Art Institute, as her power of observation was sharpened, her technique improved. Her big music room was converted into an art studio, and there Mother would paint for as long as four or five hours a day. She early discovered that she was better at landscape painting than at catching likenesses.

The first time Daddy and Mother went to Florida in the mid-Twenties, it was primarily so that Mother would be able to paint out-of-doors during the winter season and continue her study in a Florida art school.

Daddy also fell in love with Florida, but for a different reason. He was beginning to think of retirement, and now, in this enjoyable, sunny land, he flirted with the idea of actually owning a Florida orange grove after he had given up his practice. The real estate boom in Florida was going full blast, and my parents easily succumbed to the alluring advertisements and the silver-tongue persuasion of the real estate salesmen. They made some immediate investments in Florida lots and intended to make more.

In the fall of 1925, when Sterling and I were taking a late vacation at the hotel on Signal Mountain in Tennessee, Dad and Mother stopped there overnight on their way back from a real estate buying expedition. I remember how they urged us not to miss the golden opportunity to make a fortune in Florida lots, as they planned to do. They had already invested their savings and they were planning to take out a mortgage on the Oak Park home to finance some additional property which attracted them. They were so sure of the wisdom of what they had done that they found it hard to understand why Sterling would not go along. He told them that he felt the prices were far too high, and that he could not believe that the real estate would go on to double in value as my father and mother so confidently expected. But our arguments had no effect, and back they went to Oak Park to make their arrangements with the bank for a mortgage. Daddy, who had never before bought anything on partial payments, said that this wasn't like taking out a regular mortgage, it was just a loan for a little while until he could sell at a profit, as Mother's cousin, Fred Hall, had done.

But continual payments on the lots in Florida amounted to more than either one of them had realized, and the interest on the mortgage had to be met as well. The two younger children at home had still to be educated, and all of this added a new burden of worry to the strain under which my father, a busy obstetrician, always worked.

Little Grandmother Hemingway had died in February, 1923, just a few weeks after my wedding, and Grandfather Hemingway, who had been bedridden much of the time after Grandmother went, died in his sleep the fall of 1926. After Grandfather's death, Daddy began to make his definite plans for retirement in Florida. He took, with some nervousness, the examinations for a Florida State medical license, waited tensely for the results, and was delighted when he learned that he had passed and could now practice in Florida.

He also began to smoke a pipe. We found it out quite by accident, and he seemed relieved that his secret was out. He would puff contentedly while he was driving his car in solitude along the Des Plaines River Road, or while working in the back yard caring for the chickens or mowing the lawn on weekends. And now he began to smoke on his fishing trips. But we never could get him to smoke in the house at Oak Park except down in the basement by the furnace. There he had an old rocker where he would sit and relax in privacy. He had talked against smoking for so many years that he seemed to feel that it was almost self-betrayal if he now began to smoke in public.

It was in 1926 that Daddy's black hair began to turn silvery at his temples, and it was this year that we were first aware that he was looking thinner and more tired. We had become so used to his firmness of purpose and his extraordinary strength and endurance that I suppose we had come to think of him as being indestructible. Now he was sometimes cross and even abrupt with us.

One day in 1927 when my daughter Carol and I were staying at Oak Park on one of our frequent visits home, I remember that my father came back from his morning calls with a package in his hand. Even before he removed his hat, he practically threw the package on the dining room table. Mother had just emerged from her music room studio and she still had on her painting smock.

"Take a look at that!" Daddy said almost angrily to Mother and me. "I'm supposed to run my life with *that* thing from now on!" he announced resentfully. His voice was high and shrill. He did not even sound like himself.

"What is it?" asked Mother. "What do you mean?"

Daddy unwrapped the package. Inside was a black metal scale for weighing food in ounces.

"Do you know what that means? I'm a diabetic!" Daddy said in a resentful voice. I think my father had known this fact for a long time. But that was the first day he admitted it. He told Mother that a fellow physician at the hospital had examined him earlier that morning and had warned him to start dieting at once. Daddy was told to leave out all starches and sugars and limit many other foods drastically. I realized he was worried. That was probably why he sounded so angry.

We tried to reassure him. But he hardly listened.

"How can I ever do it!" he said. He wasn't asking us. He meant it was impossible.

"Why, Dad, that weighing business isn't so bad. You know you have patients who manage it all the time. I've heard you tell other people to do it. It won't be so hard once you get used to it. What's your menu for lunch? We'll get right at it," I said.

"But I've never been sick. I can't live that way," my father said.

"Of course you can. We'll all help you," Mother said quickly.

"I won't be an invalid," declared my father, and in spite of himself his face crumpled up and a tear rolled down his cheek as he rushed from the room, embarrassed. Mother followed him.

"There, there, darling," we could hear her murmuring softly from the living room. "There's nothing wrong about crying. Here's an extra hankie. It's going to be all right."

"But I'm so ashamed," I heard my father saying to her. "I think I've had it for years, but I never even made an analysis. I didn't want to know. Gracie, I can't be sick! There's too much to do. You know I've never spent a day in bed at home in my life."

"Nothing to be ashamed of in being sick," Mother's voice went on comfortingly. "Everybody has a right to feel upset once in a while. Remember all the times you've taken care of me and the children when we needed help. It's about time we helped you. You'll be feeling lots better in no time. I'm just so grateful that you finally let the hospital check you. I expect it's this diabetes that's been making you feel so tired lately."

I could hear their voices talking on softly from the other room. Soon Daddy was back in the dining room, seemingly perfectly cheerful, almost daring us to notice his previous weakness.

"Well, now!" he said loudly. "Let's have a bang-up good lunch before I go on that blankety-blank diet."

Mother spoke up. "Dear, that's a little boy talking. You know you can't say something isn't there because you won't look at it. Let's see about fixing your lunch first. Where's your diet list?"

Daddy handed her the paper and they went out in the kitchen together to consult with Louise, the cook.

My parents went back to Florida in the early spring of 1928, and to their dismay they found that their lots had not increased in value. The real estate adviser assured them that this was only a temporary lull while the "market settled" and that their holdings were sure to rise, so Mother and Daddy didn't sell as they had first thought they might do, but deferred the whole question for the time being, though they were plainly worried.

From Florida they decided to take a short trip to Cuba for Daddy's health. He loved it there and grew tanned and happy and said that he felt better than he had in years. In a photograph taken in Havana with their tour group on Easter Sunday, April 8, Mother, in a white hat, is smiling, but my father, wearing a white linen suit, looks tense.

When they returned by ship to Key West, Daddy told me he saw a hunched-over figure sitting on the dock fishing. Something about the set of the shoulders looked familiar to Dad, and he gave the family bobwhite whistle. Instantly the figure looked up and leaped to his feet. It was Ernest, and immediately he and his parents had their arms around each other. It was a happy reconciliation. Daddy wiped a tear from his eye as he told me about it. Ernest took them home to meet Pauline, who was expecting a baby. This meeting with Ernest meant much to our parents, expecially to Dad, for he had missed Ernie during the estrangement which followed his separation from Hadley and his marriage to Pauline.

In May, 1928, a letter from Ernest told of his plans to bring his family to Walloon to our family cottage for a visit in July unless he went to a political convention instead. Apparently the convention won out, for they did not arrive. Patrick was born in Kansas City that summer. his Caesarean birth enabled Ernest to finish the last chapter of the book he was working on. Ernest told us later that he rewrote this chapter over fifty times.

Another letter, in June, 1928, was so thick it could hardly fit into the envelope Ernest addressed to me. He had learned of my plan to go to Europe as the guest of Mrs. John Moody of New York City. Ernest wanted to be sure we had the right letters of introduction to the toreadors, picadors and innkeepers whom Ernest knew in the areas of Spain Mrs. Moody and I would be visiting. Though I carried the letter with me through the whole automobile trip through the Spanish Pyrenees, we did not see a bullfight. I loved horses too much to be willing to watch them wounded in the bull ring. But I did visit Hadley and small Bumbie in Paris that summer, while I was studying with Edmondo Quattrocchi, in his sculpturing studio in Passy. From Hadley and from some of Ernest's newspaper friends I learned more about the characters he had used in some of his books, especially those in *The Sun Also Rises*.

There was a change in Daddy after his return from Cuba, though he kept on with his house calls, his office hours and his daily visits to see his patients at the hospital—his patients and his family were more important to him than taking care of himself. He knew he was suffering from angina pectoris, a devastatingly painful form of heart disease, but he ignored the medical advice of his fellow physicians and Mother's urging that he rest. He lived almost as though he defied anyone to get close to him, or understand or help him.

Even before the trip to Cuba my father changed from his high-strung, active, determined, cheerful self—the self with a twinkle in his eye—to an irritable, suspicious person. He was quick to take offense, almost unable to let himself believe in the honesty of other people's motives. He began to spend long hours alone in his office with the doors closed. He kept his bureau drawers and his clothes closet locked. It was agony for my mother, who shared the bedroom with him, to think he must be distrusting her.

One of my father's few outgoing thoughts, aside from his normal professional concern for his patients at this time, was an almost possessive love for his youngest child, my brother Leicester. Daddy clung to Les even more than he had before. Les had meant almost everything to Daddy, ever since Ernest left home.

Leicester often rode with our father in the car on Dad's calls. In the last months of 1928, Daddy wanted Les with him all the time. He even seemed to resent the time away from him which Les spent in school.

Suddenly, one day in the late fall of '28, Daddy refused to take Les with him in the car. No one could ride with him any more, Daddy announced. He did not explain. There was only one car and Daddy refused to let anyone else drive it. My father pushed himself physically and nervously. He worried over his family's future and he was greatly concerned about his own health, we knew, even though he rarely mentioned it. His plans for retiring to Florida were the only happy thoughts he clung to.

"Gracie will paint her pictures and I'll just grow oranges," he told us, over and over.

The angina attacks began hitting Dad more frequently. He carried a small vial of medicine in his pocket for relief. We learned the reason he would not take anyone with him in the car was because he was afraid he might not be able to control it if an attack should come while he was driving.

Mother begged Daddy to give up his practice and go to bed and rest, as he knew he should do. But Dad would not give up his work, even though he would have made any patient of his do exactly that, in like circumstances. Mother was frantic with worry. She wrote me of her fears, but she worded the letter gently, for she always tried to make the best of things in letters. She did not want any letter of hers to add to anyone's burdens.

"It will be good when you come to visit us again, dear," she wrote me. "Bring your blessed baby, Carol," Mother said, in the late fall of 1928. "Your father always loves her so, perhaps she can cheer him up!"

In reply to Mother's letter, I promised we would all come to Oak Park for Christmas. I had no idea then how very ill Daddy was, or I would have gone to Chicago immediately instead of putting off the visit for another month.

The first of December was approaching, when the payments would come due on the Florida property Dad and Mother had acquired in such quantity in 1925. Dad was naturally worried about these obligations and his illness made him more so. He consulted his brother, our Uncle George Hemingway, who owned a real estate company and was a bank director. Dad asked for advice. What should he do? He needed a loan to cover his Florida payments before December 10. Uncle George suggested that Florida property might never go higher, that Daddy and Mother had too many lots, and that Daddy might sell some of his holdings and keep only the property he wanted to live on when he retired.

"Unload, Ed," Uncle George told us he advised my father. "Don't try to carry a burden too heavy for you. Sell now and get yourself out from under. Most of the Florida acreage values are not real ones any more."

"But how about a loan, now?" Dad asked again.

"If you can't carry the present payments you have to make now, and you add another debt to it, Ed," Uncle

George advised Dad, "you only add more to your own burden. Then you worry about another payment added to what you already have."

"But I don't see how I *can* sell those lots. They are for our family and our future," Dad insisted.

"You'll help yourself and your family more by selling now and paying up and getting yourself rested and in shape," said Uncle George. "Honestly, Ed, I know real estate. The boom in Florida has begun to slip, but you can still sell out a lot of that speculative stuff now, if you hurry. Keep a few good ones, but get out from under the rest and sleep nights."

Uncle George was wiser than he knew. But my father could not face making decisions just then. He talked it all over with Mother. She agreed that several pieces could well be sold right away. She told my father that anything he decided was all right with her. Dad thought about it, but his illness confused his thinking. He'd neglected his necessary diet restrictions.

On the morning of December 6 Daddy awoke with a pain in his foot. Being a doctor, he knew what that might mean: gangrene of the feet often accompanied neglected cases of diabetes. Dad had a patient who had lost a leg that way. Daddy mentioned the pain to Mother very casually at breakfast that morning. Mother was worried, of course, and my father promised her to have someone check him at the hospital when he went there that day on his calls.

He mentioned the pain to another friend, but he did not get himself checked. Daddy came home at noon after his rounds. He looked white and drawn.

"How's Les?" he asked Mother, as he slowly took off his hat and coat and put his black leather doctor's bag on a chair in his office.

"Oh, Les's cold is much better, but I made him stay in

bed again today. I think he may be asleep now," said Mother.

"Then I'll just lie down until lunch. Call me when it's ready," Dad said in a tired voice. He went upstairs slowly, hanging onto the banister railing. He closed the door. There was a shot. There in his room, Dad had solved all his problems.

We were all at the funeral except Sunny. She had gone down to Key West to do the final typing on a manuscript for Ernest.

Ernest received the news of Daddy's death while he was on a train taking five-year-old Bumbie, his oldest son, to Key West. He had met Hadley's ship in New York and now he was taking the youngster South for his first visit. Little Bumbie spoke a mixture of French and English.

Ernie made a quick decision. He explained to Bumbie that he must leave the train to go to Grandpère, who was sick, and that Bumbie must obey the colored porter. "Yes, Papá," the little boy answered. "I will do just as you say. I will do just as the black Monsieur says. You will find me a very big man as Mama has told me to be." This Ernest told us when he arrived. By the time he got to Oak Park, I had gone with Mother to Mr. Drechsler's to make all the funeral arrangements.

Before leaving the train Ernest had made out some telegrams addressed to Oak Park, gave the porter some money, and instructed him to send the messages at each stop the train made on its overnight trip to Florida. He was greatly worried to leave his little boy alone on a Pullman on his first day in America, but he felt there was nothing else to do. He wired Pauline to meet Bumbie at the train, and he himself came straight to Oak Park. He was a great comfort to Mother and all of us. Ernest, who had

joined Pauline's faith, told us that he had had a Mass said
for Daddy, and he led us in the Lord's Prayer in the music
room, where Daddy's body was lying, before we went to
the First Congregational Church for the services. The
whole town turned out to honor the doctor they loved so
well. The *Oak Leaves* said, "He had befriended hundreds
in distress."

All that morning and into the late evening Ernest kept
calling the telegraph company to see why he had received
no wire from the train porter. He was almost frantic
worrying. Finally the wire came. To the telegram Ernest
had prepared the porter had added, "The boy had a good
night's sleep." Ernest relaxed. He knew Pauline would
be meeting Bumbie at the train in Key West that morning.

As we all sat at the family dinner table the day after the
funeral, we were sad but relieved as people are when a strain
is over. Ernest began to talk about the book he had just
finished. He was undecided about a name for it. He mentioned several possible titles; he asked us each which we
liked best. We said them over aloud to get the sound and
feel of the names. There was one Ernest seemed to
come back to most often. I liked it too. It was *A Farewell
to Arms*.

That night, when Ernie was in bed in the front third-
floor bedroom, formerly Uncle Tyley's, he asked me to sit
down on the side of the bed as we used to do when we
confided to each other our thoughts and dreams in the
high school years. "Now tell me all about everything,
old keed," he said in his affectionate voice. "How's everything going, Mazween?"

"You know I am going to have another baby in May,
don't you?"

"I'm so glad. Mother told me," Ernie answered.

"Ernie, do you suppose that if I'd told Daddy about it before, instead of waiting to tell him as a surprise at Christmas, it would have made a difference and that Daddy wouldn't have . . ." I couldn't go on for weeping.

"No, Marce," said Ernie. "It wouldn't have made any difference at all. Dad was too sick to think about anything. Don't torture yourself with that thought. He was too sick to know what he was doing. If only he'd told me how worried he was, I could have borrowed some money, to help him." I told Ernie that I didn't know either. We talked a little more, then Ernie said, "Got to get some sleep. Goodnight, Mazween. See you in the morning." That was Ernest's last time at home; the Hemingway family's closeness had ended.

Mother Alone

MOTHER was fifty-six at the time of Daddy's death. She had two children to support and educate, Carol in high school and Leicester a boy of thirteen. Once she had gotten over the first shock of her grief, she faced up to her loneliness and problems with great courage. With Uncle George's advice she disposed of some of her Florida holdings before the crash of October, 1929, and this helped to tide her over for the time being. Some of my father's insurance was not paid because of a suicide clause.

Mother took over the responsibilities of being head of the family. She quickly learned to make decisions which she had never before been permitted to make when Daddy was in charge. Mother was forced to rent out parts of her house to finance her youngest daughter's college education and to help her younger son with his boatbuilding project, which he preferred to a college education.

But the years that followed were difficult, and she might have lost the family home had it not been for Ernest's and Pauline's kindness. Pauline Pfeiffer Hemingway had grown very fond of her mother-in-law, and she was eager to have Ernest untroubled by any concern for Mother's welfare. So it was she who first suggested in 1932 that a trust fund be set up for Mother's use during her lifetime. *A Farewell to Arms*, which Ernest was completing at the time of Daddy's death, had proved to be a great success as a novel, and it was later sold to the movies for a substantial sum. Pauline and her generous uncle Augustus Pfeiffer, the head of a large cosmetic company in New York, joined with Ernest in 1933 in establishing the fund which provided Mother with a modest income for the rest of her life. It greatly relieved all our minds. In January, 1950, at her home in Key West, Pauline told me the details of the trust fund and of her uncle's other generous gifts to herself and to Ernest.

Mother was extremely grateful and immediately wanted to do something in return. Ernest said the one thing he would like would be Windemere Cottage when Mother was through with it. Mother said she would give it to him right away, so Ernest and his sons could enjoy it as he had when he was a boy. She deeded the acre of ground and the furnished cottage to Ernest for his use with his family. She and I put it in condition for Ernest to use immediately. Even the beds were made up, but Ernest never came up or brought his family. To the end of her life my mother still kept hoping Ernest would come back to Walloon and use the family cottage she had so generously given him.

Mother learned to drive a car for the first time in her life, and in it she went on sketching and painting trips to Florida. Always on her trips she spent a few days with Ernest and Pauline and their youngsters, Patrick and Gregory, in Key West. She drove to Nantucket and even went as far afield as California, where she visited her brother Leicester and his second wife, the pianist Gertrud Cleophas. But though she could drive one, she did not have the remotest idea of what makes an automobile run.

"Have you had your spark plugs cleaned lately,

Mother?" Sterling asked when she returned from a tour of seven thousand miles.

"Spark plugs?" she asked. "What are they?"

Sometimes on her sketching trips Mother would paint from inside the car, thus avoiding the mosquitoes and the crawling creatures, which she dreaded. Though mountain driving did not faze her, she still hated bugs. She would drive her car to the exact spot she wished to paint, and then, with the view framed in the windshield, she would rest her canvas against the steering wheel, and with the windows closed except for a crack of air at the top, she would paint away happily. In spite of the heat, she followed this same procedure while she was making her desert pictures near Taos, New Mexico.

It comes as a wrench for a mother to move out of her home, which is full of family associations and in which she has spent her happiest years. But in 1936 Mother felt the time had come. She moved to a smaller, older house in River Forest, not far from the Des Plaines River, but less than half the size of the big house she was about to sell. Her new house had eight rooms. She told me she was delighted to be rid of the heavy mission furniture and dark paneled oak. She decorated the walls of her new home in light pastel tones suitable as a background for her paintings. She kept her mother's melodeon in one corner of the living room, and with it a tall table clock with handmade wooden works which had once belonged to Great-grandfather Allen Hemingway in Connecticut. She used some of her mother's Victorian furniture.

A bust of Ernest in red terra cotta stood on the grand piano, and photographs of all her six children hung in the dining room beside her breakfast table.

Mother continued to paint and to teach voice, as well as teaching painting classes. Her pictures were exhibited in a number of cities, and she had one-man shows at Marshall Field's in Chicago, at the Illinois Art Society, and at other centers like the Oak Park and River Forest Art League, of which she had been a founder. As a result of her travels in the Southwest and of her painting trips to Florida and Nantucket, Mother was occasionally called on to give talks, and this simple beginning opened up a new career for her as a lecturer when she entered her sixties. She had accumulated a fund of stories about each place, and these she pieced together with the history of the areas and with her own experiences as a traveling artist. I had acquired some professional experience on the lecture platform myself by this time, so I had the fun of helping her organize and write out most of her lecture scripts. These she used to illustrate with her own paintings of the parts of the country she was talking about.

Her first paid talk was for a Rotary Club on the west side of Chicago, and thereafter her prestige grew. Her bookings increased, and before long she was speaking to audiences all over the country and more than paying her way. Her own painting and her teaching continued during her periods at home. She was a happy woman, with a host of new, congenial friends. Several of her canvases were acquired by art museums; she won second prize in the All-Illinois Artist Show in Chicago for her painting of a hot, dusty street in Taos, and had the pleasure of seeing herself listed in *Who's Who in American Art*. Her paintings sold readily for a hundred to five hundred dollars, and one of her landscapes brought a thousand.

During World War II, Mother was greatly concerned for Ernest and Leicester and her grandson Jack, all of whom were overseas, Les as a private, Ernest as a correspondent, and Jack, Ernest's oldest son, in the Air Corps. When Jack was taken prisoner, Mother wrote frantically, wanting to send him food as she had sent food and extra clothing to Leicester overseas, but she and I both learned from Hadley that only the next of kin might send a Red Cross package to the Stalag in Germany where Jack was being kept prisoner. Naturally, Hadley, his mother, was next of kin.

Though Mother suffered a long illness during World War II, she kept on writing to all her children from her bed. When she recovered she continued to buy each new book of Ernest's, as it appeared, though I cannot swear that she read all, or any, of them. In her late seventies Mother mentioned her desire to sometime have a reply to her annual birthday letters to Ernest.

"It's not easy to be a mother," she said. "I love all my children, but at times I've had to take stern measures to do my job. It doesn't make you popular when you have to correct your grown children. Sometimes you look back and you wonder if you could do a better job if you had it to do all over again. We tried to bring up you children to be independent and self-reliant. We wanted you to be honorable men and women. It's nice if your children can be talented, but it's even more important if they are decent and kind."

We talked of a few other things, and then she said, "Do you remember how pleased and proud Ernest was when he came rushing out to Oak Park to tell us that he'd finally found a job? It was the one on that co-operative magazine. That was the first job he got all by himself. He couldn't wait to tell us, he was so happy, and we were too."

Mother expected her children to succeed. She was proud of all of us and not just of Ernest. She sent our youngest sister, Carol, to Rollins College in Florida, and was pleased but not surprised when Carol, because of her writing ability, was awarded a scholarship to the University of Vienna. When Leicester, during high school, won an award for a short story he had submitted in a contest run by *Scholastic Magazine*, this too was no more than she expected. When people asked Mother if she wasn't very proud of her son she answered quickly, "Which son?" She loved all her children.

As to Ernest's books, I can only remember her talking about the earlier ones and one other, *To Have and Have Not*. I know she read part of *For Whom the Bell Tolls*, for she told me how horrified she was about the girl whose head was shaved. Later, when Elissa Landi and her husband Curtis Thomas and I urged Mother to go to see the movie of *For Whom the Bell Tolls*, Mother glanced over the souvenir program we brought back and said, "This is disgraceful!"

"What do you mean?" I asked.

"Look," said Mother. "Right here on the first page it says the author, Ernest Hemingway, was born in July, 1896, and your father and I weren't even married until October first of that year!"

"Oh, Mother," I said. "You know Ernest always pretends to be older than he is. You can call up the theater and protest if you wish, but if I were you I would just laugh it off."

Suddenly it struck her funny, and she began to shake with laughter as her sense of humor displaced her outrage.

"I don't think Ernest will *ever* grow up," she said.

Mother also tried to read some of Ernest's earlier books again, but she gave up.

"I can't make head nor tail of such crazy people," she remarked, apropos of Lady Brett. "Honestly, Marce," she asked me, "why does he want to write about such vulgar people and such messy subjects? With the whole world full of beauty, why does he have to pick out thoughts and words from the gutter?"

I tried to explain what I understood of Ernie's subject matter and how realism and truthfulness mattered to him above all else, but Mother would have none of it. "I can't stand filth!" she said firmly.

Mother lived on for nearly twenty-three years after Daddy died. She liked to visit her widely scattered family, and wrote frequent letters, but she would never stay with any of us for more than a couple of days at a time. She loved being independent, and she continued to drive her car until she was seventy-five. Sometimes she had friends staying with her at her River Forest home, but it never occurred to her to close up the place and to come to live with any of us for her last years.

She gave the final exhibition of her paintings, arranged by her longtime friend Mrs. Harry Meehan, in 1949, when Mother was seventy-seven, just two years before her death in June, 1951. All her children had long been in homes of their own and she was proud of the creative talents of her thirteen grandchildren.

Grace Hall Hemingway did not live to know of Ernest's Pulitzer award nor of his having been given the Nobel Prize, but it would have been just like her, on hearing the news, to have exclaimed: "Good for Ernie! I always said *all* my children had real ability!"

Acknowledgments

I WISH particularly to thank Mr. Edward Weeks for inspiring this manuscript in 1955 and for assisting me to organize the memories of our family's early days, and to thank my husband, Sterling S. Sanford, for his insistence that I keep at the writing over a period of years as well as for his research work and other help which enabled me to write this book. Others who have given me valuable assistance and interviews between 1948 and 1961 are my late mother, Grace Hall Hemingway, who wanted me to write a family story for my children and whose records have been used; Miss Dorothy Connable of Petoskey, Michigan, whose sharing of her own family's letters and memories of Ernest's Toronto years has been invaluable; and the following relatives and old friends, from whom I have received many helpful facts. I thank:

Mrs. Wilbur Anglemyer, Malibu, California; Mrs. Charles Boynton, Oak Park, Illinois; Miss Frances Westgate Butterfield, New York City; Miss May Estelle Cook, Oak Park, Illinois; Mrs. Wesley Dilworth, Boyne City, Michigan; Miss Dorothy Eich, Oak Park, Illinois; Mrs. Volley Fox, Horton Bay, Michigan; Mrs. John F. Gardner, Garden City, New York; Miss Polly Gerts, Altadena, California; Mrs. Arthur Scott Gilson, Jr., St. Louis, Missouri; Mrs.

Gertrude Cleophas Hall, Glendale, California; Mrs. Anginette Hines Hatch, Wayne, Michigan; Mr. George Roy Hemingway, East Jordan, Michigan; Miss Harriet Hemingway, Evanston, Illinois; Mrs. Mary Williams Hemingway, Washington, D.C.; Mrs. Pauline Pfeifer Hemingway, Key West, Florida; Mr. William D. Horne, Barrington, Illinois; Mr. Walter Edmonds Johnson, Tamworth, New Hampshire; Miss Katherine Kester, Pasadena, California; Mrs. Chester Livingston, Honolulu, Hawaii; Mr. Otto McFeeley, Oak Park, Illinois; Mrs. Harry Meehan, Winnetka, Illinois; Mrs. Ernest John Miller, Wolverine, Michigan; Mrs. Paul S. Mowrer, Chocorua, New Hampshire; Miss Frances Pailthorpe, Petoskey, Michigan; Mr. Frank J. Platt, Oak Park, Illinois; Mr. and Mrs. Albert Reed, Oak Park, Illinois; Miss Elsie C. Roome, Santa Barbara, California; Miss Gertrude Roome, Santa Barbara, California; Mr. and Mrs. Harold Sampson, Philadelphia, Pennsylvania; Mr. Ernest Smith, Toronto, Ontario, Canada; Mrs. George Spayde, Clearwater, Florida; Mrs. Adelaide Hemingway Truesdell, Washington, D.C.; Mr. Owen S. White, Petoskey, Michigan.

FIFTY YEARS OF
CORRESPONDENCE BETWEEN
ERNEST AND MARCELLINE HEMINGWAY

Foreword

by
JOHN EDMONDS SANFORD

I NEVER met my uncle Ernest Hemingway. My search for his spirit has taken me from his birthplace, at his family's turreted, Queen-Anne-style house on a broad, elm-lined street in the Middle West; to a third-floor-walk-up flat overlooking a glistening-wet, cobble-stone street on the Left Bank in Paris; to his Finca Vigia, high on a lush green hill, with palm trees flickering in the gentle Gulf Stream breeze; and, finally, to his polished granite grave-stone set amid the dry, sun-browned mountains of Idaho.

In July 1995, on the Finca's terrace, I found myself sharing the distant view of downtown Havana with one of his sons. To make conversation, I asked, "Has the view changed much since you were a boy?"

"Hardly at all," he replied without looking at me.

I persisted, "How long has it been since you were last here?"

"It must be at least forty years," he responded softly.

Gathering courage, I probed deeper. "How do you feel, coming back after so many years?"

For the first time my cousin turned and faced me. "The house seems unchanged. A time capsule. I almost expected Papa to greet me when I opened the door."

My own time capsule experience was in the form of a book I first read thirty-five years ago—*At the Hemingways*. My mother finished writing it just a few years before she died in 1963. Rereading it today is like opening a door to Ernest Hemingway's youth.

I found myself almost smelling grandfather Abba Hall's breakfast bacon cooking in the kitchen of the house in Oak Park where Mother and Ernest were born. I delighted in the tale of Ernest's childhood exaggerations about capturing a runaway horse all by himself. I was moved to tears by the tale of Abba Hall's rescue of a horse from his junkman-owner's beatings.

As I read on, I realized that to capture a complete portrait of the complex man who wrote such timeless short stories as "Indian Camp," "Big Two-Hearted River," "The Killers," "A Clean, Well Lighted Place," "The Snows of Kilimanjaro," and the classic novels *A Farewell to Arms, For Whom the Bell Tolls*, and *The Old Man and the Sea*, one must start with the descriptions of Ernest's family and his youth from *At the Hemingways*.

This book has been out of print too long. In honor of my mother's birth in 1898 and Ernest's birth in 1899 we have designated this version "The Centennial Edition."

My good friend and preeminent Hemingway scholar Michael Reynolds has described the book as a "whitewash." From his perspective, I understand why it appears that way. I recall my mother discussing her motives for writing the book. She was "disgusted" by all the "abominable" (her favorite negative word) stories that Ernest had given out to the press about his family. As the oldest sibling in the family, she felt it was her duty to set the story straight.

She was not seeking to open dark closets; instead she

sought to balance Ernest's fictions. She was also under constraints from other siblings who threatened to sue her if she wrote anything bad about them or the family. Finally, she wanted to leave a record for her children, their children and grandchildren of a remarkably creative and dynamic family in the early part of this century. I leave it to you, the readers, to determine if she succeeded in her goals.

Recently, my older sister and I discussed our recollections of our mother's comments about Ernest as we grew up. Neither of us could remember much sentiment. I could remember seeing Ernest's picture on the cover of *Time* magazine in October 1937. My mother said something like, "He may be a successful writer but he's been a bum husband to his wives. I hope, when you marry, you'll not turn out like him." To a young boy, the idea of being a successful enough writer to be on the cover of *Time* made a greater impact.

Mother rarely discussed her relationship with Ernest with us. We heard about the "abominable" letter he wrote to her on what she described as "toilet paper." That letter, dated July 1937, and an apology of December 22, 1938, are in the "Correspondence" in this volume. Other letters, written before World War I, are almost like love letters. My favorite letter, dated October 14, 1923, announces the birth of Ernest's first son, John. It also announces (in confidence) the publication of his first two books. He calls *In Our Time* a "whangleberry." There is also a charming letter from Ernest to Marcelline written in June 1928. It is filled with his famous "expert" advice about restaurants and places to shop on the eve of his unsophisticated older sister's departure for Paris. Clearly, brother and sister were extremely close and devoted up to that point. Then something happened. As far as I know, after their father's suicide and funeral in December 1928, they never saw each other again.

When Ernest died on July 2, 1961, my mother called me in San Francisco and urged me to accompany her to the funeral. I was completely surprised at the depth of her grief. Having just taken a new job, I made a quick decision. I didn't go. I didn't go because at that time Ernest Hemingway was not important to me. He was just a name. I'd never met him. I'd never heard a good thing about him from my mother. I wasn't aware if he knew I existed. Since then, I have found out how wrong I was.

Only by recently reading the letters between Ernest and Marcelline did I discover the extent of my ignorance. Ernest knew about me. He had sent money to Mother for Christmas gifts for us children and expressed sympathy to my mother when I lost sight in my right eye in an accident at age eight. Ernest had even saved a letter I had written him while I was in college. (Of course, I know he saved everyone's letters, including letters from my sister and brother thanking him for generous gifts.)

Hemingway scholar friends often ask if I know any stories about Ernest that have not been published. My father, Sterling Skillman Sanford, was almost ninety-eight before he died in 1990. His mind was sharp, his eyes clear, and his long-term memory remarkable. He shared with me the story of his first meeting with Ernest.

It was in 1917 at Walloon Lake at the Hemingway cottage, Windemere. Dad had just met Mother at nearby Bay View, where she was playing viola in the Bay View Symphony. Dad was staying as a guest of his relative, John M. Hall, the legendary director of the Bay View Methodist summer community. Mother had invited Sterling and several other Bay View friends to Windemere for a picnic.

Doctor Hemingway was expected to arrive from Chicago in the late afternoon, and Ernest took it upon himself to be the temporary male chaperone host.

As Dad told it, Ernest accosted him on the beach and proceeded to tell him about his heroics as a football player. At the end of the story, Ernest winked and said Sterling had to keep the story confidential, because his parents disapproved of football and he had played under an assumed name. Sterling was not taken in and asked Marcelline if she knew about Ernest playing football in high school. She laughed and said, "Of course, the whole family knew he was on the team. He was just a substitute and hardly got into the games at all."

Dad also recalled the Christmas of 1923 when Ernest made an overnight visit from Toronto to Oak Park. Dad took several pictures of Ernest and family members. Even though the photos have been published frequently, I never heard Dad complain that he was not given credit as the photographer. After Mother died, Dad gave me the handprinted, numbered, limited-edition of Ernest's second book, published in 1924, which was printed under the title *in our time*. When her parents returned their copies in disgust, Mother saved hers for posterity.

The only comment that Dad made about Mother's last meeting with Ernest in December 1928 was that "sharp words were exchanged" and "both your mother and Ernest were people with strong opinions." I remember my mother being a person of moral conviction, strong opinions, and lots of advice. Years later my adored uncle Leicester said one of the kindest things about my mother I have heard from a sibling: "Your mother gave a lot of advice. I would have been better off if I had listened to some of it."

When my father died in 1990, my sister, brother, and I had the task of disposing of the many papers and letters my mother saved. (She was much like Ernest and their parents in that respect, and my wife would say I carry on the family tradition.) We decided to give the original manuscript of *At the Hemingways* to the Ernest Hemingway Foundation of Oak Park, a non-profit organization volunteer organization, which has created a jewel of a museum devoted to Ernest Hemingway's Oak Park years and which is restoring the Hemingway Birthplace.

While I didn't know the details, I remembered my mother saying there was a lot more material about the family in the original manuscript than was eventually published. Her editor cut out what he felt would not be of interest to the general public. Ginny Cassin, Barbara Ballinger, Morris Buske, Scott Schwar, and others in the Ernest Hemingway Foundation of Oak Park studied the *At the Hemingways* manuscript in detail and discovered vivid descriptions of the Hemingway house, which has since undergone many changes.

At the Hemingways provided a blueprint for the restoration of the home where mother spent the first seven years of her life, and I know she would be pleased with the work done to date. Each time I visit the house, I am honored to see that the room where my mother was born looks much as it did on that cold day in January 1898.

On one visit, I stayed in a back bedroom. By the dim light of a chilly November dawn, I wandered alone, imagining how the place might have felt to my mother and her brother as children. The ceilings are high and Mother and Ernest may have felt very small and timid. To have their parents and grandfather sleeping upstairs and their father's family living across the street must have given them a solid sense of family unity and security that few children feel today. That's how it was then—generations of relatives lived together and family ties were strong.

Perhaps, as a war veteran, Ernest had to break away from the suffocating closeness of his family to become the person who could write as he did. On the other hand, I sense that he always recreated the family closeness with his friends in Paris, Switzerland, Key West, Cuba, and Sun Valley. Michael Reynolds mentioned this in his perceptive talk "Summer People" given in Sun Valley in July 1996. On another occasion, one of Ernest's sons told me he felt his father was at his best when he was in touch with his Middle Western roots.

My search for the spirit of Ernest Hemingway has also been a search for my own identity. I, too, was born in the Middle West, I spent my early summers at Walloon Lake, and like Ernest, I had to break away from family to find my sense of self. However, unlike Ernest, I did not pursue a career in writing and have devoted much time and effort to inner discovery. Rereading *At the Hemingways*, I am struck by the relationship between inner and outer searches. T.S. Eliot once wrote:

> *We shall not cease from exploration*
> *And the end of all our exploring*
> *Will be to arrive where we started*
> *And know the place for the first time.*

In appreciation for all the fine work done to date, and in the hope that this book may inspire others to contribute to the Ernest Hemingway Foundation of Oak Park, my sister, Carol, my brother, James, and I are directing all profits from this "Centennial Edition" of *At the Hemingways* to the Foundation.

Our dream is that, one day, the Ernest Hemingway Foundation of Oak Park can complete the restoration of the Hemingway Birthplace, construct an appropriate outbuilding for a museum on the premises, acquire the house on Kenilworth Avenue, where Ernest lived from 1906 until 1919, and restore Grace Hemingway's magnificent music room so the facility may be used as an international community center devoted to the musical and literary arts.

We encourage the readers of this book to join us in this dream. For more information, to make a contribution, or to join the Foundation, contact: The Ernest Hemingway Foundation of Oak Park at P.O. Box 2222, Oak Park, IL 60303.

Foreword

by
JAMES STERLING SANFORD

THE republication of *At the Hemingways* is a tribute to the one hundredth anniversary of my mother Marcelline Hemingway Sanford's birth in 1898. Mother took great pride in her Hall-Hemingway heritage. This book, which she dedicated to John, Carol, her grandchildren, and me, is a history of our ancestors and a first hand account of her immediate family, ending with the death of her father, Clarence Hemingway, in 1928.

The letters, photographs, and interviews Mother collected for *At the Hemingways* continue to be valuable to us. Many photographs were from six albums her mother, Grace Hall Hemingway, had assembled for her. They covered Mother's life and her siblings' lives through 1917, when Mother graduated from Oak Park High School. These treasured collections of dance cards, music recital programs, theater tickets and programs, family group photos, and individual photos—all identified as to people, location, and interesting information—were lovingly saved, organized, and mounted.

Grace Hall Hemingway left us the results of her various talents. We have found many musical scores she wrote, many paintings she created, and even furniture she designed and made. She also gave Mother and us the drive to excel and the courage to accomplish our goals. She was an energetic force in our lives.

The correspondence my grandmother saved through the years was enormous. I have a penny postcard of Grandmother's written in 1897 from Bear Lake, Michigan, to my grandfather in Oak Park, Illinois. She wrote of canoeing to visit friends on the lake that summer.

My memories of Grandmother begin when I was five years old. My family drove to Chicago to see the 1934 World's Fair and we stayed at Grandmother's in Oak Park. She was sixty-two and a grand lady. She wore long dresses and large hats. Her talent and self-confidence were obvious, even to a five year old.

I remember years later when she instructed me to walk and stand with my head tilted up a little as if I were looking over a fence. Then she advised me to sing by taking a deep breath, pushing up on my diaphragm, and projecting my voice by looking at a distant object and singing to it. Grandmother's hints helped me to enjoy group singing through the years.

In 1941, at age eleven, I was allowed to take the Mercury train from Detroit to Chicago at Easter to stay with Grandmother. What delighted me was Grandmother's eagerness to take the el to the Chicago train station near the museums. Grandmother stayed in the station and read while I swiftly walked to the planetarium and museums. I was gone three hours and when I returned she was sitting on the same bench—hat on, head bowed, purse and book in her lap—asleep. On our way home she took great interest in what I had seen and what I liked best. When I look back, I am impressed with her love for and patience with her grandson.

Another generation has been born since Mother wrote

her book of family life as she knew it in Oak Park and Walloon Lake. With publication of this Centennial Edition, Marcelline's great-grandchildren can now read what life was like growing up in the Dr. Clarence Hemingway family from 1898 to 1928—"The Years of Innocence."

Foreword

by
CAROL SANFORD COOLIDGE

IN the twenties, when genteel women devoted themselves mainly to home and church, my creative mother, Marcelline, was a woman ahead of her time. She expressed herself through the fine arts—sculpture, pottery, writing, acting, reviewing theater productions, and lecturing. In the summer of 1928, Mother studied sculpture in Paris, producing some very graceful nudes. Later she learned the art of pottery at Pewabic Pottery in Detroit. She supplied us with bowls, cups, and plates, beautifully glazed. Writing came easily to Mother. She carried on a large correspondence with family and friends and co-authored a one-act musical comedy with Dorothy Coolidge, who would one day become my mother-in-law. *Be Seated!* was performed by theater groups for a number of years and Mother delighted in receiving the occasional royalty checks from her publisher, the Samuel French Company.

The theater was her main love. She acted in little theater groups, attended touring Broadway shows, and reviewed plays for the Women's City Club magazine monthly. Later in life, she became a professional lecturer and traveled around the country, letting women's groups have intimate "Backstage Glimpses" of New York productions. As background for this lecture series, she went to New York twice a year and attended the theater almost every afternoon and evening for a week. I heard her speak once and was so enchanted that I forgot she was my mother. I was told that Mother played the viola in her youth, but I never heard her play. She and my father were very fond of music, though, and attended the Detroit Symphony regularly. They occasionally took me along, to my delight.

I remember my mother at home. She read to us with great expression and was always attentive when my brothers or I were ill. When I was a young girl, she and I took cooking lessons by mail. We had some delightfully messy sessions in our family kitchen trying out new recipes.

But like her mother before her, my mother occasionally had a great need to be alone. She treasured her springtime visits to her cottage on Walloon Lake. There she puttered around by day and read murder mysteries to relax in the evening. She painted furniture and planted sweet peas for us to enjoy later in the summer.

Although it has been over thirty-four years since my mother's death, I remember her vividly as an interesting individualist who left my brothers and me a legacy of her own years growing up in *At the Hemingways*.

[POSTMARK] Jun. 9, 1909, Oak Park, Ill.

[ENVELOPE FRONT: written in the handwriting of
Clarence Hemingway]
Miss Marcelline Hemingway
Nantucket, Mass.
c/o Miss A. C. Ayers
45 Pearl St.

Wed June 9

Dear Marc,
   Our room won in the field day against Miss Koontz
room. Al Bersham knocked two of Chandlers teeth out in
a scrap and your dear gentle Miss hoad had Mr. smith hold
him while she <u>lickt</u> him with a raw hide strap.

Lovingly, Ernest

———

MEMORANDUM

<u>You poor</u> boins caput how in the name of all things just and
unjust did you get in the story club. If I couldn't write a
better story than you I'd consign myself to purgatory.
Congratulations.

Thine eternally,
Ernestum

To Marcelline from Ernest on hearing that she had
"made" the Story Club. 12 out of 100 candidates accepted. <u>Crazy Nuts</u>. May 5, '15.
[The note above is in the handwriting of Grace Hall Hemingway.]

[POSTMARK] Jun. 24, 1916, Boyne City, Mich.

[ENVELOPE FRONT]

Pinehurst Cottage
Horton Bay
Boyne City, Mich. R. F. D. No. 2

Miss Marcelline Hemingway
27 West Avenue South
La Crosse, Wisconsin
Tender Care
Miss Emily Goetsmann
207 West Avenue South
La Crosse

[ENVELOPE BACK]
From Rev. E. M. Hemingway
HellanBack, New Jersey

June 20, 1916
Dear Antique Ivory—;

Well old soak I suppose you have had quite the "Te su pas" time as it were. While commencement was going on Lew and I were fishing all night on a pool of the Rapid River 50 miles from no where. Murmuring pines and hemlocks, black still pool, roar of rapids around bend of river, devilish solem still, dammed poetic.

When 9 bells came I arose and gave a skinny wow wow. Then I gave a masterly oration in my best English French and Ojibway. Just when I had reached the part telling of my touching boyhood friendship with Mac, Lew landed a big rainbow out of the pool into my face. "Oh shut up," quoth he. "Here's your diploma." So having received my diploma I shook hands with all the balsams—bowed to my trout basket—kissed my flyrod and murmurred x "____ ____ ____ ____." x deleted by censor.

Then we had the alumni banquet. It was about 12:30 and I opened the sacred can of apricots that I had packed about 200 miles. You know you always carry something like that for constipation. We ate the apricots and I made another speech which was spoiled by the log I was standing on rolling over. Lew didn't appreciate my oratory a bit and ate most of the apricots. Did you see France? Are my pictures any good? I'll bet you have some rare time at Emily's. Did old Coxy come across with the necessary bid? I would wager a tuppence that Sammy looked foolish when he grasped his diploma in his hairy right mitt and stalked across the stage looking like a cross between Charlie Chaplin and Lord Kitchener. I caught so many trout that it was bushing. We got so that we would throw all back under about 9 inches. We gave several big ones away. Ivory dearest you should have seen the old brute doing a rain dance in the costume of Adam enveloped by a cloud of mosquitoes on top of a bluff about 300 feet high at night while my clothes were drying on a rack of cedar poles in the driving rain. One hand moved a shoe aloft the other helped me swear. The calm and quiet of the abysmal wilderness of the Boardman river were violated by the old Brute. Lew nearly died of paroxysms. You see it was about ten P.M. and it would have furnished quite a sensation to any one within a mile or so. I was singing Ban-Ban-Bay. Nuff sed. We didn't go anywhere but what the people asked us to come back and visit them again. Gosh but we made a lot of folks happy with giving them big fish. We gave an old couple two great big suckers—the first they'd had in ten years—and they darn near fell on my neck. I was glad they didn't because the old woman smoked a clay pipe and she might of busted it. Go to a lot of dances for me and eat some civilised food.

I suppose you saw Lewis. He would forget to tell you any of the interesting things tho. Tell Emily for me that some time after she gets fairly graduated and every body else is dead and it is raining and she has also goldarnlutely nothing else to do to write to me. You can tell her to that I've got a picture to send to her after I hear that she is <u>still alive</u>. Bet you have some rough time without me to guide and protect you?

So Long
Yours Sin Searely
O.B.

Nutty P.S.

P.P.S. For John's sake write (not Emily's John).

[POSTMARK] Sep. 6, 1917, Oak Park, Ill.

[POSTCARD FRONT: Picture of "The Cages in Lincoln Park Chicago"]

[POSTCARD BACK]
Mr. Ernest M. Hemingway
Boyne City Mich
c/o F. W. Dilworth R. F. D. #2

Beloved Little One,
   "<u>We are</u> having a fine time and wish you were here."
Lessie weeps for you and the 'Raugataug nightly and I—
oh-oh-I can't express it but—"you know what <u>I</u> mean."
                                        Love and kisses
                                        Marc Ivory
P.S. Did you tell G. A. W.?

———

[POSTMARK] Sep. 15, 1917, Boyne City, Mich.

[POSTCARD FRONT: Picture of "Pere Marquette Park
and Station, Petoskey, Mich." Ernest Hemingway
handwritten X on edge of Bear River and note
"Cross shows my room"]

[POSTCARD BACK]
Miss Marcelline Hemingway
Barrows House
Oberlin, Ohio

WK Hell—;
   <u>This</u> shows my room. Fine time. Wish you could be
here. Maybe you will sometime.

                                        Aunt Grace

Write me often. <u>Don't</u> join any fraternities. It's lonesome
as hell.

                                        Love and kisses,
                                        [Drawing of beer stein]

[POSTMARK] Sep. 18, 1917, Oberlin, Ohio

[POSTCARD FRONT]
E. M. Hemingway
Boyne City, Mich RFD #2
c/o James Dilworth

[POSTCARD BACK]
207 S. Professor St.
Oberlin Ohio

Dear Eoinuts,
    Your P.card created una riot with my room mate. She's
from a 13000 acre ranch in Colo. Some girl. P. Rea met me
at the train. "Boy!" Sam comes here today. Joy! I'll write
you longer later.

Love,
The Iverian

———

[POSTMARK] Oct. 12, 1917, Oberlin, Ohio

[ENVELOPE FRONT]
Mr. E. Monstrocity Hemingway
600 N. Kenilworth Ave.
Oak Park Ill.
Very Private Personal + Urgent

[ENVELOPE BACK]
From M. Hemingway
Barrows-on-the-Plum
Oberlin-near-Heidelburg
Ohio-near-Lake Erie-U.S.A.

207 S. Professor
Oberlin Ohio

Dearest Eoints,
  <u>Why</u> won't you write to the old Ivory? I've been looking
for a letter for weeks & I've written you at least 4 times—
no fair—woman—no fair! I'll say "you horrid cat" with the
true Walter Grover inflection in a few moments if you
don't pep up pretty soon.
  Gee—Eoin—you'd like this "Review" work here. The
senior fellows know so much about the stuff and are not
the P. Rea variety in the least. "Nat" Howard the Ed. is a
peach, as far as I can tell, but this paper hasn't the "go" that
we achieved with our little ol' "Trap."
  No siree!
  You see, these poor creatures haven't any sweet Fannie
to inspire them. I wish they had you, Hux, The "Blight"
Cohen & Fanny with perhaps a few Bobbitts once in a
while & then it would be <u>some</u> little sheet—Leopold
Godowsky, the pianist, gives a recital here next Tuesday
and our Cons. Orchestra gives part of the great Dvorak
"New World Symphony" at the Weekly students' recital
next Wed. night.
  My dear, bro, I long so to see an honest-to-goodness
man! Why most of the callow youths here have never seen
a coffin nail except in picture books & their idea of heavenly bliss is a glass of milk & a doughnut on Sat. afternoon.
Aint it H___? It are!! My roomie isnt that kind, tho, & lots

268 / AT THE HEMINGWAYS

of the other girls in the house have other methods than looking at a mag's back cover in order to scent the sweet odor of Fatimas. Understand this letter is to be strictly private.

What do you hear from Annette? & How are K.s Meyer & Bagley? Tell the family to give S. Capps a wedding present for me because I can't buy anything in this burg.

<u>Write soon.</u>

Your loving & kissing,
Marc.

P.S. Isn't this cons. stationery slick?

[POSTMARK] Oct. 26, 1917, Kansas City, Mo.

[ENVELOPE FRONT]
Kansas City Star [Stamped over Postmark]
Miss Marceline Hemingway
Barrows House
Oberlin College
Oberlin, Ohio

[ENVELOPE BACK]
E. M. Hemingway
3733 Warwick Boul.
K.C., Mo.

No. 4 Police Station
2:25 P.M.

Dear Old Ivory,
   And how is it at that most dear Oberlin huh? I also am working hard. Yesterday morning I had six yarns in the sheet and 1 on First Page. A veritable reporter the old Brute. But nix on Fatimas for even they have went up to 18¢. Carl Edgar and I jazz forth with frequency. On Sunday last at St. Joe we were and one Ada Lyon sent to you her love also that Helen and this Auryllus. In truth it is the life at this place.
   All cops love me like a brotherhood. I am Editor of Public Mind like Vox of the Pop. but am now promoted and edit mine with less frequency. This is copy paper. On it is written with a typewriter solely. Poor handwriting has not handicapped me yet. At St. Josephine I was and have chance to work on St. Josephine Gazette. But the salary! Merci! It is nought. A mere pittance! Here I receive 60 of them per month. A princely stipend. And why is it I hear from you not? Loneliness consumes me theoretically; practically I am all business and have no time but at the office there is a frequency of the tempus. Write me care the Star Ed department and you will be answered I swear it. Are there any he men with pants at that your school? Write me concerning them. I think not of damsels but when the spring cometh when no man can work; ah then. It is! [Drawing of 3 tears] = Tears.

Yours,
The Brother

[POSTMARK] Nov. 6, 1917, Kansas City, Mo.

[ENVELOPE FRONT]
Miss Marcelline Hemingway
Care Barrows House
College
Oberlin
Ohio

Written 1 week before being mailed

Dear Old Ivory:

Of course I wont say anything you old abysmalite. Sure I run the Public Mind, Honest to Godfrey. Glad you could have such a rare time in Cleveland—it must be quite a burgundy. Tonight Carl and I go to Turn To the Right. What show did you see in Cleve? Does Red Milliken play on the O team? Today was pay day and I just dragged down $30 for the first two weeks work. I got the negatives from G. Al Walker today of those two pictures he took and am having a print made today. The Blight and Jock and the Mick have all written me this week. Jock is at Michigan and is having a rare time. Blight is still at Allentown, the Mick is working at Western Electric.

I am having a good time down here old kid and hope you get lots of joy out of the Alum Mattress. But take it from the Brother; be muchly careful and exercise discretion if not absolute conformance to all rules and regulations. Carl is a good guy and not a suds downer, he smokes the pills, as you are aware, but he is 27 and I believe his life will not be ruinated thereby. Your kid brother leaves the fiery stuff alone and is about the only one down at the office that does not work with his face equipped with one of the filthy weeds. His vices are buying an occasional magazine and going to the debasing theaters ever and anon, also eating apples. I intend to enlist in the Canadian Army soon but may wait till spring brings back Blue days and Fair. Honest kid I cant stay out much longer, the Canadian Mission Down here are good pals of mine and I intend to go in. Major Biggs And Lieut. Simmie are the officers in charge. If you enlist in the Canadian forces you are given as much time as you specify and then go to either Toronto or Halifax and then to London and in three months you are in France. They are the greatest fighters in the world and our troops are not to be spoken of in the same breath. I may even wait untill the summer is over but believe me I will go not because of any love of gold braid glory etc. but because I couldnt face any body after the war and not have been in it.

You probably cant get me but cheer up because I am next to myself anyway. None of the above is for Family consumption, you know me Al.

Your old Brute
Ernie.

A week later.

Hey old Brute. Glad Mother was there. Kiss all your room mates for the Stien. I joined the Mo. National Guard for State service only. Have a 40 buck uniform and 50 dollar overcoat. Some youth.

The Heming Stien

[POSTMARK] Jan. 31, 1918, Kansas City, Mo.

[ENVELOPE FRONT]
Union Station Headquarters
Soldiers and Sailors
Kansas City, Mo.

Miss Marceline Hemingway
600 N. Kenilworth
Oak Park, Ill.

[ENVELOPE BACK]
From E. M. Hemingway
Care K. C. Star
Editorial Dept.

Two Days before Pay Day

Dearest of Ivories—:
    Tickles and pleasings enveloped me to get your sun
dried and windblown epistles. Gosh I am glad to know the
old Al is coming down. I love him like a brother! Tell him
to write me tho will you! How long is the dear lad going to
step around that dear dump.
    If the parents get rough explain to the old Al and he is a
peach and will understand. Give him my love.
    Say kid this newspaper business is the life. Since being
here I have met and talked with Gen. Wood, Lord
Northcliffe, Jess Willard, V. Pres. Fairbanks, Capt. B.
Baumber British Army, Gen. Capper of Kas. and any
amount of others. Tis the life. Also I can distinguish chianti, catawba, malvasia, Dago Red, claret and several others sans the use of the eyes. Some days when I review
shows I see three shows in a single day, all theaters very

close. Show of Wonders, Orpheum circuit vaudeville and Gayety Theater. I can tell mayors to go to Hell and slap police commissioners on the Back! Yeah tis indeed the existence. Today got a letter from old Bill Smith. He speaks muchly concerning that joyous day the first of May on which we flea unto a far country.

I haven't written a soul except one slight epistle to the Fambly for a week. There is a devil of a big political fight going on and I haven't had a minute even to think. Lucile and K will be mad as the stuff they make the malt from. If you see any of them tell them the darn stien has been so busy that he hasn't even writ his family! will you? Tell them that is the straight stuff. Damme kid did you know they call me Hemingstien down here too? Even the boss! Also Stienway and Hamstick. Also Hopkins the city ed of the Times addresses me as Mr. Goldfish! Reason unknown. Most of them call me the great Hemingstien of Hospital Hill. That being one of my hang outs. There are a swell bunch of birds here ivory. Almost as good as the old gang. They are all abit to the wild but a peach of a gang. That Mrs. Hunter stuff seems all to the rosy. Do what ever you think best my dear!

Do you know I have to pack a Colt gat? Don't spill it to the folks they might worry. Wm S. Smart or Bug Faced Bareshanks have nought on me.

Fare well
Your true love
The Old Brute

[POSTMARK] Mar. 2, 1918, Kansas City, Mo.

[ENVELOPE FRONT]
E. M. Hemingway. The Press Room
Hotel Muehlebach
Kansas City, Mo.

Miss Marcelline Hemingway
315 S. Ashland Boulevard
Chicago Illinois.

Daer Kid Swester.
    Love from the great Hemingstein to you all. And how is all with you? and that Sam how is he? Fall not for any such as Sam, Ivory, because there are far better fish in the world than yon sucker, any way, think of the great Hem-----y acting as brother in law to such. Far better Al or someone or the real jazz. I can hear you rave, but the Kid brother, while a mere infant, has been out in this old sphere considerable lately. And has seen many and various types. Also he has had many and varied experiences, it is the truth for a fact. No kidding, kid. Think twice about Sam. I have seen his breed before. Of course if he likes and loves you, there must be some great good in him, that stands to reason. Aint it. Sure, but there are so many that are such a Damn sight Better Kid. Take it from the Great HemO-----y. That is the way all my copy is signed. It takes too darn long to write out Hemingway. Any way Kid that was no idle Jest about the Great none other than that Mae Marsh, whom you and Sam glimpsed. If she would ever become Mrs. HemOOOOOOO----y joy would reign supreme. Such is the state of affairs. Maybe she will love me enough some day. What did you and the Sam think of the Beloved

Traitor? I haven't seen it yet and so cant tell if it is up to her former standard. But I dont care if it is poor because that makes no difference by me. Did you tell Sam that I was in love with she who you were glimpsing? And what did he say? Have you slipped any one else the glad news? If so, let me know the results. I am glad that L. Dick is bats about the Grimes if that is what you intended to infer. Ashes to ashes and dust to dust if the Whiskey don't get you the cocaine must. etc. That means nothing to you aint it. Any way did I tell you that I was enlisted as an Ambulance driver for the American Ambulance service in Italy? Yes it is an fact. Mit me my love but say nought to the fambly. They might worry and I probably wont be called for some time. Any way it is a big relief to be enlisted in something. I enlisted for immediate service but got gypped on the immediate end of it. You see it is like this there are only five jobs for immediate service and my telegram got in sixth so I and the great Ted Brumback, who drove on the Aisne for Six months will be next in line. The St. Louis Headquarters said that our enlistments were received in response to our wire they sent blanks, and that they would let us know when they should avail themselves of our services. The rank of a first Lieut. expense paid, an officers Italian uniform, and a probable Fifty a month for spending money. Aint it the life. Any way promise on your word of honor not to say ought to any one as I want not to be gypped. I now study French and Italian and have learned to drive an ambulance. right jazzy. Pull for the old bird. Isn't Mary M. a wonder? HuH?HUH?HUH? HU? HUHU? Oh Boy. Brumstein and the Great Tubby and the stupendous Hix all envy the gt. Hem--y. Is it not an just cause? h man. Dale Wilson, has not yet left for Gt. Lakes and he is the bird that I yearn to have you have out?

H is? But they are filled up there now and so he is delayed leaving. I yet hope to have a part of next summer up North. Maybe, Maybe Not.

So write me right away and Good Luck with your Amours.

Old Kid it is none other than the great Hemingstein what signs this.

The Antique Brute

———

[POSTMARK] Mar. 8, 1918, Kansas City, Mo.

[ENVELOPE FRONT]
Miss Marcelline Hemingway
315 South Ashland Boulevard
Chicago, Illinois.

[ENVELOPE BACK]
From E. M. Hemingway
care Editorial Department
Kansas City Star.

Daer Kid Sister:

Well Kid let me slip you an ear full. First I have not to my knowledge got the Big Head? I was just trying to let you know how I was getting along. Every time Hicks and Wilson and I get our pay checks it effectually fore stalls any tendency toward the big head. Secondly old Sweetheart, incline an ear, I dont want you to tell the family because I may yet get gypped on the Ambulance Service as it may be taken over by the U.S. Govt. tho not probably, and this is the point, You dont get any service flag until it is for sure, and I am not going to have any tears shed or letters written and then be gypped. Do you get me? HUH? And I will let the folks know as soon as I am certain, if you think I am jesting or as it were kidding with you, why I will enclose my correspondence with the St. Louis and Washington depots. I did think kid that you had a little more faith in me than that. Uncle Tyler is out of the City but I told Aunt Arabel and got a letter of recommendation from Capta. J. B. White, the noted lumber hound and relative. Also from Boss R. E. Stout, and Boss C. G. Wellington. would I idly jest with the Boss Stout one of the greatest newspaer men in the world or trifle with my boss to send letters? Also the W. K. J. B. White. However if you think that I am kidding and it makes you any more happy why go ahead. Also if you dont like Mae Marsh, why go plumb to and take a long leap and see if it affects me in the least. I am in love with her and while as I usually do I may get over it yet she right now is the most wonderful in the world. Also in the Beloved T. she was if you remember playing a character part and in real life, there is a just a bare possibility that a wonderful character actress looks a trifle different from playing the part she played in the Beloved Traitor. I only have pulled one boner in picking them and that was the late lamented D Davies. In other respects, fer example, Annette DeVoe, Frances Coates, my judgment has been fairly sound. And Mary Marsh, is far from an error in judgement. Also what did you tell me that Frances Coates wanted to hear from me for? I had no intention of writing her beyond the impression that you gave me. But going under that assumption I did write her about two weeks ago, which was a darn poor thing to do if she didnt want to hear from me and also you might say a trifle humiliating, under circumstances, about which you know nothing, not being home while I was. And she has not re-plied to the letter. It makes no difference to me except maybe a matter of pride. And so dear old kid in your sheerful manner you have caused the beans to roll forth frae the pot.

This is indeed a cheerful epistle. Any way I yearned to tell you about any amount of things here but fear to because of a fear that you will think that I have the Big Head or that I am kidding you. And so dear old thing write me an epistle and see if you can ease my mind, and dont kid me sweetest.

Thanks for asking Hutch out to the house. Wilson is still down here. also dont get the Big head.

———

[NO POSTMARK: envelope hand delivered]

[ENVELOPE FRONT]
<u>My Buzz</u>

600 N. Kenilworth
The night you are leaving

May 11–18

Dearest Old Kid In The World,

It's great that you can do it, old fellow, m'lad, but its just plain necessary, isn't it? Personally this "hero courage" stuff tires me with entirety, but when you come down to brass tacks, I'd be furious if you didn't go.

Good luck, Old Sport.

Remember I'm always your

Same Old
Ivory

P.S. You'll write more often won't you kid?

So long,
Marc.

———

600 N. Kenilworth
Oak Park, Ill.

July 5, 1918

Dearest Old Buzz,
 I've tried to get time to write to you at least 50 times in
the last 2 weeks, but all in vain.
 To let you know just how busy the old Ivory has been
here's a straight fact:
 I didn't even answer Sam for a week!
 And the dear lad writes to Ivory every other day.
 I haven't heard from Al W. for almost a month. Perhaps
he has been transferred or has gone across.
 Sterling Sanford gets his commission in the Engineer
R.O.T.C. at Camp Lee, Va. on July 7th. He's a nice guy,
Eoin Bones, and he does write such sensible letters.
 Mighty different from the "mash notes" one receives
from the Jackies.
 By the way, said Jack Eyes are as numerous as ever.
We are going to have two here tomorrow nite for dinner.
As Ursula flew the coop for Pine Lake after the boys
were invited, I have asked Melrose Wilson to "help me
out". She's awfully sweet Ernest. (Even if you don't
think so.)
 Gee, Buzz, the Old Ivory has been leading a gay exis-
tence for fair & warmer. Every Sat. for 7 weeks I have gone
to a dance somewhere & lots of other nights beside.
 Lucille Dick and I see quite a bit of one another lately.
She & George G. are still as thick as butter. (Gooey, you
know) I suppose you heard the Frances Coates & Jack
Grace are engaged? It was announced the day after you
left! (Wise Frances!)
 K. Bagley invited me to go canoeing last week. They

have a jazz boat and K. is good at paddling. <u>She wants you to write to her.</u>

Next week K. takes a job as an analytical chemist for the government. Isn't that slick?

I work at Hyde Park Center (farther south than Chicago U.) two afternoons a week & I take typewriting at OPHS summer school every morning.

Did Muzzie tell you that Dorothy Board was at the Presby. Hospital studying to be a trained nurse? She is so sweet. Ernie, you would hardly know her for the same girl who visited us at Walloon some years ago.

Sam was very eager to have me come up to La Cross to visit him for a week or so but I <u>turn</u> him down, Buzz. I turn him flat. I'm not going to engage myself to him nor any one else until I get good & ready & that will probably be <u>never.</u>

Bill Hutchins wrote me from Italy. He is in Sec. 587 American Ambulance Service, A. E. I. Italy, so you <u>may</u> (very improbably) run across him. He can toss Ivory the merry flattery but the hard hearted woman does not fall. Next week I'm to tell stories to kids at the Municipal Pier. Aunt Grace the-Second—what say?

Write to me, dear, if you get time.

Your loving,
Ivory Marcelline

———

[POSTMARK] July 27, 1918, Mad., Wis.

[POSTCARD FRONT: Picture of O. Hammon Pub. Co., Chicago]

[POSTCARD BACK]
College Camp
Williams Bay, Wis.
July 27, '18
Mr. Ernest M. Hemingway
Italian Am. Service
Section 4
Milano, Italy
American Red Cross
c/o The American Consul

Dearest Old Buzz,
    Alice Corbin and I are here vegetating and taking in some marvelous lecture courses. There are 100 men here preparing for Y.M.C.A. overseas work. You ought to hear them serenade us at night. I have blood-poisoning in my knee so I can't do the gay stuff as much as usual, and yet I get there. Oh Boy, Yes! Hope you are loads better.

Your
Marcelline

Alan Ingulls is to take us riding tonight (youngsters!)

———

[POSTMARK] Milano

[ENVELOPE FRONT]
American Red Cross
Croce Rossa Americana
3, via Bocchetto Milano

Miss Marcelline Hemingway
600 North Kenilworth Ave.
Oak Park, Illinois U.S.A.

[ENVELOPE BACK]
Soto Ten. Ernesto M. Hemingway
Sezione IV Ambulanze
Croce Rosa Americana
Milano Italia

Ospedale Americana
Aug. 8, 1918

Cara Mio,
    Perche non scrivere a ev? Numero giorna niente Epi-
stola! Au altro tenente amata. Come? Dearest Ivory the
fore-going is but to illustrate a sample of the letters I am
compelled to write daily. Translated it means my dearest;
why my love have you not written. Many days I wait and
nothing of letters. Is it that you love another Lieutenant?
Tis thus that the old master learns the Italian language. He
can speak it with great fluency and on my return we shall
journey to Italian restaurants downtown where I will
demonstrate when I tell of the many Austrians that have
fallen at my hammy feet. They will feed us free. Serving
any   ment [?].

Why oh bright beam of an August moon have you not written me? Is it that you love me not? Or is it but neglect? If but the girls of our village could see me in my dress uniform. I am of a great fear that the men would be   [?]. However for them to appreciate my scars it would be necessary for me to wear no pants (i.e. trousers) or else to have flaps sown the length of the knees that they might be unbuttoned at will to show the marks of valour which be many and various. Ah Hah! I will wear nothing but my tank suit! Then will all be revealed. N'espa?

Dear Ivory call up on the telephone all my former sweet hearts! Tell them that the master woodsman, now known as The Hero of the Piave, loves them with an undying love, coming to them my undying fealty and fillial devotion.

Tell them that I will return, God willing and woo and perhaps wed them all. Inform them that it is only lack of interest that keeps me from writing them. Write me their replies.

Also call up Frances Coates and tell her that your brother is at death's door and that she will please, no excuses, write to him. Make her repeat the address after you so that she will have no alibi! Tell I love her or any damn thing! You know me Ivory Sweet sister, why not do you not dip the quill and sling me a screed yourself? Merely because I am a great man do not stand in awe of me! I am democratic or nothing. Si! Mostly nothing. Here are my kisses.

Arevedechi, Bon Giurno!

I kiss again—

                                                    The old Brute

[POSTMARK] Aug. 25, Chicago, Ill.

[ENVELOPE FRONT]
Lieut. Mr. Ernest M. Hemingway
Section 4
Italian Ambulance Service
c/o Croce Rosa Americana
via Milano, Italia
c/o American Consul

[ENVELOPE BACK]
From M. & U. Hemingway
600 N. Kenilworth Ave.
Oak Park U.S.

600 N. Kenilworth Ave.
Oak Park, Ill.

¡Mi Amigo Cara Magnificos!

Darlingest Heroine of the Peeve,
    I have inscribed at least 6 (or is it 7?) epistles to you,
m'love. Is it possible that you have received none of them?
    I weep at the thot. Dad has sent you the O. Leaves every
week too. Haven't you received anything we sent you?
Gosh I was glad to hear from you, Buzz. It was my first
word except the love to the "The Ivory," via Ted B.
    I met a darling Jackie named Freemont Jones, of K. City
who knew T. Brumback there. He goes to sea next week.
Lucille is very much in love with him. (You know G.
Grimm is canned from the Dick residence.)
    I am all thru with my knee trouble, thank the Lord. I
certainly had a sympathetic feeling for you my love. You
see I was in bed 4 weeks with a cast on. Will Lyon (you

remember him—Marion Hines beaux at med. college) took care of me while I was at Lake Geneva. He has a wife and an infant now. (How time aviates along.)

Sam Anderson is a cadet in the Naval Aviation School at Dunwoody Institute, Minneapolis.

I suppose Dad told you that Hap was coming to the Ensigns School on the pier and that Bill Smith has enlisted at Great Lakes.

In my previous letters I told you about Frances Coates engagement to Jack Grace but I'll tell her to write to you anyway. She isn't wedded yet, y'know.

Al Walker is on his way across by now. He is in the 57th Engineers as I told you. He promised that his sister would send me one of the pictures he had taken in Philadelphia but it hasn't come yet.

Gosh, Buzz, the Ivory is proud of her young friend Eoin bones. Think of getting an Italian V.C.! Do remember that all men are free & equal over here. We can't give you a peerage, m'lord, but we love you just the same.

Bill Hutchins, the guy who thinks he loves me, is in Italy now also. He arrived there about a month ago and says he has been hunting all over spaghetti to find you. He was a Junior at Yale when he enlisted. He is in Section 587, United States Army Ambulance Service. Bill's section were the first American troops to land in Italy. I hope you'll meet him. He's such a clever chap. Old Tofe, dontcha know!

Bill Wilson is coming out to spend Sunday with Ursula, Sunny and I.

It's doggone lonesome with out the folks but it certainly is great to go to the old movies without begging 2 bits from the reluctant parents. I have had some good sized pictures taken to give to my devoteds in various places.

Joe Armstrong, an Annapolis man, is very garrulous with

the pen and ink lately. Maybe I'll go to the Annapolis "prom" before I die! Oh Boy, would not that be heaven indeed?

Ursula is cutting sand"witches" for the Jackie supper-dance at the Tennis Club tonite and Nun-bones is bicycling with the omnipresent Curley Wolf.

My school is moved to Chicago University so I'll be near Ida Noyes Hall next winter.

Sergt. Fritz Wilcoxen was in O.P. on furlough this week. He looks great. He is in tank service now in Pennsylvania. DeWayne Clinton, Chuck Dunning and mobs of others are in the Marines. "Karrie" sends love and will write soon. Jane Nissen asked about you & so did Helen Condron & K. Meyer. Gordon Shorney & Catherine M. are very thick just now. If this dog-dog letter does not get to you I shall give a demonstration of the Kaiser in 2018, gnashings of teeth, you know my dear.

I am learning international code, for wireless, signalling, etc. Sam and I write it exclusively for practice. He is good but I am horribly slow. Babs is going up to Horten's to be with Mother & Carol for the month of September. Dad & Leicester return to us next Friday. They will have had ten days of rest anyway.

Bob Preble is a 1st Lieut. and so is Herbert Shorney.

Almost every body from Oak Park (there are almost 2000 men gone now) are commissioned. Don't kiss too many Italian dames. You will use up all the energy you might spend in writing to your adoring Ivory Jane.

Ura & I must bathe now, preparatory to the Tennis Club dance. I leave you, loved one of the Peeve'd, so that I may perform that act of all acts most heroic; — the lighting of the tank.

Adoringly and everlastingly yours,
Marc.

P.S. I made the best Hermits a little while ago. How I wish I could send you some. I will send some magazines under separate cover.

Your own, Iverion

Write!
Write!
Write!
[Drawing of bar of music]
To the tune of "Smile, grin, giggle!"

––––––

[POSTMARK] 23 IX 1918, Milano Centro

[ENVELOPE FRONT]
American Red Cross
Croce Rossa Americana
10, via Manzoni, Milano

Miss Marcelline Hemingway
600 N. Kenilworth Avenue
Oak Park, Illinois
Estati Uniti

[ENVELOPE BACK]
Da Tenente Ernest Hemingway
Croce Rossa Americana
Ospedale Milano, Italia

Sept. 21, 1918

Dear Ivory and Nun Bones;
    Your epistles of Aug. 25th just arrived and oh women I was glad to hear from you! I'm still in the hospital and

probably will linger for about 3 weeks more. Believe me kids, the old master is an authority on hospitals. Darn near three months already.

It's funny that I've only had two letters off you since the war started. Aug 19 and 25.

There isn't a thing to relate. I know where your friend Bill Hutchins is and will try and look him up. The Captain in charge has invited me to come and visit him so I'll strive to lamp Bill.

You know Milano is some town, about 690,000, good opera and everything. I go out and walk around town almost every aft and sure know the old burg. After the war I'll be qualified to run a rubber lunch wagon through Italy. When I walk it looks like I had locomotor ataxia but that will all clear up. My right knee bends a little now. Gee but I get anxious to get back to the front. I don't know exactly what I will do now that I have been commissioned at 1st Lieut. but know I will have charge of a front line post somewhere. Aren't things going great in France? Next fall will see the Germans smashed completely and the Italians will anihilate the Austrians. Now Ivory I will give you a full list of the old master's titles and other stuff. Tenente Ernesto Hemingway! Properto Al Medaglia D'Argento, (volore) proporto per Croce D'Guerra Fento D'Guerra Da Prima Linae Promotzione for mento D'Guerra. Translated that means that the old jazz hound is a First Lieut, cited for the Silver valour medal, cited for the war cross, wounded in the first lines and promoted for merit. Now aint he stuck up? He aint though, I hope. I've only got one ambition though, but then I better not tell it. Huh?

Thank everybody that asked about me and give 'em all my love. I know a wonderful American girl over here so

I'm not a bit lonesome for any of the X ones. None of them have a prayer, which reminds me of a good yarn. A nigger recruit was talking to a nigger veteran. "Say! what does this going "over the top" mean Boss?"

"It means just this nigger, just this, Good mournin' Gawd!"

Not bad ah? I'll bet you kids had a rare time while the parents were away, what?

Well be good and write me soon and don't break too many Jackies hearts! What do they do anyway besides go to dances?

So Long Kids,
Ernie

[POSTMARK] Moltarone, Italy

[Date of 9/26/18 is based on a reference regarding Ernest Hemingway's holiday in Stresa, September 24-30, 1918, in *Hemingway in Love and War: the Lost Diary of Agnes von Kurowsky, her Letters and Correspondence of Ernest Hemingway*, Henry Serrano Villard and James Nagel, eds. (Boston: Northeastern University Press, 1989), 276.]

[POSTCARD FRONT: Picture of Grand Hotel Moltarone, Kulm]

[POSTCARD BACK]
Miss Marcelline Hemingway
600 N. Kenilworth Avenue
Oak Park Illinois
Stati Uniti

Dear Ivory—;

We are here for the day. It is of a great beauty. Above the clouds in sight of Switzerland—right next door. I am here on a permission at the Lakes. Fishing Bathing.

I love you Ked
Ernie

———

[POSTMARK] Oct. 3, 1918, Chicago, Ill.

[ENVELOPE FRONT]
S. Ten. Ernest M. Hemingway
Section 4
Croce Rosa Americano
Italian Ambulance Service
Milano, Italia
c/o American Consul

[ENVELOPE BACK]
From M. D. Hemingway
315 S. Ashland Blvd.
Chicago, Ill. U.S.A.

315 S. Ashland Blvd.
Chicago, Ill.
Oct. 2, 1918

Caro Buzz,

Buon giorno, signore! Come state?

I am beginning Italian today, so I know you will enjoy a real letter in the language of your adopted mother-in-law. Siete voi il padre degli scolari? No, eglino sono i fratelli dello straniero? Come a il corpo senza anima, tale a l'uomo senza amici.

I was going to finish this in spaghetti but it takes too long. Don't you think I have quite a grasp of the language for the first day? We agree.

Well, old man, the Beloved Ivorian is back at 315 S. Ashland Blvd. taking up many religious subjects so that she may be a real inspiration to all your friends "When the Boys Come Home."

Doggone it, Eoinnts, I want you and all the other chaps to come back, but, oh boy! It will be a rare sight if you should all come at once! Al is sure I love him and so is Bill Hutchins, and you know what Sam thinks! Gee I hope they don't all come at the same time because I do hate to have the parlor carpet all messed up.

Anyway I love 'em all so tell them so if you see them before I do. Bill is going to try to get to see you. He is in active service now with the Americans. He sent me four pictures of himself in a letter, last week. Honestly Buzz, you would like him a lot.

Sam is at the Naval Aviation Ground School at Dunwoody Inst. Minneapolis but he expects to fly, at Pensocola, in 5 weeks. Edith Walker sent me a wonderful picture of Al taken just before he sailed. Neither of us have heard from him since he boarded the transport.

Marion Vose stayed 5 days with me, before school opened yesterday. We both wanted to go to Chicago University but our dear families have not quanti pestos to send us this year. There are 1500 students A.T.C. men at U. of C. and 350 Selected men besides. It would have been gay, all rite, but I'll do more work here.

Say, oh Brother, harken to my plea.

Won't you get some nice, peppy, safe, sane Italian chap to write to me in English and I'll write to him in "Wop" so that we can both learn to perfect our studies. Do you hear a baby's prayer at twilight? (That's me.) I send devotion to your newest love. She must be a corker or you wouldn't fall. With the exception of D. Davies, I'll hand it to you for picking winners!

My room mate is a good old sport, Vera Watson b' name.

Helen Gody died yesterday from the spanish flue. Mobs of people have it in Oak Park.

I'll send you some pictures of "Min" Vose and I pretty soon.

Write to me here at school, old top. Believe me Buzz, I am your onty-donty

Marc.

P.S. Is it a Red + nurse? I won't tell!!

[Drawing of Marcelline studying, with her roomate, Vera, sleeping in the background]

After the bell for retiring!!

Who said all art treasures come from Italy??

[POSTMARK] Oct. 26, 1918, Chicago, Ill.

[ENVELOPE FRONT]
Da Tenente Ernesto M. Hemingway
Section IV
Croce Rossa Americana
Italian Ambulance Service
Milano, <u>Italia</u>
c/o <u>American Consul</u>

[ENVELOPE BACK]
From Marc. D. Hemingway
315 South Ashland Blvd.
Chicago, Illinois
Los Estados Unidos
U.S.A.

315 South Ashland Blvd.,
Chicago, Ills.
U.S.A.
Oct. 24, '18

Dearest Buzz,

Gee, dear old Brute but the Ivery was thrilled with joy to receive a letter, via the pater familia da voi!

Honestly, Ernie, I have written to you every two weeks and some times oftener, since you left in May. Didn't you ever get all the letters I wrote in June, July and the 1st part of August?

I must seem like a beast to you, but really, dear, it is the P.O. dept and the German subs which are to be blamed for your failure to receive letters from me.

I'll write oftener from now on, Eoinuts, and perhaps some of the letters may get across to you.

Your letter telling about your wounding in detail, ending with "Leave us keep the house fires burning" was printed in last night's Chicago "Herald."

The faculty pinned it on the bulletin board here at school today, so I am the object of many congratulations. Bill Wilson called up today to tell me how splended she thot it was. Ah you are a peachy old court. Can you still read inglese? If you find it difficult I can write in Italiano but I think it is good practice for you to try to decipher a little literature in your native lingua once in a while ne ce's pas? Al Walker is in France. I heard from him last week, and he is <u>very</u> anxious to hear from you, as I have told you in the last 5 or six letters which you may have received by now. His address is Pvt. G. A. Walker Co "D," 57th Engineers, A.P.O. 716. American Ex. Forces.

Did I tell you that I had a splended picture of him which was taken just before he sailed?

Sam graduates from the Naval Aviation Officers School in three weeks and will then be sent to Florida for active work. Gordon Shorney, and Eddie Noel (whom you don't know but a good old sport) are also at the U.S.N. Aviation School at Dunwoody Institute, Minneapolis. Sam knows Gordon and one other Oak Pk. fellow there.

You ask, dear young brother, what we sisters of yours do except go to dances? I will answer for myself first:

I am at the C.T.S.W. where I am taking 22 hours of work per week not counting the 8 hours I give at the First Cong. Church as Mrs. Hunter's asst. I also teach a Sunday sch. class of <u>eleven</u> husky 4th grade girls every Sunday morning and go on Sociology field trips every Friday afternoon! Boy! This is a busy life. We hardly have time to sleep or eat.

"Waltie," my room-mate from Ottawa, Ills., is a peach and so is another new girl, Alice Millard of Detroit.

Those two, Marion Vose (the tall girl from N.H. whom you met last spring) and I practically live together. We play hard too, Ernie and last week 3 of us, "Waltie," Marion and I had 3 Jackies out and had a regular house party at 600 N. Kenilworth Ave.

As I write this we are just thru having a class meeting at which I was elected School President and Waltie School Treasurer. Looks like job politics, doesn't it?

My Italian professor Senore De Luca is a perfect dear. He shrugs his shoulders, talks with his hands, and lifts his

eye-brows so expressively for every conjugation, or translation, that any one would be sure that he was dramatizing
"Hamlet" or "Macbeth" at the very least.

Sociology is fascinating stuff, and I have 5 chapters in
Dealy, "The Family and its Sociological Aspects" to read
before ten o'clock.

Theoretically we go to bed at 10 PM and arise at 6:25 AM
but practically we are still boning at 11 or 12 PM and often
times I, thy W. K. sonella, am up with the milkman (I can't
say with the chickens because there are none either at the
school or near it) to study "Life and Teachings" etc. or
Hebrew history.

Now do you think we do some thing else besides dance
with fascinating sailor boys?

You know that poem dedicated to Great Lakes, don't
you? I can't recall it all, but it begins like this:

"I want a little sailor boy,
A dainty little Fontleroy.
He sure must have a pedigree
A tall and stately family tree.

etc. etc.

. . . .
And he must dance and walk & sing
And hold my hand an' every thing!"

[Drawing of two hearts]
ne ce's pas?

But really, Buzz we are very kind to them. Two of my
best friends died at Great Lks. during the recent epidemic. Over 900 died during 4 weeks there. Sam was terribly
ill, but he is better now. I hope he will stop with me for a
day on his way to Florida in a short time.

Oh Boy! Oh Joy!

Ernie Kester writes <u>great</u> letters from naval base 18 which is somewhere in Scotland. I do hope you will see Bill Hutchins; he is a great chap and I think a lot of him. Tell me about your new girl. I am very confiding to you.

Always, your own,
Marc.

P.S. Address me here at 315 S. Ashland. I only go home for 2 or 3 hours on Sunday usually.

P.S. Al Dungan is at the S.A.J.C. at Illinois University. Mussie is there too. Melville Crandell is a 1st lieut.

———

[POSTMARK] Nov. 18, 1918, U.S. Army Milano

[ENVELOPE FRONT]
Miss Marcelline Hemingway
315 S. Ashland Boulevard
Chicago, Illinois
States Uniti

[ENVELOPE BACK]
Da Ten. Carvesle M. Hemingway
Croce Rosa Americana Ospedale
No 4a Via Cesare Canto
Milano - Italia

La Croce Al Merito Di Guerra
[Drawing of a three banded ribbon over the Red Cross]
Milano, Nov. 11.

Dear Ivory—;

Noted sister it is with a feeling of deep humiliation and esteam that I write these few words? Your sympathetic if not over ample ears. Your effluence in Italian greeted me with all the joy of a man drowning in a sea of Schlitz (t.h.t.M.M.F.) on having a bottle of beer flung to him. Oh why, beautiful and handsome creature, must you write me in Italian when sempre giorni I eat, drink, sleep, drink some more and have my being in it? Also you are learning the lofty brow type of Italian while I speak the common or garden variety. However on my return, which may be expired within 3 or 4 or 5 or six months, we will hie us to a spaghettery and try our respective linguistic abilities upon the chianti vender. Capito? Tesoro mea ho piace le tanta! Il scuolo sta melia?

In regard to the question you asked I will reply. Yes. She is a Cross Red Nurse. Further more I cannot state I am of a dumbness. However, Frances Coates, A. DeV. and all others can take a back seat.

However from long experience with families, etc., I don't talk about things anymore. So guess anything you want to. But I don't wear my heart on my sleeve anymore. But all Oak Park damsels are going to have to show something. I'm off of them the whole bunch. I'm afraid to come home and have 'em pull this blooming 'live stuff. All the fair maidens that wouldn't give a damn about me before you write what drag I have. Child, I'm going to stay over here until my girl goes home and then I'll go up north and get rested before I have to go to work in the fall. The doc says that I'm all shot to pieces, figuratively as well as literally you see. My internal arrangements were all battered up and he says I wont be any good for a year. So I want to kill as much time as I can over here. If I was at home I'd either have to work or live at the folks. And I can't work.

I'm too shot up and my nerves are all jagged. So I'll stay over and then can rest up all summer and be fit for fall cause I'm going to work like a dog for I want to make good. Got a lot of reasons to. All kinds of secrets. Nothing to revue though. Nothing definite, but I want to knock them for a loop anyway.

Well Kid, have a good time and take care of yourself and steer clear of the Flu and I love you a lot Kid. Also you wont know me. I'm about an 100 years older and I'm not bashful and I'm all medalled up and shot up.

So So Long Ivory Old Kid,

Yours (partially) ever,
Ernie

[POSTMARK] 25 XI 1918, Milano Centro

[ENVELOPE FRONT]

Ten. Ernesto M. Hemingway
Croce Rossa Amerci OANH
Milano Italia

Miss Marcelline Hemingway
318 S. Ashland Boulevard
Chicago, Illinois
Stati Uniti

Nov. 23

Dear Old Sister;

Well Kid yesterday I got your letter and today I met your friend Bill Hutchins. Bill is quite an estimable youth although slightly fussed at meeting the Old Master. We found him quite cold and chisly and took him up to the hospital and gave him one of our knitted sweaters and a pair of heavy sox. He is a very nice kid but has had hard luck and a bunch of mean jobs. He thinks a lot of you and especially as a correspondent. Don't marry him but be very nice to him because he likes you a lot. Maybe he loves you, I didn't ask him. He has a mustache that looks kind of discouraged. I approve of him. He will probably write you about me so I can see myself as others see me.

From your letter Kid you surely must be working. I never thought you were pulling the butterfly stuff. Don't worry. I only wish you could.

Salute your Italian teacher for me. Tell him your kid brother is tre volte ferite, decorato due volte per valore ance promosso Tenente per merito di guerra and see what he says. Tell him <u>Ciaou</u> for me. Pronounced <u>chow</u>.

I'm sorry you are so strong for Sam Anderson. He seems an awful simp to my humble view. But Al Walker is a peach and you have lots of time. You aren't more than 21 yet are you? I don't know what I've written you about my girl but really, Kid Ivory I love her very much. Also she loves me. In fact I love her more than anything or anybody in the world or the world its-self. And Kid I've got a lot clearer look at the world and things than when I was at home. Really Ivory you wouldn't know me. I mean to look at or to talk to. You know those pictures we took at home before I left? Well showing them to Ag the other day she didn't recognize me in them. So that shows I've changed some.

Really Kid I'm immensely older. So when I say that I'm in love with Ag it doesn't mean that I have a case on her. It means that I love her. So believe me or not as you wish. Always I've wondered what it would be like to really meet the girl you will really love always and now I know. Furthermore she loves me—which is quite a miracle in its

self. So don't say anything to the folks because I'm confiding in you. I'm not foolish and think I can get married now
but when I do marry I know who I'm going to marry. And
if the family don't like it they can lump it and I never will
come home. But don't say anything for I'm not going to
get married for two years.

Oh Ivory but I love that girl. Now don't ever say not
confidential—for I've written you what I wouldn't write
anybody.

Now Kid who in hell is giving all my letters out for publication? When I write home to the family I don't write to
the Chicago Herald Examiner or anybody else—to the
family. Somebody has a lot of gall publishing them and I
will look like I'm trying to pull hero stuff. Gee I was sore
when I heard they were using my stuff in Oak Leaves. Pop
must have mal di Testa.

The wife is up at the front in the invaded district dis-
pensing medication from an ambulance and is awfully
lonesome. They are going to shut up the American
Hospital here shortly. Then I'll probably live at a hotel. I
have to continue the mechanical treatments on my leg if it
is ever to be any good. Two months more of that. Then in
a couple of weeks I'll be blowing back to the States.
Probably get in some time in February–March maybe
sooner. Frances Bunsleval [?] wrote me a letter, also Alfred
Dick and Aunt Grace. All were full of bull. Give my love
to the family and anybody else I ought to.

And I still love you Ivory Old Jazz.

The W.K.Brother,
Antique Brutality

[POSTMARK] Nov. 26, 1918, Chicago, Ill.

[ENVELOPE FRONT]
Da Tenente Ernesto M. Hemingwail
Sezroue IV
Italian Ambulance Service
Croce Rossa Americano
Milano, Italia
c/o American Consul Milano

[ENVELOPE BACK]
From Marcelline D. Hemingway
315 South Ashland Blvd.
Chicago, Ills. U.S.A.

C.T.S.W.
315 S. Ashland Blvd.
Chicago, Ill.
Nov. 25 '18

Dearest Buzz,

It is way after bedtime and all the others are fast asleep like good children. But I have just finished answering a most beautiful, but rather disquieting letter from Sam, and not feeling sleepy, I turn to you, my best beloved.

I am wondering, dear, how your knee is getting on. Can you bend it all right now? "Hop" said that in your last letter to him (we haven't heard for 3 weeks) that you were still taking treatments for it. By the way, dear, I suppose Dad has written you that "Hop" is at Great Lakes as a 2nd Class Seaman, the Ensign School refusing to take on more men since the armistice has been signed. We hope that he will be with us for Thanksgiving dinner. Marion Vose is coming out and Ursula has invited her special Joe from Great

Lakes & also Mr. Dent, who is wild about Marion. This bunch, with Uncle G's familiar, & Gram & Gramp will be the merry mob, what say? Gee, Buzz, don't we all wish you were going to be with us. I'll say so! I got a P. card from you a week or so ago which you doubtless sent about 2 months ago, from a lake near the Swiss border. Many thanks, old Brute. The Ivory appreciated deeply to have sent on said P.C.

Eoin bones, I had the most gorgeous time last Saturday! I must tell you about it.

Friday nite came a telegram from Sam saying that he would be in Chicago Saturday on his way to the Advance Naval Aviation Sch. in Miami, Florida. Gee, excitement in the camp! Muzz had 4 Jackies invited for dinner & the dance Sat. eve & Marion was coming out too so I was all upset. But, Sam, (whether you fall for him or not you must admit he has a pull with our mother) well he just phoned her that I would stay in town to dinner & Marion also with one of his aviator pals. And the dear Muzz was <u>pleased</u>, actually!

We had luncheon at Field's with his two sisters, went to see Laurette Taylor in "Happiness" in the afternoon, and then all of us went out to the Bismark Gardens (rechristened "Marigold Gardens") near the Edgewater Beach Hotel and had a gay time until we had to dash madly back to the Dearborn St. Station in time for Sam & Tom to catch the "Dixie Flier" for Florida. Honestly, buzz, the W. K. Sam has improved so in looks and everything. And then the U.S.N.R.F. Aviation uniform of forest green & gold is wonderful looking too. (Girls <u>will</u> gaze at uniforms, armistice or no!) Sam expects his commission at the Miami School & then he is going to get an aerial mail route next summer and maybe take me for a <u>flight</u>. Oh Boy! Have you ever been up? I suppose the thrills of the clouds are old

stuff to you, Ernie, but the Ivory is young and unsophisticated <u>in some ways</u>! Give my affectionate greetings to all
the senoritas who have been so sweet to you & the
American girl, or girls, who have been ditto. I love 'em all.
Tell 'em so. Tomorrow I have about 5 hours of recitation
and an evening lecture by Harriet Viltim of N.W.
University settlement. I'm crazy about sociology. You may
return to find me the matron of a police court. Who can
tell?

Write to me, dear, and come back as soon as you can
honorably.

Your own,
Marcelline

P.S. I hope you'll go to college next year.

————

[POSTMARK] Oak Park

[ENVELOPE FRONT]
Tenente Ernest M. Hemingway
Italian Ambulance Service
American Red Cross
Milano Italia
c/o American Consul Milano

[ENVELOPE BACK]
Da Marcelline D. Hemingway
315 S. Ashland Blvd.
Chicago, Ill. U.S.A.

Jan. 2, 1919
"The Old Homestead"
Oak Park, Ill U.S.A.

Dearest Eoin-bones,

The family all enjoyed your letter of Nov. 28th which came on New Years day. You beat us to it by having a turkey dinner on that day. We had a greasy goose, fat and ferocious but good, withal, like unto a bite of as luscious a bird as ever thou didst taste. Shakespeare is hard on my sentence structure. I'll refrain from further man slaughter.

I wrote you about two weeks ago in reply to your letter about "Ag" and Bill Hutchins visit to you. Have you seen either one since then? I'm awfully anxious to see Bill and Agnes too, for that matter.

Mussie asked me for a date last Monday so he came over, spent the evening with me listening to our new vic ($60 baby) which Uncle Leicester gave us for Xmas, and discussing you and Pickles and all the other O. P. notorieties. We had a gay time prophesying how long Agnes Hecox (Gosh, this ink is heck!) and Gene Tallman would stay married & also what the marital fortunes of Lawrence Brink & his wife (both of the class of '19 O.P.H.S.) will be.

Katherine Shockey is engaged and so are Laura Conade (to a N.W. University "medic") and Clarice Hutchins (of '14) to a handsome Lieut. in the Army. I suppose you heard of Bob Prebbles marriage, didn't you?

Well, dear, I'm not trying to give you Doris Blake stuff, but this two-hearts-that-beat-as-one seems to be the only winter sport in Oak Park.

We, that is I, at least, have had a terrifically gay Xmas vacation. Dates with Bob Mansfield, Pete Brereger (1st Lieut. of Aviation) & Hop as well as the theatre, dances and all the regular pre-war stuff. Hop & Min Vose were with us for Xmas dinner & Pete & Bob, as well as Elaine Smith & Mrs. Marsda came over after dinner and stayed for tea. We danced all aft. and at about 8 bells we beat it over to Eliz. Warrs where Lucille & other kids (most of whom you never heard of) awaited us. Hop is a pretty good dancer & an awfully nice guy but he gets too doggone serious, Ernie. Bob & Pete are both wonderful dancers & so were the other boys so we had a grand & glorious time. Yesterday, New Years, Tom Temme, a Jackie, Lib Warr & Bob came over to call while Mother & Dad went to see your W.K. friend Mae Marsh at the movies. This gay couple of parents then went to Hodgson's for dinner & so Bob & I had a little party, joyfully attended by Ursula, Sunny, Carol & the young terror, all by ourselves.

[Smudge on page] Sorry 'scuse us please.

Then we went to see Mae M. She was pretty good but very care worn & wrinkled. I imagine that her hair & coloring must be the greater part of her charm. School begins tomorrow but I'm just going in for one class in the AM.

"Hop" went home for a furlough last Fri. expecting to be back here at noon today but his train is 7 hours late, due to these awful blizzards, so I don't know when I'll see him next. He has to be back at Camp Wilson at 8 AM tomorrow. However I have had a number of letters & telegrams sent from all along the line, so I don't feel quite so desolated as I might. Lucille & I spent New Years eve at the Raymonds & had a beautiful time. Bob wanted me to go down town but Mother & Pafather said "nix." We all know that the lid would be off, & it surely was, but I wanted to see a really wild time. However all the people who went said it was just one long guzzle because everybody knows this is the last chance for a legend N.Y. eve before the old U.S.A. goes bone dry.

P. White was home from his ship for Xmas day. He looks years older & horribly hard boiled in his Jack uniform. I wish "Hop" could get out of his sailor costume. It's so sloppy on all the men that it makes them act as they look, sort of "Darn the Devil, I don't care what I do!"

Mother, Jo Taylor & her sister & I are going to see Lionel Barrymore, Ethel's brother, in his great success "The Copperhead." Mussie says it's the best thing he has seen & believe me, Ernie, Mussie has been seeing everything in town.

I have had two letters from Al W. this vacation & an adorable embroidered N. Year's card from him too. He hopes to be back soon. Have you written to Ernest Kester at U.S. Naval Base 18, Scotland, yet? I hope so.

Dad has been working like the deuce & is cross, but Mother is awfully sweet ever since Uncle Leicester arrived in this country. Ernie, we have been fooled about him all our lives. He is a peach, a pip, a ring dinger, etc. etc! He just can't stand Dad, that's all! he would like you, & you him immensely, if you ever met.

Write me soon & often at 315 S. Ashland Blvd. Chicago.

I love you still kid and am yours (partially),
Marc.

————

[Date of 1919 is approximate, based on Marcelline Hemingway Sanford's address.]

South Congregational Church
3978 Drexel Boulevard
Chicago

Dear Ernie,

Wallie says you and he spent the night together last week and that he told you of our engagement.

I was going to tell you myself but I was afraid you wouldn't care; or be interested, and it has all been so beautiful that I could not bear to take the chance of having anything spoil our joy this summer.

But I'm very glad that Walter told you himself. He promised me that he would as soon as he could after I left. I should have gone over & told you myself the last week, but you and Al left before I had a chance.

Ernie dear, I do hope you will love Wallie. He is such an all around person and so splendidly manly and wonderful. I have had lots of people to choose from, Buzz, but Walter is the <u>only</u> one who has ever fitted all the requirements I want to find in the man I love. He <u>thinks</u> a great deal of you and admires you tremendously. I hope you won't tell anyone else or anyone in Oak Park about our engagement because I want to have it a surprise when I give a regular announcement party at Xmas time. Wallie & Jo Travers are both going to be in Oak Park for the holidays, and I hope you can arrange to be there too.

I know you and I haven't gotten along so well the last few times we have been together. But believe me, Ernie, I want to love you—and I want your love too. Do try to think kindly of me, even tho you don't approve of my work. It seems the biggest thing, and the most necessary that I can do now to contribute as my share to the world.

I know <u>you</u> will do something splended, Ernie dear, and I'm looking forward to the time when you and I can be pals together, as we used to be.

Do write to me. I am very lonely, living as I am, absolutely alone, in one room without a friend in the neighborhood. My room address is 4011 <u>Lake Park Ave.</u> Always your devoted sister,

Marcelline

[POSTMARK] May 17, 1921, Evanston, Ill.

[ENVELOPE FRONT]
Mr. Ernest M. Hemingway
100 East Chicago Ave.
Chicago, Ill.
c/o Y.K. Smith

[ENVELOPE BACK]
Marcelline Doris Hemingway
23 Warwick Road
Winnetka, Illinois

The Nite Before the Day, May 17th

Dearest Old Buzz,
  Scribe a bit to me at the O.P. Hospital. I'm going to have the glossary & appendix taken from the book on Thursday AM. So I'll look forward to words from thee, & if thy friends have moments of idleness induce them to recollect that the Iverian thinks mightily of them all & will welcome them, both in person & by mail.
  <u>Note</u> All dandelions, copies of "Life" & "Snappy Stories" accepted, but <u>no</u> lilies, <u>American Beauties</u> or other <u>cabbages</u>, or biblical tracts will be admitted. <u>This is going to be good!</u>

                                        Love,
                                        Marc.
Address Anasthesia Anne the Appendix to the vol. of
M.D.H.—O.P. Hospital

[This letter previously published in Ernest Hemingway *Selected Letters 1917-1961*, Carlos Baker, ed. (New York: Scribner, 1981), 44.]

[POSTMARK] May 20, Chicago Ill.

[ENVELOPE FRONT]
Special Delivery
Miss Marcelline Hemingway
care Oak Park Hospital
Oak Park
Illinois
(A Patient With The Appendix Out)

May 20, 1921

Dearest Carved Ivory—

Hope the'domen is feeling in good shape. Gee I was sorry when I heard that you were to go under the knife. There's nothing bothers me like having a dear old friend or relative go under the knife.

Conversation with the male parent, however, ellicited the information that you had come out from under the knife in nice shape.

The men are going to screed you and I will be out shortly to see in what shape you have come out from under the knife.

Tonight the Carper, i.e. Mr. La Fever the Carper and Yenlaw Smith and the writer are going to be seated at the ringside while Frankie Schaeffer—of the Stock Yards—and Gene Watson—the Pacific Coast demon—maul ten rounds at 130 lbs. ringside. It should be a good brawl. I look forward to viewing it.

I think that Al had a good time with me here. Hope so— I took your tip that he was without seeds and financed the entire entertainment—food drink etc. It must have schocked Al to learn that you were going under the knife.

Does Douglas Wilde know that you have gone under the knife? He ought to come through with something pretty handsome. Think of what you might have rated from him if you had only permitted kissage. Your going under the knife would then have rent him in such bad shape that he would probably have smothered the hospital in onions like a steak is smothered in onions.

All the men were broken up to hear that you had gone under the knife.

Last night Issy Simons and I had a swell party. Went to four of the best places in the city and while I was saddened at the thought of you being under the knife I managed to assume a certain false Gayety. We had a peach of a time. Issy is a priceless kid. It was a glorious night. We'd come out of some place where we'd been waltzing and into the outer air and it would be warm and almost tropical with a big moon over the tops of the houses. Kind of a warm softness in the air, same way it used to be when we were kids and we'd roller skate or play run sheep run with the Luckocks and Charlotte Bruce.

I'm, and Horney's, going down to St. Louis next Friday night and stay three days at Hash's domicile. Ought to have a swell time—

The new Domocile is a wonder—much larger than the old one—and with an elevator and a view from my front window looking down over the queer angled roofs of the old houses on Rush street down to the big mountain of the Wrigley building green of the new grass along the street and trees coming out—wonderful view. Bobby's going to New York for good pretty soon—did you know that? Horney's working hard.

We've a fine song—wrote by me about the men—

Bobby strolls round on La Salle street
Carper spends money on sin
Horney'll write ads for a quarter
My Gawd how the money rolls in!

Gee I'm sorry that you had to go under the knife. But still if a person has to go under the knife they might just as well go right under the knife without struggling. Sleepy as the deuce this aft—hot you know—and I didn't get in till all hours this morning. Gee had a good time—more fun to go out with Is than any body I know in this town. Youghta a seen us in the Grottenkeller waltzing round and round and all germans around and a fine beery, smoky, cheerful pound on the table with a stein for more music, atmosphere.

Scuse the rotten typeage and the probably tousands of errati—that's on account of me typing by the touch system—just learned it recently and it's faster but more inacurrate. Kate sent you her love and said that you were the last person she would enjoy having go under the knife. Me too I hate to think of you going under the knife—did you have 'em take anything else out too? I'd have had everything out at onc't. Coming out Sunday I think and will cast an optic on you—

Best love to you, dear old swester—and hope you're comfortable—

ever,
Ernie

[POSTMARK] May 25, 1921, Chicago Ill.

[ENVELOPE FRONT]
Miss Marcelline Hemingway
The Oak Park Hospital
Oak Park
<u>Illinois</u>

Hemingway

Dear Ivory Tower—
Enclosed is a biological missive from Yenlaw written at the Crear library—there is nothing to report. The maternal parent came up last night and she and the enditer placed away a chow mein at the Royal Cafe—it isn't hot any more—but you probably know that. Yen cut the end off his thumb with a razor but the writer, asssuming for a moment the role of a physicist, fixed it back on again and it is growing in nice shape.

Horney and I are shoving off to SinLouis on Friday nocturnal. As you surmise I will be glad to clap my deadlights onto Hash. There is nothing of any moent at the office of the enditer. I have been laboring hard and it has been terrible hot—but a cool breeze from the lake has swept the heat away like a bad dream.

You are probably in pretty good shape by now. Is a present indicate in the event of our attending the wedding of the Passionate Blight and Cousin Maggie? In such an event I feel that my attendance may be difficult to obtain.

Gee I wish it was Friday night—two entire diurnals to get through somehow before the evening cometh. It'll only be worse when I'm back again tho—that's the hell of it—to coin a phrase.

How's the 'domen?

Pardon the brevity and also the assiniinity of this screed and believe me always your devoted brother and sincere admirer—

your good friend,
Ernest Hemingway

[WESTERN UNION TELEGRAM] PORTSMOUTH NH
1220P JULY 23 1921

ERNEST M. HEMINGWAY
CARE Y K SMITH
100 EAST CHICAGO AVE
CHICAGO ILLS

ILLNESS PREVENTED MY WIRING YOU BUT DID NOT FORGET YOUR BIRTHDAY LOVE
MARCELLINE

[POSTMARK] Aug. 11, 1921, Chicago Ill.

[ENVELOPE FRONT]
From Ernest M. Hemingway
100 E Chicago Ave.
Chicago, Illinois

Miss Marcelline Hemingway
7 Essex Road
Concord
New Hampshire

Dear Diseased Ivory—

The maternal parent has informed me that you are Haywired in New Hampshire. Gaw. The letter came today, revealing for the first time your address, and I hasten to crouch over this chattering Corona and with terrific speed and thousands of errors advise you of my undying fire of love for you, which at the moment of writing, courses through my veins like nigger gin.

So you're haywired Eh ¢. That is supposed to be a question mark, which I will now insert? You see this is a Corona, the gift of she who, I keep telling her, in a temporary lapse of all good sense, is to assume the difficult role of Mrs. Hemingstein. The Corona, however, is as yet too small for my hands which daily caress the bigger mills of commerce. Therefore pardon the multitude of mistakes which mar its marvelous melody.

The enditer is to become man and wife on September the 3rd at Hortense Bay, Michigan, as yet I do not realize all the full horror of marriage, which was plainly visible on the Blights face, you recall his face?, and so if you wish to see me break down at the altar and perhaps have to be carried to the altar in a chair by the crying ushers, it were well that you made your plans to be on tap for that date. It is a Saturday.

Come Ivory, for Gawd's sake, come. Be there. A choice array of young males will be present. Horney, the Ghee, The Carper, Art Meyer, others, Hoopkins I hope, Odgar I crave, Come at once and by all means. Be there. Answer at once in the affirmative that you will be there. I can count on you can't I? I will do everything in my power to make it as pleasant a wedding for you as possible.

Really it ought to be a high grade affair. Hash is in excellent shape. She is training in Northern Wisconsin and press reports say that she has never been better. I am working out daily at the Ferretti Gymnasium with a capable corps of sparring partners and Nate Lewis declares that he'll put me in there in the best shape of my career.

Naw Ivory, seriously you know, come to this wedding. Please, Please, Please! You gotta come. I may call it off if you don't.

September 3rd is the date at 4 o'clock in the afternoon. My love to youse and get well. Tanks for the birthday wire. Dear love to you—and be on tap.

Immer,
Oui

———

[POSTMARK] Aug. 16, 1921, Concord, N.H.

[ENVELOPE FRONT]
Ernest M. Hemingway
100 East Chicago Ave
Chicago Illinois
Important

[ENVELOPE BACK]
MDH
Merriewold Park, N.Y.
(Sullivan County)
c/o Mrs. J. Moody

7 Essex Street
Concord, N.H.
Aug. 16, '21

Ernie old darling,
You simply can't fancy the joy & rapture which were

produced in the bosom of the Ivory over our receipt of your urgent invitation to the nuptials of Our Hash, et our Eoins!

I've been wild to come all along, old dear, but you didn't write, & the family said nothing, so I thot perhaps you all didn't need my beaming smile to make the ceremony complete.

I'm in a mell of a hess, old dear. I leave Marion's home in Corcord for Mrs. Moody's in Merriewold Park, New York. She expects me to stay until Sept. 10 & has a house party planned for me. <u>What to do</u>? However I'd rather come to your wedding than to all the house parties under the solar body, and if I can fix it up with the family, & <u>you'll help me</u>, I'll do it. Will you assist me, my brother? <u>Get the family to ask me to come, immediately</u>. If I should leave on September first I'd get there on the eve of the second, I think. Do you know where I could stay? Would the family stake me to Dilworth's hospitality for four or five days?

Oh Ernie I'm so happy for you! You are a lucky person (not that you haven't realized it, been told so by probably a thousand people), but if you had ever been in a tight spot like I am you'd realize it more.

Purely <u>not</u> for publication is the news I am about to impart. You were once left out until the last, when Gig Rover & I almost committed some thing, but I am resolved, oh my dearest, that you shall be the very first to even surmise the present romance of the ancient sister. <u>Please don't tell the parents</u>. I want to write to them first. Just keep this under your cuticle for a while.

The Ivory has committed a promissory entanglement with the most wonderful person (of course <u>he would be</u>!) and I'm crazy to have you meet him. Can you fancy me as the sister-in-law of Marion Vose? Well that's the idea exactly. <u>Milton it is</u>! Actually you are the first I've written to, & it gives me little thrills down my back to even say the words. I know you'll like him, Ern. He's athletic, a graduate of N.H. State, a Theta Xi, good looking, sensible, has a sense of humor & <u>gosh</u> how I love him! He's a lot like Horny Bill & somat like Robbie. A good combination, what?

Now this is to be entirely secret because Milton is only starting in business & we couldn't do the deed for two years or maybe more. So you see how it is, don't you Ernie. Don't even tell the gang. I'm crazy to see them all up at Hortens & I wish Milt was coming too.

My love to Hash. Where can I address a scribe to her?

Always your <u>own</u> devoted sister,
Marcelline
P.S. (over)

Please be sure to answer soon. Gosh, Ernie, I want to come to the Bay, but I can't unless you fix it up with the family or some body, so I can stay there. I'm wild to see the place again. It's been two whole years since I viewed it, but having been sick all summer I am a pauper, sabe?

Write to me at Merriwold Park, Sullivan Co., New York, c/o Mrs. John Moody

———

[POSTMARK] Chamby Sur Montreux

[The Jan. 15, 1922, date is based on Marcelline Hemingway
Sanford's birthday.]

[ENVELOPE FRONT]
Miss Marceline Hemingway
600 N. Kenilworth Avenue
Oak Park Illinois U.S.A.
United States of America

Chamby sur Montreux
Les Avants
Sonloup
Chateau Chillon
Montreux Oberland Bernoise Rail
Railroad Switzerland

Dear Ivory—

I send you this on your birthday from Suisse where we
are very happy and wishing for your good health and continued prosperity. I broke my hand in a couple of places
yesterday and it is swoll big as a pumpkin so there will be
no highgrade, and perhaps not very much, typing.

Switzerland is a swell place. See my articles in the
Toronto Star. Where we are it is lousy with English Lawds
all of whom we go to tea with. Hash is getting to talk
English to beat hell and will constantly say something like
"Run me a tub Ahthuh, for the glass is falling and I'm off
to the cinema." We have a bob sled with a steering wheel
and two hand brakes and a foot brake and ride up the
mountin in a fine little train like the Peto-Walloon
dummy, climbing, winding, climbing, winding, till we get
way to hell and gone above everything where the train

stops and you get into another one that runs on cog wheels to the top tip of the mt. Then we shove the bob into the road and go down a drop that makes you're heart hit the roof of your mouth for seven kilometers. All through thick pine forests on the most wonderful roads. We get up to fifty miles an hour and Hash, who is now called Binney, and I take turns steering. The one who doesn't steer breaks. The Mountain is called Sonloup and it is in sight of the Dent du Jaman, the Dent du Midi, The Wetterhorn, the Jungfrau and lots of big snow covered ones.

We eat nice and are both getting as healthy as mt.goats. Been here ten days and going to stay about ten more and then go back to our apartment in Paris. It is a fine place. My hand hurts too much to type or I'd write you about it. I'm doing a lot of work and writing some good stuff. Sherwood Anderson's introductions didn't harm us any. This is the best country I was ever in for simply living. You have so much fun, out-doors all day, that you don't think at all, nor worry, nor do nawthing but a days work about four mornings a week and eat up the air and the swoops on the bob.

Again wishing you renewed prosperity and a continuation of your remarkeable career.

I am,

Your affect. Bro;
Ernie

[POSTMARK] 2-5, '22, Paris

[POSTCARD FRONT: Picture of Genova—Via G. D'Albertia]

[POSTCARD BACK]
Miss Marcelline Hem'gw'y
600 N. Kenilworth Avenue
Oak Park
Illinois
STATI UNITI

Dear Ivory:
    Leave here tomorrow for the old home town; worked hard as compatable with temperament and will be glad to see Hash again.
    This isn't a bad town if you don' hafta live in it and travel to it and from it on the trains.

Ernie

––––––––

[WESTERN UNION TELEGRAM] CABLE MONTREUX
JAN 2 1923
MRS. STIRLING SANFORD
600 NORTH KENILWORTH AVE
OAK PARK (ILL)

BEST LOVE AND CONGRATULATIONS
HADLEY ERNIE

––––––––

[POSTMARK] Oct. 14, 1923, Toronto, Ont.

[ENVELOPE FRONT]
Madame
Sterling Sanford
8100 E. Jefferson Avenue
Detroit, Michigan
U.S.A.

Dear Ivory—

I wanted to wire you and Sterling but couldn't remember the address. Thought of wiring Next Door To Edsel Ford. but at the last minute decided against it. Well young John Hadley Nicanor weight seven pounds and a half and no trouble to anybody was born on the morning of the 10th. Two oclock to be exact. I was on Lloyd George's special train enroute from Montreal at the time. Hadley is absolutely well and getting better every day. Young J.H.N. Hemingway is beautifully built, very dark, very good looking and very hungry. He is going to talk a little English in the home and then we hope he will correct his parents French accent. As he's ski-ied in Switzerland and the Dolomites, raced in the Bob Racing championship of the Canton of Vaud, seen three world's championship fights, Siki-Carp, Siki-Nilles and Carp Nilles and seven bull fights you can understand him having a useful build for ski-jumping, the ring or the Arena. Nicanor Villalta, his godfather, is from Zaragossa. Which as you may know is on the Ebro riber but has nothing to do with the Ebrews.

Hadley has not yet received your packages because they are in hock at the customs house but is crazy to get them and very excited. I will outhock them excustoms. She thanks you for the letters and begs you to accept a screed from a mere brother in reply.

Why don't you and Sterling drive up here some Sunday? It is no distance at all from Detroit to Toronto you know. You can see us, we can see you, confidences and felicitations will be exchanged. A pleasant time indicated for all the young people present. Start some Sat. Stop here Sat night and if you have to be back on Montag leave here the noon of the Sabath day, remembering of course to keep it holy. A pleasant plan for pleasant people.

Write the elderly brother about all things. Your great wealth, of which I hear stirring and conflicting reports, your numerous trips, your successess while treading the boards and all like triumphs. Remember that a brothers love never dies. Remember that always Marcelline dear, that a brother's love never dies. A brother may dies it is true. In fact they die like flies. But their love. Never.

We have a very lovely place here just on the edge of the country across a ravine from the Hunt Club. It is very beautiful, new, light, airy, beautifully and tastefully furnished by ourselves, full of electric fixtures and bath tubs. We hope not to have to stay here long as we are both homesick for Paris where there are few bath tubs, no electric fixtures, but very nearly all the charm, all the good food, and most of the good people in the world.

CONFIDENTIAL

One of my books, THREE STORIES AND TEN POEMS, pooblished by the Contact Publishing Company is out and all sold out the first edition. I took great care to keep this from reaching relatives due to the first story which is a whangleberry but would simply shock and give them that familiar I'd rather see you dead and buried in your grave than—feeling. It is a corking story and I am very proud of it but there is no sense making trouble. If you give me your solemn pledge that it will not fall into the hands of any of the family, your solemn pledge on your word of honor, I will put you into the way of obtaining a copy.

Book No. 2 IN OUR TIME—originally announced under the Title of Blank—which I believed you have ordered. Is in the printers hands now. It is a whangleberry and I don't care who sees it. It will give them a jolt but mores the good. You should get it in a month or so. The illustrations and borders are taking time. Just received a cable about it from Paris yest. There is, I believe, a frontispiece of the yauthor painted by Mike Strater who is miles ahead of all the rest of the pigmenters. This book is published by THE THREE MOUNTAINS PRESS.

If you want to see some more of my stuff k THE EXILES NUMBER OF THE LITTLE REVIEW—just out—Price $1.00 and obtainable in Detroit I believe. Has the Leading thing by E.M.H. and another. The stuff that opens the number are the first six chapters of IN OUR TIME.

There is also a very good thing by Gertrude Stein, some nice drawings by Leger and a story by Bob McAlmon. The number is worth the paper seed.

Now remember that the above in regard to Three and Ten is given you absolutely confidentially. Let the family in on les autres.

So Long old dear. My love to Sterling. Write me care THE TORONTO STAR TORONTO CANADA. OUR HOME ADDRESS IS 1599 BATHURST STREET.

Immer,
Bruder.

[POSTMARK] Oct. 20, 1923, Oak Park, Ill.

[ENVELOPE FRONT]
Mr. Ernest M. Hemingway
"Toronto Star"
Toronto, Canada

600 N. Kenilworth Ave.
Oak Park
Oct. 20
At the old domocile for 10 days—after that Detroit as usual

Eoin-bones, m'love,
It was good to get the splendid screed and to know why Nicanor, and how is Hash and all the other good & much appreciated dope. True to form I reserved the last page for myself and husband, and signed a spurious initial "E" to the end of the first page because, having received it in the parental home & all that, I knew that it would not be kept away from the father's eye. SS & I are already thinking out dates & schemes for coming to Toronto & would care to do it in the extreme. Indeed yes!! However we have an open vehicle, and I am subject to freezing on the slightest pretext (tho Sterling will testify that I am <u>not entitled to Robbie's epithet</u>, <u>the C.P.</u>) So unless the weather shakes off this icy blast of the moment we may not get there until spring, <u>but</u> we shall see, we shall see!
My voluminous love to Hadley and her namesake. I'll bet he's cute, even if young, which is quite a lot to say for any baby. Lucille Dick's son is quite cute, & Herrick Goodwillie's son is likewise, but this long named nephew of mine is not to be compared to mere babies. He is <u>ours</u>! That makes the difference. You intrigue me with the

sketchy and mysterious reference to "Three & Ten". I do want a copy and also copies of the other things. I hope my nervous order for "blank" will come true all right. Do tell me how & where to get the sold out edition, & mums the word to the family.

SS sends affection & I devotion, gobs of it, old kid.

Marc.

————

[POSTMARK] Dec. 18, 1923, Detroit, Mich.

[ENVELOPE FRONT]
Mrs. Ernest Hemingway
1599 Bathhurst St.
Toronto, Canada
Ontario

[ENVELOPE BACK]
Mrs. Sterling S. Sanford
8100 East Jefferson Avenue
Detroit, Michigan

Dec. 17th, 1923

Dearest Hashley,

Here's hoping this will get you before you start for Chicago. We are all so thrilled at the idea of having you all there for Christmas! Sterling, Sunny and I are coming back here Christmas night so the day will be the big thing for the parents. They are positively living only for the happiness of having all their family together.

They are so pathetically eager to see you both and the baby!

I've taken such a chance on your coming that I've sent our small helps to Santa to O.P. instead of to Toronto. Please don't think that you are supposed to give us anything, dear heart. Just the sight of yourselves and the dear infant will be the loveliest Xmas gift in the world.

Lots & lots & lots of love,
Marcelline

————

[POSTMARK] Jan. 4, 1924, Detroit, Mich.

[ENVELOPE FRONT]
Mr. and Mrs. Ernest M. Hemingway
1599 Bathhurst Street
Cedarrale Mansions
Toronto, Ontario, Canada

Jan. 4, 1924

Dearest Hashley and Eoin,

Mother sent us the lovely and most useful gift of the seedlings and Sunny and I proceeded to buy ourselves what we really wanted. It's been loads of fun having Boney up here. The piano has resounded every moment. We had a gay dance on Jan 2 to usher in our first anniversary. I wish you could have come. There's a tremendously nice chap named Quillet, of the Edison Co. is going abroad in Feb., I believe to travel and enjoy the continent for a year or so, and I'd like to have him meet you. "Quill" is much like Bill Horn and Jenks, and he also, adores the liquids. May I give him your Paris address?

I'm afraid that my plans for getting up to Toronto before you sail are not going to go thru. The time is so short and the allowance so low that we just can't make it. But do send me some pictures of "Snocker." I'm terribly sorry I can't do it for I'd planned on it. Again my thanks for the Xmas gift and lots of love to you both.

Marcelline

———

[POSTMARK] Sept. 25, 1925, Detroit, Mich.

[ENVELOPE FRONT]
Mrs. Ernest M. Hemingway
113 Rue Notre Dame des Champs
Paris, France

[ENVELOPE BACK]
from Mrs. Sterling Sanford
2941 Field Avenue
Detroit, Michigan

Sept. 25

Dearest Hadley & Bumbie,

I hope this gets there in time to wish Bumbie as happy a second birthday as any little boy ever had. Carol Sanford had her first one last Saturday and had all the thrills & ice cream and one candle & a pink teddy bear and all the other trimmings. I'm enclosing a snap taken at 10 months. She's running all around now and putting 2 words together and making life generally exciting for her parents.

Ura's wedding was very lovely and she seems delightfully happy. I hope Jap is everything she thinks. He's so quiet it's hard to know him very well. We left Carol here with a nurse & had 3 days pure vacation. She's such a darling (the daughter not the nurse) that I hate leaving her, but it is nice to sleep after 6 AM once in a while!

Many happy returns to Bumbie and lots of love to you all.

Devotedly,
Marcelline

[HANDWRITTEN GIFT CARD]

Merry Xmas.

Happy New Year.
to Marcelline
with love from

Ernie & Hash
Xmas 1925.

[NO POSTMARK]

[ENVELOPE FRONT]
Mr. Ernest M. Hemingway
c/o The Guaranty Co. of New York
Rue des Italiens
Paris

2941 Field Ave.
Detroit
Feb. 7, '27

Dear Ernie old thing,

I am introducing to you, thru this letter, Mr. A. C. Valentine, who is a publisher, and eager to meet you. Mr. Blake, of the White Star Line, and the John Moodys of N.Y. are friends of his, and asked me to pen you this note of introduction, even tho I haven't met Mr. Valentine myself.

He is one of the heads of the Oxford University Press, and was a Rhodes Scholar, and a rugby player at Oxford, and a worth while friend, as well as charming, from the accounts of Ernest Moody, whose letter I hold before me.

I hope this note will serve to bring you near to another publisher, and to connect Mr. Valentine with the World's Greatest Writer.

All kidding aside, dear, he is undoubtedly someone you will really like to know and I am glad to send him to you.

Mr. Blake has offered to get me a position on one of his White Star boats so that I may get over to Europe some day before too many years elapse. I hope I can come.

We were surprised at the latest new dispatches about you and the family, but life is so perplexing to all of us that one should never feel surprised. I am modeling on at a great rate and hope to study in Paris someday. Let me hear from you.

Love dear,
Marcelline

[POSTMARK] Feb. 21, 1928, Detroit, Mich.

[ENVELOPE FRONT]
Mr. & Mrs. Ernest Hemingway
No. 1 Rue des Italiens
Paris, France
Guaranty Trust Co.

[ENVELOPE BACK]
From
Mrs. Sterling Sanford
2941 Field Ave.
Detroit, Mich. U.S.A.

Feb 20
2941 Field Ave, Detroit

Dear Ernie & Pauline,

It was nice to hear that the Xmas pkg. came thru & that you are coming over next summer! My friend, in whose house in Paris I would live, is not able to go to Paris this summer, so I guess my plans will have to be postponed to gibe with hers. I hope I can stay 2 or 3 more nites when I do come (if she wants me that long).

We have had quite a gay winter here and I feel quite like a Detroiter. It takes about 4 or 5 years to get acclimated to this city if you have no introductions. So many thousand people come each year that one can't blame the old residents for being clanish.

Here's a pathetic lot which Ernie will want to see (clipping [not included]). I think they are the same Boltons that Nick fathered in the logging camp near Windemere.

Won't you visit us when you come over here? If you are in Detroit we'd love to have you here, or if not come to our cottage "the Skidway" at Walloon. We have a great urge to go up to Eagle Harbor (up above Houghton & Hancock) to part of S.S.'s hay fever season. It is great being between Superior on that tip of land, not a pollen in a thousand years!

Beefish is growing up, Ernie. She is simply a peach in looks and mind and I think you'll like her a lot, Pauline. Mom is still in California but expects to come back via K. City next week. K is as sore as ever at life in general. Do discount any of his screeds. I'm so glad we are going to see you before long. Now you'll both be   [?] get any glimpses of you.

Love to you mes enfants,
Marc.

[Written on or before 6/8/28. See cable of that date.]

Dear Ivory—

I lost your fine letter on a fishing trip. It dissolved in the pocket the 4th time I went in the water—so I didn't realize how soon you were going—wrote the family and am writing now—will send you a wire to the boat.

Hadley's address is 98 Bd August Blanqui, Paris XIII. She can tell you thousands of places to eat, buy clothes, etc.

If you want a tailored suit go to O'Rossen in the Place Vendome. Millions of citizens will recommend places to you—it is some peoples main life to get people to go to the wonderful attractive little places they found themselves. So I wont bother you with many. However—

Eat outside at the Pavilion du Lac, the restaurant of the Parc Montsouris, get fresh trout—tournedos and aspera-gus—and drink Pouilly (white) and St.Esteple (red) with the tournedos. It's grand there on a warm evening.

Eat at the 4 Sergents du La Rochelle 4 B<u>d</u> Beaumarchais (on the Place du Bastille). Eat anything but drink <u>Richebourg</u>—the best burgandy in town. They have it in magnums if youve any friends with you. But for Christ sake dont tell people to go there because there are only five magnums left. All their wines are lovely. Try the Margaux (red bordeaux.) Tell the wine waiter your my sister.

Go to Brasserie Lipp on Bd Saint Germain opposite Cafe des Deux Magots for beer, potatoe salad and choucroute garnie. Best beer in Paris.

Eat to spend money at Foyots, Tour D'Argent etc. But still spending money you can eat better at Laperouse and if you want to get your hair cut or a permanent go to <u>Antoine's</u> in Rue Cambon, only decent coiffure in Paris.

If you want the best perfume there is, get <u>Chanel's</u> Gardenia at Chanel, also on rue Cambon.

Go to the Ritz for a cocktail and see the fraternity pins. I wish to God I was there to take you to the real places but we're not. Mrs. Moody will know all the places but they aren't my places. Best love and good luck.

I've no friends in Paris in the summer time so am not giving you any letters. Everybody is out of town. If you want a fine place to go, go to Saint Jean de Luz on the Basque coast. Swimming and everything else.

If you want to go to Pamplona—it is the 7th 8th 9th 10th 11th and 12th of July—go to Don Juan Quintana at Hotel Quintana and tell him you are my sister and he must get you tickets. Give everybody my love.

So long kid and I hope you get this.

Love always—
Ernie

———

[WESTERN UNION TELEGRAM] PIGGOTT, ARK 8 1031A

MRS S S SANFORD
STEAMSHIP OLYMPIC SAILING MIDNIGHT
JUNE 8 NEW YORK NY

SENT LETTER TO BE FORWARDED TO GUAR-
ANTY TRUST PARIS IF MISSED BOAT STOP
HADLEYS ADDRESS NINE EIGHT BOULEVARD
AUGUSTE BLANQUI PARIS THIRTEEN STOP LOVE
AND LUCK

ERNIE

[POSTMARK] 15 June 1928, Southampton

[ENVELOPE FRONT]
Mr. Ernest M. Hemingway
Ruth White-Lowery
6435 Indian Lane
Kansas City, Mo.

[ENVELOPE BACK]
From Mrs. S. S. Sanford
Bankers Trust Co.
5 Place Vendome
Paris, France

[Postcard mailed in envelope]
[POSTCARD FRONT: Picture of unidentified ship]

[POSTCARD BACK]

June 14, 1928
26 hours out from Cherbourg

Ernie dear
    Your letter & telegram arrived in time and I was thrilled to get them. I do hope Hash is in Paris. I haven't seen her since you both left for France the first time. I've consumed a lot of liquor & cigarettes on this boat & am rather tired of both today, but haven't been seasick a bit. We met a couple of nice Americans who were in Paris & hope to go about a lot. Only I will miss you. We write again later. My love to Pauline & very best of luck to her next month. Many many thanks dear.

Marc.

[POSTMARK: illegible]

[ENVELOPE FRONT]
Mr. Ernest M. Hemingway
c/o Mrs. Clarence Shepherd
1500 Sante Fe Road
Kansas City Mo. U.S.A.
Les Etats Unis (Please Forward)

[ENVELOPE BACK]
Mrs. S. S. Sanford
Modern Hotel
Saint Jean De Luz
France

July 2, 1928

Dear Ernie,

We took your good advice and are here at San Jean de Luz for a few days. I'd like to go to Pamplona but Anna wouldn't so naturally I can't dash off by myself. However, we are going to take several day trips to Lourdes & San Sebastian etc. I adore the ocean here & its so quiet & peaceful after Paris. Met some of the people who knew you at a cocktail party Hash gave for me on Sat. afternoon and they were all awfully nice. The Carlos Drakes took me home to dinner with them. They are slick people.

I'm simply amazed at myself. I do not feel any queer effects from liquor at all. Even at first I wasn't ill nor have I ever had a morning after effect. Such I had fully expected. It must run in the Hancock & Hall blood to "drink like gentlemen". I always remember that everyone got squiffy but you, at the Italian parties in the old days. We are to be here about 10 days, counting the trips, and then go back to Paris for 2 weeks. I'm to be staying at Mr. Quatrocchi's studio during that time.

Bumbie looks marvelous. He is absolutely the handsomest child I ever saw. He said to me "I like you & Marie & Mother & my fine papa in America." So I'm let into the inner circle.

I hope you had a swell time at Aunt Arabell's palace. I must look it over some time soon while I still have the good wardrobe for & from this trip.

Much love & my best to Pauline,

Marcelline

Address me c/o Bankers Trust Co., 5 Place Vendome
We sail back July 25 on the "France".

[WESTERN UNION TELEGRAM]

KEY WEST FLO 24
MR AND MRS STERLING SANFORD
600 NORTH KENILWORTH AVE OAKPARK ILL

VERY MERRY CHRISTMAS TO YOU ALL
    ERNEST PAULINE SUNNY BUMBY AND PAT.

————

[POSTMARK] Jan. 3, 1930, Detroit, Mich.

[ENVELOPE FRONT]
Mr. Ernest M. Hemingway
Gen. Delivery
Key West, Florida

[ENVELOPE BACK]
If not called for in ten days return to
Mrs. S. S. Sanford
1503 Seyburn
Detroit, Michigan

1503 Seyburn Ave.
Detroit
Jan 3

Dear Ernie,

The surprise and delight your check occassioned is still registering. Carol, in consequence, is the proud owner of two new dresses which she picked out herself, and Jimmie has a darling new yellow sweater (with elephants on it), mittens and a rattle. You were a dear to be so very generous to us, with all you have to take care of besides. I think you are a peach to be so generous to <u>all</u> the family! Mother certainly appreciates it.

I hope you didn't have duty to pay on Pat's toy pup.

We've loved reading all the splended reviews of your book, but "Farewell" its self is so splended that the reviews are pallid beside it. (I was dissolved in tears at the end).

I also had a grand time reading Dorothy Parker's shout in the "New Yorker". She certainly is fond of you, brother.

I gave away several copies of "Farewell" to my <u>discriminating</u> friends for Xmas.

Much affection to you all. I'd love to see your Patrick. Hash sent a lovely picture of Bumbie for Xmas, does Pat look like him?

Always your old
Marcelline

P.S. I found this notice in this mornings "Trib". I wonder if it is Bud Ault's father or his uncle. Poor guy, if it is either of them.

Love,
Marc. Ivory etc.

Did you hear from Ernie Vector? He said he wrote to you from Base 18.

I can't find the clipping now, but it said that H. P. Ault of Cincinnati O., the millionare dye maker, had committed suicide last Sat. because he did not get a high commission in the Army which he was expecting in the G.M.C.

[POSTMARK] Dec. 22, 1931, Key West Fla.

[ENVELOPE FRONT]

Box 406
Key West
Special Delivery

Mrs. Sterling S. Sanford
1503 Seyburn Avenue
Detroit, Michigan

Dec 20, 1931
Box 406
Key West

Dear Marce:

Merry Xmas to you and Sterling and all your outfit! You were very sweet to write Pauline in hospital and send presents and she would have answered if she could—but was on her back. She will write you and is very grateful. I should have written but was finishing book and between that and hospital no could do. Then the joys of travelling with new born child etc. You probably know them.

Hope everything goes well with you. Splended weather here. Greg weighs 11 lbs 6 oz—not fat just big. Pat well—Pauline now too. Carol expected here today or tomorrow.

Best to you and Sterling and your children from Pauline and me and all of us

Always
Ernie

[NOTECARD]

[Date of Dec. 1931, is based on Gregory's birth and Ernest Hemingway's letter of 12/20/31.]

Dear Ernie,

The special, with its simply grand enclosure, arrived at 11 o'clock Christmas eve, and was much appreciated. I'm glad Pauline is herself again and that Gregory is gaining so well. Carol is going to have her part of the check for her bicycle fund. It is now about half way to the $25 mark she aims for, for May. I never had one, but I remember how I longed for one so I'm glad that she is heading the right way. If Beefish is still there tell her that the fruit arrived in perfect shape & is being enjoyed daily. I'll write to her at college later. We expect Ura & Jap here tomorrow.

Much love & tremendous appreciation,
Marcelline

[POSTMARK] Dec. 20, 1933, Oak Park, Ill.

[ENVELOPE FRONT]
Mr. and Mrs. Ernest Hemingway
c/o Barclay's Bank
Nairobi, British East Africa

Wed Dec 20

Dear Ernie and Pauline,

Mother is resting a little better today. She's very weak and spits blood continually, but she isn't in nearly so much pain. Dr. Pond says she has a fifty-fifty chance. The next few days will tell. I think she's looking better this afternoon. All the neighbors are very kind, bringing in soups & flowers etc. Of course she isn't seeing anyone who calls. Les writes every day or so, and his letters cheer Mother tremendously. If she's better I'll go to Detroit Xmas eve to be with the children. If not I'll stay here.

Sunny takes turns with me when she's not at the office. I'll keep you informed, even tho you'll not get these letters for some time. Of course I'll cable if there's any need.

Uncle Frank Hines is not getting better Aunt Anna told me yesterday. This is just a bulletin, not a letter. Sorry it's all so doleful.

With affection
Marcelline

[POSTMARK] Jan. 2, 1934, Oak Park, Ill.

[ENVELOPE FRONT]
Mr. & Mrs. Ernest Hemingway
c/o Barclays Bank
Nairobi
British E. Africa

[ENVELOPE BACK]
From Mrs. S. S. Sanford
c/o Hemingway
600 N. Kenilworth Ave.
Oak Park, Ill. U.S.

Oak Park Jan 2

Dear Ernie and Pauline,

I told you that I would keep you informed about
Mother's illness. I don't think I'll have to write again after
this, because she's so much improved that she sat up in bed
for New Year's dinner yesterday, and will undoubtedly be
out in a chair in a day or two. If all goes well, I expect to
go back to Detroit the end of the week. My family needs
me pretty badly.

Mother had a relapse Monday (Xmas night) so I dashed
back here Tues. AM. I've been here 3 weeks now, not counting Christmas day in Detroit.

I wish Beef could come out to stay part of the time while
Mother is getting stronger. Louise is so crabbly, & of
course Sunny is at her office most of the time, tho she's a
great help in an illness.

Beef is derateo to her Jack! So derated that she worships
his every breath and gesture. She says she's perfectly happy,
but it's a strange slave-like happiness. Anyway, I'm glad she
likes him, because he seems to me the most superficial and
conceited young egocentric I've encountered in years!
Perhaps he's just young and may improve. Well, everyone
to his taste!

I hope you'll find lions, if they still have them in Africa
(which a radio lecturer denied in a debunking lecture the
other day.) And that you'll see few ants at close quarters (he
admitted that there were ants and mosquitoes). and that all
in all it will be a grand trip! I'm celebrating my 11th wedding anniversary by writing letters today. Ura writes that
Greg had a lovely Xmas & Beezer too. Mother was thrilled
with your cable. Les was sweet & telephoned to Mother

long distance, on Xmas, too. Again many thanks for all your generous gifts.

With affection & a happy New Year
Marc

Write to Mother whenever you can. She loves letters and will be house-bound for many weeks yet until her leg and ankle are strong.

MHS

[POSTMARK] Aug. 30, 1934, Detroit, Mich.

[ENVELOPE FRONT]
Ernest M. Hemingway
Key West, Florida

[ENVELOPE BACK]
From M. H. Sanford
1503 Seyburn
Detroit, Michigan

1503 Seyburn
Detroit
Aug 31 '34

Dear Ernie,

I keep wondering what news you have of Les. It's such a long time between letters, and between stops on his journey too, that I get pretty restless just waiting for second or third hand "Did-you-know" type bulletins from some friends or relations. You ought to be the very closest to the source of radio and cable news. I heard he had reached Havana but thats all.

We were all pretty disappointed that Les didn't get his trip in during the summer so he could go to the U. of Mich. this fall, as he had so definitely planned. But if all goes well he'll have a wonderful year of adventure to look back on when he does settle down.

We keep enjoying your "Esquire" stuff and other things when ever I find them in the magazines, but I wish you'd do another novel that would pull us to pieces emotionally as "Farewell to Arms" did. How was the African adventure? Much different from the travel books? There certainly is room for a new slant on Africa with a non-trader Horn—non-white woman tempting men from the right—aspect. Those two types, the game and native poisoned arrow terror one & the white vamp stuff, have been done pretty thoroly, and nothing much else that I've known about.

We had a good three weeks at Walloon this summer and our boys expanded under the influence of space and freedom from traffic perils and taboos on noise. Jim got to be quite a canoeist and fisherman and, John, who was in a boat and the water for the first time, was really happy.

Carol, my daughter, is quite an adept at swimming, paddling, and rowing and is now at a girls' camp near Grand Rapids, riding & enjoying life a lot.

I wish Ura & Beezer could have been with us too. They certainly had a grand winter with your children last year.

Sterling is doing well with his air conditioning & cooling business. He's the consulting engineer on this aspect of the Det. Edison Co.'s business, you know. This was a grand season for expansion of the business too. The weather cooperated splendidly!

As to your ancient sister I am mostly a mother, but in between I garner a sheckel or two doing bits for a local movie co. My last role was a banker's wife with a group of theatre guild people. Chevrolet gets the picture, and I have corn starch on my hair and am supposed to between 40 & 50. Very impressive with pearl earrings etc. The picture before that, I was supposed to be 25, and did that too. Make up is a marvelous thing!

I'm enclosing a snap or two of our group taken at the lake. I'd love to have some of you and Pauline and the boys too.

We thot of you on July 21st. Beefy had a birthday tree on the 19th at Windemere. Warren Sumner sent regards to you, by the way.

As always,
Marcelline

––––––––

[POSTMARK] Dec. 27, 1934, Detroit, Mich.

[ENVELOPE FRONT]
Mr. and Mrs. Ernest Hemingway
Piggott
Arkansas

[ENVELOPE BACK]
Mrs. S. S. Sanford
1503 Seyburn Ave.
Detroit, Mich.

1503 Seyburn
Dec. 26

Dear Ernie and Pauline,

We were so happy to get the telegram, via Sunny, yesterday afternoon.

I hope the little packages for the boys arrived when they should, early in the fall. I didn't know where to send Bumbie's gift. Is he in France with Hadley at the same address 98 Blvd. Auguste, Blanqui?

It must have been a great Christmas for you, with your boys, after missing it last year. Our boys are such a grand age for thrills too.

John is four tomorrow and Jim is 5½. Carol is quite the older sister at 10 years.

We read your Jan. Esquire article out loud last evening (the young John Drieskes of O. P. were here) and had a grand time with it.

It sounded so exactly like you talking with the gang of Bill Smith, Horny Bill, Yenley etc. on Chicago Ave. in the old days!

A happy new year to you all and love to my nephews.

I hope that if you have any news, or an address for Les, you'll send it to me. I haven't been able to send his Christmas present because no one has seemed to have an address since Cuba, in October.

Affectionately,
Marcelline

P.S. Am having swell time making pottery this year.

[POSTMARK] Jan. 26, 1935, Key West, Fla.

[ENVELOPE FRONT]
Special Delivery
Mr. and Mrs. Sterling S. Sanford
1503 Seyburn
Detroit, Michigan

Dearest Marcelline:

Much love and a very Merry Christmas to you, Stirling and your fine children from Pauline, Bumby, Pat, Greg and your affect. Bro, Uncle, and Bro. in law

Ernie

Dear Marceline,

This is a pretty belated Christmas present. Ernest got it all ready and then we couldn't find your address, and in the rush of getting off to Arkansas for Christmas, it got left behind and then it disappeared and suddenly turned up this morning. I'm going to mail it Special Delivery so you'll get it without further delay.

The children thank you for the fine Christmas presents. I was certainly impressed when they came last fall. Do you have your whole life organized like that? I certainly envy you. And I think you're pretty fine to pick out presents for nephews you've never even seen.

Good luck to all of you.

Pauline

January twenty-second

———

[POSTMARK] Jan. 30, 1935, Detroit, Mich.

[ENVELOPE FRONT]
Mr. Ernest M. Hemingway
Key West, Florida
Box

Dearest Ernie & Pauline,

Your special caused plenty excitement on <u>Monday</u>

Morning. It was delivered at 7:30 AM just in time to start the day right!

You were very generous, Ernie, and we are all planning things to do with our respective parts of the check. We particularly liked the belated Christmas card, Ernie. It's the first word I've had from you in over a year.

Is Bumbie with you. I had sent him a gift to Paris in care of Hadley.

We follow your doings from pictures & paragraphs in "Esquire". I hope your Christmas in Arkansas was as happy as ours in Detroit. It was probably our very nicest year. Lots of people entertained at egg-nog parties and "at homes". It was a gay season after three very quiet years for this city.

I'd like to see my nephews. I expect they are almost as grown up as Carol, James & John.

Affectionately,
Marcelline

[POSTMARK] June 18, 1935, Detroit, Mich.

[ENVELOPE FRONT]
Mr. Ernest M. Hemingway
Key West, Florida

Dear Ernie,

I thought you might like some of the prints of the family taken Memorial Day weekend in Oak Park. Everybody was keen about your Bumbie. It was quite fun to see the grand children together. I wish we might have had your family too. Ura looks better & I hope she'll continue to improve. We're enjoying the African story tremendously in Scribner. In fact they got a whole new years subscription from me just on your account.

I had supper with some people who admire you greatly yesterday. Not until the evening was almost over did we discover that Prof Maier, of Ann Arbor, was writing a book which includes you. He's an interesting person.

Affection to Pauline & the children.

As always,
Marc.

[POSTMARK] Jan. 9, 1937, Detroit, Mich.

[ENVELOPE FRONT]
Mr. Ernest M. Hemingway
Key West, Florida
Box 464

Jan 8, '37

Dear Ernie,

Your generous check was here when we got back after having Christmas at Mother's house in River Forest.

Thank you, and Pauline too. The children are delighted. Carol is eager for a small radio for her room and will use her part of the money toward that project.

We had our 14th wedding anniversary last week. It hardly seems possible that so much time has passed. We had twenty guests for a buffet dinner and charades afterward (<u>Fun</u>!). Tell Pauline that I enjoyed meeting Marjorie Hollis who used to work with Pauline on Vogue. Miss Hollis is getting a tremendous kick out of the success of her "Live

Alone" and the new series she's doing for the newspapers. I like her very much. Bumbie was a great success the day he came to Grandmother's. He looks amazingly like you, Ernie.

Much love always.
We're eager to see the new book.
Marc

P.S. I hope the game and the photograph got to you.
Marc

———

[July, 1937, date based on Michael Reynolds, *Hemingway: An Annotated Chronology* (Detroit, MI: Omnigraphics, Inc., 1991).]

Telecable address
Cat Cay, BWI
mail after Aug 1 to Box 406 Key West, Florida

Dear Marce—

Thanks for your charming letter. Reading it made me slightly sick. Windemere happens to belong to me and if you wanted me to let you use something out of it you could have done so without writing a hysterical letter full of insults. But I suppose people do not change much. I had planned to go up there this summer but have to go back to Spain instead.

The keys to Windemere are in my workroom in Key West. The workroom is locked and I am here at Cat Cay B.W.I. where your letter took ten days to reach me. Getting the keys to you is out of the question. It is absolutely impossible.

I am therefore enclosing ten dollars in the letter for Sunny to get a locksmith to open or cut the padlock off wherever her canoe is, take out the canoe and replace the padlock with another equally good one, and when she goes, lock it and send the keys to me at Key West marked hold. If Sunny is still there she can live in Windemere but must lock it up and see that it is cleaned and fully shuttered when she leaves. If Sunny is <u>not</u> there you may use the row boat but I do not want you to use the house or anything else. Please remember that what is my property is my property as much in Michigan as in Key West. Because you would like to have it does not change that. Nor did your way of writing me make me feel friendly toward you. Windemere is not for rent nor is to be used for your guests.

Ura is welcome to use it at any time for herself and family. I know Ura and how careful she is of things. If she wants to use it write me and I will have the keys sent her when I return to Key West. I haven't seen Sunny for a long time but the last time I did see her she was no one to trust a house with, being careless. If I let her live there I am relying on her haveing changed and takeing the necessary responsibility to keep things decent and close it up properly.

Thank you for telling me about the repairs which are necessary to the cottage. When I am up there I will have them attended to.

The question of why mother deeded Windemere and contents to me does not arise. As I told you before it is as much my property as our home in Key West. I give Sunny permission to live in it this summer if she wishes. Leicester and his wife are very welcome to stay there this summer if they wish. Ura and her family can go there if they wish. I expressly forbid you to enter or use it in any way except in the matter of using the row boat which you offer to repair and return in good condition in return for this use. If you go into the house for any other purpose, except if you go there as a guest of any of the people that I have given the right to use it, I will regard it as trespass and proceed accordingly.

Yours always,
Ernest

[Handwritten note by Ernest Hemingway.]

They must write me first for permission
Excuse torn letter—had only ½ hour to catch the weekly plane
I just received yours today

[Handwritten on back of letter by Marcelline Hemingway Sanford.]

Note. Later Ernest wrote an apology—this letter came in answer to mine asking if he could not let younger children use Windemere. Especially Sunny & Ursula & because I told him Mother had said we might use the family rowboat—we had our own cottage & did not wish to use Windemere at all. Other children did.

[POSTMARK] July 31, 1937, Petoskey, Mich.

[ENVELOPE FRONT]
Mr. Ernest M. Hemingway
Box 464
Key West
Florida

[ENVELOPE BACK]
M. H. Sanford
"The Skidway" on Walloon Lake
R. F. D. No.1, Petoskey, Mich.

July 30, 1937

My dear Ernest,

On rereading your terrible letter for the 5th time I find that I must add a few facts to the letter I wrote to you a few days ago. I do not wish to write again but my husband is as hurt at your insults as I am at your cruel letter. There was no sarcasm intended by any statement in my 1st letter asking for your permission to use your old boat. Also I thought you would be glad to know that renters were available, since you did not use your cottage. The place has never been used or entered by me or any of my family at any time since Mother left it excepting once. I have not taken nor would I wish to take anything from it ever. You have a strange attitude toward me. I have nothing in my own cottage but what I bought & paid for except a few things from Grace Cottage which Mother did not think worth while shipping to River Forest. She took all the nice things she wanted from Grace Cottage & left me some useful articles—2 cots & 3 chairs and an old couch, a broken tea cart which were just about the only things left by prowlers who had taken all the mattresses, bedding, lanterns, stove, etc. from Grace Cottage. I am grateful for them & use them all.

The only time, as I started to say, that I have ever been inside Windemere was to take out & return the old row boat last summer which we used, with Mother's permission last summer for two weeks, & returned in exactly the same condition in which we found it. I wanted Mother to ask your permission at that time but she said not to bother you as you were not in Key West at the time. I opened Windermere last summer by the simple method of a 10¢ pass key which Mrs. Bacon had. I am glad it is not available to pass keys now as Mrs. B. said couples had used it over nights at other times she was sure. I hope you will now get the Windemere situation clearly in your mind and will understand that because it was the family home I thought you would care as much as I did about having it <u>used</u> & <u>kept up</u> so that the general impression which is now prevelent around here, that it is an "old unused place where anybody can go & use the old fence for fire wood," as I heard one crowd of picnickers say, will soon be changed by your ownership. My suggestions, which I am sorry that you resented, that since you were <u>not</u> coming up yourself, you might <u>like</u> to offer it to your less fortunate brother & sisters, were not sarcastic, but were motivated by a feeling of kindness toward the others who have no summer homes, & were suffering in the intense heat at this time of year at which I wrote. I have just 4 bedrooms here for my three children & a helper, my husband & self. I will not, of course, give any permission to any one in your name. If you ever wish to let any one occupy it, I am sure you will deliver your own messages. No one has asked me to write to you, except that my husband felt that I should say these obvious things to you. I had taken for granted that you would <u>know</u> that I would not hurt or use your property. I hope that you will stop being so unkind & suspicious, Ernest. I believe in kindness. There is too much war every where in the world. Why should we encourage hatred in families?

As always,
Marcelline

[POSTMARK] Dec. 22, 1938, Key West, Fla.

[ENVELOPE FRONT]
Mrs. Sterling S. Sanford
2941 Field Avenue
Detroit Michigan

[ENVELOPE BACK]
If Mother's with you please give her my love and tell her
I wrote her to River Forest. E.

Dear Marce:

So sorry to hear your ill. Hope your better now poor
Masween. Much love and Merry Christmas. Am awfully
sorry I wrote you such a rude and boorish letter about
Windemere that time.

Love to you and Sterling and all the kids from us.

Ernie

Key West Dec 22, 1938

————

Havana
May 29, '39

Dear Marce:

I'm so sorry to hear about the accident to John's eye.
Poor, poor kid. I hope so it will be all right.

Mother sent me a letter of yours in which you mentioned a row boat. I would be very glad for you to use the
Windemere boat. Write Les about boat house keys. He
was there last.

Best to you and Sterling.

Ernie

————

[POSTMARK] Dec. 31, 1940, Habana, Cuba

[ENVELOPE FRONT]
E. Hemingway
Ambos Mundos Hotel
Havana Cuba

Marcelline H. Sanford
1503 Seyburn Avenue
Detroit Michigan
Estades Unidos

Merry Christmas and Happy New Year to your three kids from all of us

Ernie

———

Grace Hall Hemingway
Studio 551 Keystone Avenue
River Forest, Illinois
Sept. 9, '43

Dear Ernest,
Mother is much better & getting stronger every day. I hope you are well and Martha too.
Mother was terribly ill but she came out of the coma and pleased us all. Mrs. Beich, Mother's friend cabled you when she thought it was necessary (as the doctor had asked her to notify all of us.) I came right down from Walloon & got here Tuesday A.M. to find Mother much improved. She had had "strep & uremic poisoning which had affected her heart. We will all have to arrange some way for her to have some one live with her after she gets well. I'm doing all the

nursing & housekeeping since I got here. She has an excellent Dr. (Dr. Finley John of 6 N. Mich. Ave.) who really saved her life. Mother sends love to you and Martha.

Affectionately,
Marcelline

[POSTMARK] Apr. 18, 1945, Detroit, Mich.

[ENVELOPE FRONT]
Ernest Hemingway
c/o Scribners Publishing Co.
(Charles Scribner & Sons)
5th Ave.
New York City, N.Y.
Important Please Forward

[ENVELOPE BACK]
From (Marcelline Hemingway Sanford)
Mrs. Sterling S. Sanford
279 Hillcrest Road
Grosse Pointe Farms 30, Michigan
U.S.A.

April 7 '45

Dear Ernest,

I don't know where to reach you, but I thought you would want to know that your "Windemere" property at Walloon Lake has been advertised for sale at the Public Tax Sale for unpaid taxes & penalties for 1942, '43 & '44.

Mother just heard about it in a letter from one of the Bacons. The sale takes place May 1st—in 2 weeks. Mother telephoned me long distance about it. I, in turn, telegraphed to Dan Ernst, R #1, Petroskey, the Township Treasurer to please send me the am'ts owed so Mother & I can pay it up & save the property before the sale of May 1st. I have not heard from Dan Ernst yet.

Mother says she will pay all she can & I will forward what I can. I hope we can cover the am't & save it for you.

It's a shame to let a valuable property like that go for just a few hundred dollars in taxes. The ground is worth at least 15.00 a front foot, plus the buildings. Please write to Mother about it. She feels very upset about it.

I wrote to Scribner & asked for your address in order to write to you last fall when we could send Xmas boxes overseas but they said they had no address except the old one in England which they doubted would reach you in France. They said your cable address was private to them & I could not use it. We are all waiting news of Jack. Hadley has promised to let us know any news she gets, or where he is imprisoned, as soon as she hears. It must be terribly hard for her and for you to be waiting so long with no word from your boy.

We have been at this new address since last November. I hope we can stay here the rest of our lives. It's a wonderful feeling to own the place we live at last, after all these years.

All the best to you, Ernie. I'll be glad to do anything more you suggest about your property. I will be up at my own cottage in June & July, I hope.

Always & affectionately your sister
Marcelline

279 Hillcrest Road
Grosse Point Farms 30, Mich.
Oct 9, 1950

Dear Ernie,
    Poor old Wes is gone. He'd been ill for quite a long time.

Affectionately,
Marcelline

Wish I knew Pats address. I have a wedding gift waiting for him.

MHS

———

Mrs. Sterling S. Sanford
279 Hillcrest Road
Grosse Pointe Farms 30, Mich.
Jan. 21, '51

My dear Mary,
    May I tell you how much I enjoyed reading your article in the Jan. "Flair"? It was a delightful surprise too. I had a two hour wait for a train back to Detroit (following a lecture on the Theatre I had given for a club in Kalamazoo) last Monday. It was my birthday, and a dull way to spend it, sitting on a platform. And then I came upon your article. Since cooking is one of my enjoyments too, I felt a tremendous interest in your achievements in that line. I only wish I knew half as much about seasoning. Food in Key West last winter, gave me a lot of new ideas. Having met Toby & Betty brought the story closer, also.
    We haven't seen Ernie for so many years (and you, not at all) that I should expect all of us to have quite an up-to-

date mental picture of one another by now! Your writing helps me to clarify mine of you and Ernest. I enjoyed my brief glimpse of Havana.

I have wondered about Bumbie's expected baby and what happened.

Please tell Ernest we all read his "Over the River". In fact I've read it twice. A lot of the first part reminded me of stories he told us when he first came home in 1918.

Sincerely,
Marcelline H. Sanford

———

[POSTMARK] 1951, Habana, Cuba

[ENVELOPE FRONT]
CORREO AEREO—AIR MAIL
Mrs. Sterling S. Sanford
279 Hillcrest Road
Grosse Pointe Farms 30, Michigan
Estades Unidos

FINCA VIGIA, SAN FRANCISCO DE PAULA, CUBA

Dear Marcelline—

Thank you so much for your sweet letter. Ernest has had so many wives that, not unnaturally, I feel a little shy about his family. But perhaps time will dissipate that. When Sunny and young Ernie came down a couple of years ago, we had a delightful time—or at least, I did. And now we hear from Ura (she IS the Hawaiian one, I hope) that she and her husband are coming down for a bit in April, and I shall doubtless be amazed again how much the family are look-alikes.

Bumbie's and Puck's baby was born last year—May, as I recall—in Paris, a fine, healthy and handsome girl. And now they are expecting another one whom, the doctors assure them (medicos are so omniscient these days) will be a boy. They are still in Berlin but Bumbie is doing his utmost to get himself transferred to Paris, for obvious reasons. We saw them both last December, a year ago, in Paris and they seem to be a fine harmonious couple. Bumbie has retained all the sweetness of his youth while maturing and I thought Puck had grown out of many of the provincial mannerisms which she had when we first knew her in Idaho.

We had Patrick and his wife, also Gigi, here for Christmas, sweet children all and now that the holidays are finally finished, Ernest, who's in good health, is working hard and extremely well.

Sometime we must exchange some recipes.

Best wishes,
Mary (Hemingway)

February 1st

"The Sanfords"
Skidway Cottage, Route No. 1
Petoskey, Michigan
July 16th 51

Dear Mary and Ernest,

Perhaps Sunny has written you about Mother's funeral in Oak Park. I hope so. I wrote Ursula and Uncle Leicester's widow. You know how grand Ruth Arnold Meehan was to Mother thru many many years. I know Mother wanted to leave Ruth something equal to our shares in her will. She often talked of it, but Ruth said Mother should not do it. At the funeral we suggested that perhaps each of us might want to give Ruth (who will lose her home 551 Keystone at her age of 60 & who only has 2 days work a week in a hand sewing place) when the house is sold in River Forest) one of the $100 bonds, 5 of which I had put in each of the 6 childrens names when the Florida lots were sold some years ago. The bonds were Mother's & she had the interest of course but each group of 5 were designated P.O.D. to one of the children by name. Louis Clarahan suggested this to me when I asked his advice, as I frequently did, about Mother's affairs at the bank.

Mother put the house in my name, long before she told me about it, with the thought that it would obviate taxes & instructed me (& her lawyer) that I am to sell it & distribute the proceeds to Sunny, Ursula & myself. She thought she had given me her car but she had not, so I paid her a sum for it 2 years ago when she could not drive it (it was 10 years old then) & she gave me a bill of sale for it so it could have a license. I am driving it now, as I drove it for her for some time previously after she could not. She liked to go up here summers & loved the movies & going to church & calling on friends, none of which was possible without a car, nine miles from town. I am extremely grateful to her. (It is the first car I ever had.)

I want you to know how wonderful Sunny was during Mother's last illness. We are very grateful to Sunny. Up to last Nov. (Thanksgiving) Sunny & I had shared Mother's time & care as Ruth had but Sunny was marvelous during last winter & spring.

We all missed you very much during the sad time in River Forest. The lawyers have asked me to come down soon to appear at Probate Court to represent the children (which I will do). It was good to have four of us together again. I hadn't seen Les in many years. He is a dear. Very changed in appearance from the slim blond boy we used to know. Carol Gardner & Sunny I see oftener, of course, and of course Ura had just returned to Honolulu. Ruth did more for Mother through the years & with selfless unpaid devotion thru many years than any of us. She seemed so pleased to have "her children" together again for the few days recently in River Forest.

Many of your old friends, Tubby Williams, Bill Horne, & Jenks got in touch with us very kindly. We appreciated it. As Sunny may have told you I arranged for a stone at Forest Home for Mother & Sunny forwarded the money for it from some you sent her. We all appreciated that kindness.

With love to you, & I'll be thinking of you on your birthday, Ernie, July 21. We used to have happy times with your Beefy up here in those old days.

Marc

[POSTMARK] Oct. 2, 1951, Detroit, Mich.

[ENVELOPE FRONT]
via Airmail
Mr. Ernest M. Hemingway
Finca Viglia
San Francisco de Paula,
Cuba

279 Hillcrest Road
Grosse Pointe Farms 30, Mich.
Oct. 2, '51

Dear Ernie,

Just an hour ago I read a notice of Pauline's sudden death. She was such a darling. Tho' we had only known each other thru letters until 2 years ago, I was so very fond of her when we had a visit in Key West in 1950. She meant a great deal to you, I know and she told me she had never ceased to love you. My affectionate sympathy, Ernest. (I heard from her 2 weeks ago.)

Lovingly,
Marcelline

———

[POSTMARK] Dec. 20, 1951, Habana, Cuba

[ENVELOPE FRONT]
Mr. and Mrs. Sterling Sanford
279 Hillcrest Road
Grosse Point Farms, 30
Michigan
Estados Unidos

Merry Christmas to you all. Thanks for the letter about Pauline.

Ernie.
Dec 1951

[PRINTED CARD]
Muchas Felicidades
y los
mejores deseos
para el
Ano Nuevo
Habana–Cuba

Ernest and Mary Hemingway

———

279 Hillcrest Road
Grosse Pointe Farms 30
Michigan
Jan 5, '52

Dear Ernie,

Since the things, including family photos will be devided when the O.P. Trust Co settles Mothers estate, I had some copies made of the pictures of some of our parents pictures. I did not know whether you had a copy of this one of Daddy. It was taken in the 20s, as I recall and was the one Mother liked best. His last photo when he had the heart disease and diabetes was not that of a well man, naturally so I did not think you would want it in preference to this one.

The photos hanging on the walls at 551 Keystone are largely framed ones. I had the copies made in Oak Park last fall (Ruth Meehan took them to and from the copy place for me when I was on tour) and I meant to get these to you and others in the family before Xmas.

If you would like one of Mother in her earlier years I can get one made also. Sunny tells me she was promised many of these. I dont know. Anyway it is nice for us each to have copies before the family things Mother had are separated and the estate devided. Ruth Meehan (Bobby) is taking good careful care of everything in the house. I am sorry Sunny changed her mind about buying it but since she only offered to buy it for $100 over what I would be offered and since she withdrew her offer less than 3 weeks after she wrote me, there was no time to receive offers from others which were pending. Sunny would have liked to move right in with her things on top of Mothers very full household of furniture etc all of which the Lawyers for the Trust

Co told me would HAVE to be put in storage, if the house was sold to any one. That was their written word to me. They are responsible for the care and settling of the things in the house. All I do is pay the bills for utilities and upkeep until the house is sold, I told Sunny I thought by spring it would be available or certainly more chances of a good sale. Sunny either would not or could not wait to give me the chance to get a decent offer. She benefits of course when it is sold as does Ursula and I do too, as I wrote you long ago. Mother arranged this means of being sure the house was sold to advantage and that each of her three older daughters would have something in proportion to what others had thru your Trust fund or like the cottage at Walloon. You really ought to see that home at Windemere Ernie. It is so much nicer since Sunny arranged for and helped with the remodeling and repairs you authorized. You have a lovely place there now, and the most desirable location too.

We put a floor furnace, small one run by tank gas into our Walloon place last year. We will be living there many months a year when Sterling gets to Retirement age in six more years.

My lectures are a god send. I could not keep up the 551 house to give Ruth a home and hold the place for sale and to be shown unless I had this lecture income.

I have tried to help Patsy and the boys and Beefy too in their recent difficulties. John is better and Linda may not have permanent scars they think. The accident was nearly tragic for the Gardners . . . . I'm glad Beefie wasn't in the car nor the baby . . . .

We are a scattered family but I want us to keep in touch and love one another. Dad and Mother would have wanted that. Life is too short for unkindness even in our minds.

You and I who are the oldest know this especially. . . . Love dear. I'll get any other photo copies you wish . . .

Marcelline

---

279 Hilcrest Road
Grosse Pointe Farms 30, Mich.
Jan. 26 '52

Dear Ernest and Mary, perhaps this clipping [not included] one of my friends sent me the other day (she had kept it all these years) may be of interest to you. That party was such a happy one. I was not able to be there when Mother gave that interview, tho Carol was at home to let in the "News" representative who came to interview Mother about <u>herself</u>, (not about you or any of us.) The news reporter thinks that <u>this</u> interview, picked up by a TIME reporter, and vastly changed and distorted, must have been the basis for a very untruthful "quote" supposedly by Mother, in Time a few weeks after this about some percent of people liking or not liking your writing, Ernest. I was eager to write to Time, for Mother, and <u>deny</u> that <u>supposed</u> quotation at the time. I knew Mother could <u>not</u> have said it, but Mother said, "No, People will forget a mis-statement faster if you do nothing to bring it to their attention, and anyway, any one who knows me knows I never would talk about percents of anything like that since Mathamatics is a closed subject to me and always was. . . . In case you saw or recall, that fantastic little item, credited to Mother (of more than two or three? years ago) I thought you might care to know the straight of it even at this late date. "Time" apparently does what it likes with so-called news, and takes a chance on being corrected later on distortions of truth.

The Birthday party, referred to in this article, was a very happy occasion. I saw that she had another one each year after that, but this was the best one because Mother was thinking brightly and was so gay and enjoyed it so much. . . . Later on, she did not even remember this at all, nor any of the fifty people or the gifts. That was the very sad part in her last year or so.

Mother looked beautiful & her coloring was always lovely.

Affectionately,
Marcelline

"The Skidway Cottage"
On Walloon
Route 1, Petoskey, Mich.
Sept 5-'52

Dear Ernie,

We have read with appreciation your "Old Man and the Sea" and all of us want to tell you how fine it is, (which you know) and how proud we are of you. It's nice to have you in the stride which reminds me of some of your earlier short stories (tho this is even better) and I'm delighted that you too feel that this is the way you wanted it to come out.

Sunny left last Sat., with her son Ernest, for Chicago. We have had four days of rain but a pleasant day yesterday and today makes the week not quite a total loss. Our John goes back tomorrow and Sterling and I follow in a day or two.

You might be interested to know that both news stands in Petoskey mentioned that they have sold more copies of Life than ever before, this week.

Lets hope the published volume does the same.

Congratulations and good luck. . . .

Love Mazaween
Marcelline

I thought much about our father yesterday, He would have been 81 on his birthday . . . .

———

[RETURN ADDRESS NOTE]
MHSanford
c/o Mrs. Leicester C Hall
1205 N. Louise St.
Glendale, California
Until Dec. 4

Mrs. Sterling S. Sanford
279 Hillcrest Road
Grosse Pointe Farms 30, Mich.

5 AM Sun 23rd of Nov. 1952

Dear Ernie,

I am flying to California today. Its my first trip out there and I'm very excited about going especially as I'll see a lot of our family out there.

I have several things to tell you but first I want you to know how thrilled I was, and that really is the word for it, when I read in a Louisville paper about the class of school children all writing to you recently and your very kind and charming reply to a boy in the English class. Your letter was reprinted in full and it sounded like you, Ernie, in the days I remember you before so many years and ideas came between . . . I just wanted you to know how happy it made me . . . .

Next I wanted to tell you that I had a very nice letter from Patrick, early this fall. He said he was so sorry to be late in signing the paper which the executor of Mother's estate, (Mr. C. R. Preiss, of the Oak Park Trust Co) had sent him. He said that with all the problems he himself had had, in being executor for his own Mother's estate, he knew what it meant when one person or another held things up. He also urged me to visit Hennie, in N.Y., when I went in October . . .

I did so, and it turned out that her apt and my hotel were in the same block, tho I hadn't realized it until I looked her up. Shes a darling, Ernie. And such a happy person. I just loved her. A sister of her father's, Mrs. Peter Pund of N.Y., and I saw Hennie off on the boat to Africa in late Oct. What guts that child has to recover so quickly from her great disappointment at losing the baby, and to sail off alone on the little freighter, the "African Grove" to Africa. She's so crazy about Pat! Hes a lucky man. Hennie arranged for some of Pat's pictures to be shown on 58th st before she sailed. I met the Broyles family too. They seem very fine people. I liked her Dr. father especially well. . . You are lucky in your daughter-in-law, brother. I wish I had son-in-law or daughters. Time will grant my wish, I feel sure. . . .

Now I hope to be seeing Gregory and Jane, and their baby, when I'm in Los A. next week. I'll be headquartered with Aunt Gertrude, (Mrs. Leicester C. Hall (his widow) but my lecture business will take me many other places during the short 10 day trip. Our son Jim is a navy airman electrician at the navy Air station at Moffett Field near San

F, and I'll have Thanksgiving with him. . . . He works on the big bombers in from Japan & Korea.

But one of the things I thought you might care to help in, is this. . . Uncle Tyley Hancock's grave is in the plot with the Ernest Halls in Forest Home cemetery (Ills.) near CEH's. I didn't even know it was there until I looked up records there last spring. It is unmarked. It seems a shame that it should remain so. Mother, I recall, worried about that. When I see uncle (really cousin) Dr. Clarence Tyley-Roome, in Santa Barbara, where he lives, I'm going to ask about whether he (and perhaps you?) and I can't have a stone of identification put on that grave. Would you like to be part of that plan? (It would be about $125 I think). I'd have done it before, if I could have financed it alone. I'm so lucky to have found this lecturing, Ernie, at my time of life. I had worked part time in a Dept store for seven years and when they let me (and many others) out because we had reached 50 (the policy is to have no "Old ladies" because pension time comes at 65) I was so discouraged I thought the end had come. Then I thought hard about what I might do. Luckily I've always been able to get on my feet, before a meeting, and for years I'd talked (free) to Garden clubs and I knew everybody likes a sense of humor-So, when one club I belonged to asked me to get up a program on the N.Y. Theatre (which Ive always adored) I did one they liked enough so that other clubs began asking me, too. (I did the 1st one just from Reviews) and by the next season I got a chance to go to N.Y. with Sterling on a business trip of his to see some plays. I'd missed being there for 8 years during the war and my long illness, and then this "business" was on its way.

Last year (and I booked myself entirely thru requests coming in to me or sending out the brochures) until this season (now I'm with the the Roxeme Wells Bureau) I spoke in 33 cities and they even included Town Halls. I make very little actual money, but I do carry all my personal clothing and other personal expenses & plays etc. and I've helped SSS put all the children thru college. John will graduate next June (God Willing!). We couldn't carry it another year I'm sure of that. Sterling was sick for two months this fall and out of his office for more time than that, but he's fine now, and we are holding tight and hoping that Jim will be out of service in time to finish his last year or so of college (he was a junior when he enlisted in the Navy) before Sterling has automatic retirement in a few years. That's a rule of the Det. Edison Co. (all out at 65). People in the creative arts are lucky. They can keep going as long as "it comes".

I want to tell you again how much we love "The Old Man and the Sea". People congratulate ME on it everywhere I go, as tho I could take credit. But I'm so delighted for you that what you wanted to say came out so exactly right. Even to very talented people like you, and ones who are great craftsmen, (again like you,) that only happens once in a long time. I'm neither of these things, but I know.

It happened to me just once when I was doing sculpting and it makes you feel that God has been very good to let you in, even a tiny bit, on his province. . . .

Because Mr. Preiss, of O.P. Trust, keeps writing to me so frantically that he cant possibly settle the estate until he finally gets yours and Greg's signatures, I hope a personal visit from me will help Greg to want to sign for the picture of Mother's making which he received months ago, and the receipt for which is necessary for the probate court before the estate can be finished. Its so silly to have it drag on forever. Sunny put $1000 in herself, repaying a loan, so it should not be used up in fees.

There are still three small pieces of Florida property some one ought to investigate before they are sold or let go for taxes. They were almost sold for taxes, but the notice came to me and I sent it on to Mr. Preiss in time for him to cover it. Its such a waste to have this tiny bit going into lawyers fees and Executors added fees, just because the necessary signatures arent there for the court from Gregory and you, Ernie. . . Sunny could use the little one sixth and so could Les, I'm sure. Beefie is teaching school, (her 4 yr old is at home) full time to help with her 2 older children being at a private school she feels is necessary for them. I know she could use what is coming from the estate, if it isn't all used up in these fees, due to delay. Patrick was so understanding. I guess that comes from having to be responsible for an estate himself. . . .

It would mean a lot to me if my small part, equal to your share, could come to me in time to help our John thru his last semester bills at Yale next Feb. . Sterling's recent illness took all our savings. . . I hope my Calif trip will result in enough bookings for next season to make it worth while to go out there now. I feel sure, now that you know that it is only yours and Greg's signatures that are lacking, that you wont hold it up longer. . . . If the papers Mr. Preiss sent you have been lost or misplaced, Im sure he will send another set to sign. I hated to have to add this business note to the letter about other things. But I know that it has to be finished some time (the executors work on the estate I meant). I told Mr. Preiss, when he last implored me to please write, (and I think he's been after Sunny too,) that I was afraid you'd misunderstand. . But now I've done as he asked me.

To return to other things. . You are a lucky man to have Grandchildren. I can hardly wait to be a Grand Mother too. Ura gets such a kick from hers. . . . Here's <u>hoping</u> <u>sometime</u>.

> Affectionately always your sister
> and with love to Mary
> Marcelline

P.S. Cousin Walter Johnson who teaches at Princeton says he saw Hadley & Paul last summer. They are fine.

Marcelline Hemingway Sanford
279 Hillcrest Road
Grosse Pointe Farms 30, Mich.

Dec. 23, '52

Dear Ernie,

When I was in California recently I talked to cousins Elsie & Gertrude Roome about the headstone for Uncle Tyley Hancock's grave (which is not yet up at Forest Home Cemetary tho' he was buried there years ago) and they said they would gladly pay part of the cost of erecting a granite stone similar to the ones on Dad's & Mother's graves there (if I'd make the arrangements). It is the only unmarked grave in our family plots (either Hall or Hemingway). They said they felt sure Dr. Clarence Tyley Roome, their brother, (who was away that day) would help too. Would you care to be part of this project? It was very close to Mother's heart. She talked about getting that stone very often, & you loved Uncle. I wish I could do it alone but I can't. I hope you have a Happy Christmas. I just loved your boy Gregory. The baby looks like him.

> Affectionately,
> Marc

P.S. I am writing to Mr. Gray, at Forest Home, Forest Park Ills. He's the one in charge of monuments. I did all arrangements for Mothers headstone, thru him in 1951. He has access to all records there.

———

[POSTMARK] Jul. 28 ,1954, Detroit, Mich.

[ENVELOPE FRONT]
Mr. Ernest M. Hemingway
Finca Viglia
San Francis de Paula
Cuba

[ENVELOPE BACK]
Mrs. S. S. Sanford
"The Skidway"
R. F. D. No. 1
Petoskey, Mich.
until Aug 1st
then 279 Hillcrest Rd.
Grosse Pointe 36, Mich.
This was written but not stamped until July 28, sorry!
MHS
Many Happy Returns!

July 21 '54

Dear Ernie,

Its a shame we aren't better about getting birthday letters out further ahead of the day itself. I wrote to Beefy <u>on</u> her July <u>19th</u> day too. Shes having a happy summer at Merriewold Park, in a house that has been given to the school of which her John Gardner is also a professor at

Adelphi College in Garden City too. (Merriewold gave me many good times years ago). I'm so glad Beefie and some of her three children can have a real vacation.

Sunny seems happy and busy and the old cottage looks attractive with all the improvements. Young Ernie M. goes to summer school. I'm varnishing floors & painting window frames etc. at my cottage now that my family have left until Sept.

Always, your affectionate sister
and love to you and Mary
Marcelline

I hope you got the invitation to our Carols wedding last Dec. I know you were in Africa & had much else on your mind. Hope you both are <u>well now</u>.

———

Marcelline Hemingway Sanford
279 Hillcrest Road
Grosse Pointe Farms 30, Mich.
Oct. 30, 54
Room 534 (S) Harper Hospital
Detroit Mich

Dearest Ernie,

I'm so glad the Nobel finally came to rest in its proper place, in your possession. I know you have so many friends and admirers now that you never could have time to reply to all. But Congrats! I didn't even use the Hemingway name at the time of my recent accident where a Mrs. Reed of Vernon Mich hit me a rear & side blow. Anyway all the facial cuts have healed & the big "contusions" like apples on neck & head are almost gone. Just the fractured hip & pelvis have to heal. This is my first accident (when I was driving) and it surely has played havoc. My car completely smashed (the only one I ever had new) & all my income gone since I've had to cancel all lectures up to Feb 55. But I am getting on well, & they got me onto crutches for the first time on the day your wonderful prize was told to me by this Times reporter.

Few people knew I was here. I carefully didn't say Hemingway at the time of the "crash" because I remembered the awful time when we were told you were dead (Just Jan) while I was in Philadelphia.

At that time, Ernie all the distance & apparent misunderstandings faded away (that have come with the years) & you were my darling little Ernie whom I loved, the one I grew up with and who sat beside my bed (or I on yours) & exchanged secrets about girls or boys we liked. The brother I loved above anyone in the world who fished with me in Hortons Creek & shared fun in OPHS.

Lovingly your sister

Marcelline

P.S. Ura is in the hospital in Honolulu too for operation. You see I haven't seen you in 25 years, since Daddy died & all you know of me is some one's else somewhat greeneyed version & all I know of you is thru Hadley & Greg & reading it in the papers. You don't look well to me in your picture, Ernie. Isn't it time, now that you are 55 and I am 56 that we loved each other again? Mazween

[POSTMARK] Mar. 22, 1955, Grosse Pointe, Mich.

[ENVELOPE FRONT]
Mr. Ernest M. Hemingway
c/o Charles Scribner & Sons Co. Publishers
Fifth Avenue
New York City, N.Y.

[ENVELOPE BACK]
Mrs. S. S. Sanford
279 Hillcrest Road
Grosse Pointe 36, Mich.

[Postcard mailed in envelope]
[POSTMARK] Mar. 17, 1955, Saint Petersburg, Fla.

[POSTCARD FRONT]
Grace H. Hemingway
c/o S. S. Sanford
279 Hillcrest Rd.
Grosse Point Farms 30, Mich

[POSTCARD BACK]

March 15, 1955

Are you the owner of Lot 7 & 8, Block 6, Shore Acres,
Shore Acres Center, in city of St. Petersburg, Fla.
Do you wish to sell. What is your asking price. May we
hear from you at any early date. Our commission is 10%.

James D. Dowling Realty
120-107th Avenue
St. Petersburg, Fla.
Phone 21-1471
A. L. Major

[Handwritten note on postcard by Marcelline Hemingway Sanford.]

I believe this is your property, Ernest.

Marcelline

———

[POSTMARK] Jan. 11, 1961, Grosse Pointe, Mich.

[ENVELOPE FRONT]
Mr. Ernest M. Hemingway
St. Mary's Hospital
Rochester, Minnesota
(or Care Mayo Clinic)

[ENVELOPE BACK]
Marcelline Hemingway
Mrs. Sterling S. Sanford
279 Hillcrest Road
Grosse Pointe Farms 36, Michigan

Jan. 10, 1961

Dear Ernie,
    Sterling woke me at midnight to tell me he had heard, via radio, of your hospital stay. I am so sorry. We didn't know where you were at Christmas so we sent our greeting to you and Mary via Scribners. It was so wonderful to know your Jack and Puck and our son John & his Helen & their baby, had Christmas dinner together in Mill Valley. John's new house is fairly near Jacks (in Tiburon, Calif.). Pat and Hennie's Christmas card photograph with their adopted daughter was a happy note too. It's good to see the next generation growing as they want to do. Our Carol

Coolidge will join her husband David (& Davy Jr. too) in Garden City in Feb. They've sold their house here. It was nice to have a birthday card from Ursula this week too. I hope you'll be well soon.

Love to you both, always,
Marcelline

New Acknowledgments

THIS Centennial Edition of *At the Hemingways*, together with Fifty Years of Correspondence between Ernest and Marcelline Hemingway, could not have been produced without the encouragement and support of numerous individuals. I especially want to thank my sister and brother, Carol Sanford Coolidge and James Sterling Sanford, for providing letters from Ernest Hemingway to Marcelline Hemingway Sanford and for their personal remembrances of our mother and her family.

The John F. Kennedy Library generously permitted us to publish the letters from Marcelline to Ernest in the Hemingway Collection. Stephen Plotkin, Curator of the Hemingway Collection, and Megan Floyd Desnoyers, Supervisory Archivist of the John F. Kennedy Library, and their staff were extremely helpful in copying several letters and leading me to others and allowing me to copy them.

Permission to publish the Ernest Hemingway letters to Marcelline was given by the Ernest Hemingway Foundation. My special thanks for facilitating this to Allen Josephs, President, and Ted Striggles, attorney.

My daughter, Sarah Hemingway Sanford, assisted me by searching out and making the copies of the Marcelline

Hemingway Sanford letters at the John F. Kennedy Library. Both she and her brothers, Eric Drake Sanford, M.D., and Walter Edmonds Sanford (who also provided invaluable software advice and counsel), have been extremely encouraging and supportive throughout this endeavor.

It was Charlene Murphy, a fine Hemingway scholar, who first alerted me to the Marcelline Hemingway Sanford letters in the John F. Kennedy Library and then copied the relevant pages of the catalog. Susan Beegel has been a patient editor and a wise counselor. The staff of the University of Idaho Press has lead me through the publishing process. Joan Bekins, who has provided valuable encouragement and support, proofread my mother's text, and offered helpful comments on my foreword. Jeannie Smith introduced me to Nancy Klussman, a brilliant, creative, and talented computer typist, who deciphered and typed all the letters. Beatrice Maifredi helped translate Ernest Hemingway's Italian. Elena Scanu at Ram Insta-Print, also helped decipher the Italian and handled my copying needs in a cheerful and efficient manner. We are also grateful to Professor Kazuo Shimizu for his meticulous research which unearthed a number of items that have been corrected in this reprint edition of *At the Hemingways*.

Over the years various family members have provided friendship, help, stories, and insights that contributed to this book. Thanks to Carol Hemingway Gardner, the late Madelaine Hemingway Mainland Miller, the late Leicester Hemingway, the late Patricia S. Hemingway; my cousins Jack, Patrick, and Gregory Hemingway; Ernest Mainland; Hilary Hemingway Freundlich and Anne Hemingway Feuer, with their late mother Doris Hemingway; and my nephew, David Coolidge Jr.

Scholars and writers Robin Gajdusek, Sheila Johnson, Morris Buske, Lucille deView, and Marybeth Bond Sheppard provided helpful comments on my foreword. Michael Reynolds, by his meticulous research, helped in ways that he never knew in this production. Thanks are due to the many Hemingway scholars in the United States and abroad who encouraged me to take on this project, including, but not limited to James E. Nagel, Linda Wagner-Martin, Robert Martin, J. Gerald Kennedy, Scott Donaldson, Frederic Svoboda, H. R. Stoneback, Donald Junkins, Richard A. Davidson, Kim Moreland, Janice Byrne, John Weser, Ann Putnam, Jenny Lee, Paul Helfer, Aletha Kramer, Gladys Rodriguez Ferrero, Mary Cruz, Mary del Pino Cruz, Esmeralda Avila Vazquez,Rose Marie Burwell, Bernice Kert, Bickford Sylvester, Arthur Waldhorn, Max Naenny, and Roger Asselineau. Scott Schwar and Virginia Cassin, officers of the Ernest Hemingway Foundation of Oak Park, also provided information, encouragement, and inspiration. My special appreciation goes to Judith B. Sanford, my wife, for her help, understanding, and emotional support.

J.E.S.

1998

EDITING NOTES

Anyone who works with the letters of Ernest Hemingway is indebted to Carlos Baker for setting such high standards in *Ernest Hemingway Selected Letters 1917–61*. I have attempted to follow Baker's lead in keeping "Hemingway's endearing and exasperating idiosyncrasies of spelling, punctuation and paragraphing." The same applies to the forty-eight letters of Marcelline and the one letter from Mary Hemingway. I have joined Baker in making occasional brief deletions in order to not hurt feelings of living persons. Like Baker, "obvious errors in typed letters and slips of the pen in longhand have been silently corrected; punctuation has commonly been altered or added only where the sense of the sentence appeared to require clarification." Where possible, I have included postmarks and inside and outside addresses to give a sense of place and time. Where I could not ascertain an exact date for a letter, I have given my source for the date assigned to the letter. Where I could not decipher the handwriting, I have shown a two-em space and a [?]. Further editorial interpolations are denoted by brackets. Copies of the Ernest Hemingway letters have been donated to the John F. Kennedy Library, Hemingway Collection, by Sanford family members. All the Marcelline Hemingway Sanford letters are from the Kennedy Library. I leave it to qualified scholars to provide footnotes in future editions.

Index